The First Muslims

History and Memory

Asma Afsaruddin

ONEWORLD
OXFORD

A Oneworld Book

Published by Oneworld Publications 2008
Copyright © Asma Afsaruddin 2008

All rights reserved
Copyright under Berne Convention
A CIP record for this title is available
from the British Library

ISBN 978–1–85168–518–9 (Hbk)
ISBN 978–1–85168–497–7 (Pbk)

Typeset by Jayvee, Trivandrum, India
Cover design by Design Deluxe
Printed and bound by The Maple-Vail Book Manufacturing Group,
Braintree, MA, USA

Oneworld Publications
185 Banbury Road
Oxford OX2 7AR
England
www.oneworld-publications.com

For all those who strive against malevolence in truth and dignity

Contents

Preface

When Oneworld Publications first approached me about writing a short history of "the First Muslims," I had not fully envisaged this book. I had expected to write a fairly straightforward account of the major events and key figures of the early formative period of Islam. In the period of gestation, the current book evolved against the crisis-ridden backdrop of today's world. Hardly anything involving Islam and Muslims appears to take part in a vacuum anymore in the post-September 11 milieu. What influential Muslim intellectuals, politicians, and activists, whether in the Islamic heartlands or the West, choose to say and do often become the focus of intense scrutiny and commentary in intelligence-gathering and policy-making circles in the United States and Europe, as well as in academic communities. The actions of the global purveyors of terrorism originating in Muslim-majority countries appear to have tarred all Muslims with the brush of suspicion. Muslim public discourses of self-validation and empowerment today provoke anxious unpacking and deconstruction among both Muslims and non-Muslims. Such Muslim discourses often point back to the generations of early pious Muslims, the *salaf*, and seek to discover the relevance of their lives and thought and establish their resonances today.

Thus I came to realize that writing about the earliest Muslims and their communities could not be accomplished today without writing about contemporary Muslims as well, on account of the historical and mimetic continuities between the two. This is why my book is as much about the present as it is about the past and why after spending more than the first half of the book talking about the first three generations of Muslims, I then switch to a discussion of today's Muslims and their issues. The concluding chapters establish how the *salaf*, as seen through different lenses, continue to shape the world-views and consciousness of many contemporary Muslims in many parts of the world, and why they will – and must – continue to do so.

A word about the method of dating used in this work. When a single date is used, it always refers to the Common Era date, unless specifically stated to the contrary. The infrequent double dates separated by a slash lists the Islamic Hijri date first followed by the Common Era date.

A number of good-hearted people read the whole or part of the manuscript and offered concrete suggestions for revisions and improvement. They include valuable colleagues and friends like Richard Serrano, Masood Farivar, Sebastian Guenther, and Walid Saleh, as well as the anonymous readers of this manuscript, to all of whom I record my thanks. My husband, Steve Vinson, not only read the manuscript and made valuable suggestions for improvement, but also provided critical moral support throughout this undertaking. I owe him a special debt of gratitude. My student assistant, Kendall Hannon, provided special assistance in compiling the bibliography, for which I am grateful. I would also like to thank the faculty and staff, particularly the director, Professor Muhammad 'Abd al-Haleem, at the Centre for Islamic Studies, School of Oriental and African Studies, London, England, where I spent part of my sabbatical year (fall, 2003), for providing a congenial environment in which to start this project. Thanks are also due to Mike Harpley of Oneworld Publications, who proved to be an efficient, wise, and patient editor. It goes without saying all remaining mistakes and shortcomings in the text are mine alone.

Introduction

WRITING ABOUT THE "FIRST MUSLIMS"

Who are the "First Muslims?" From a Qur'anic and general Muslim univer-salist perspective, the very first Muslim was Adam, the first human being fashioned by God from clay into whom He breathed His spirit (Qur'an 15:29; 38:72; 32:9). He was also the first prophet, beginning a line of prophecy and prophethood that ended with the mission of Muhammad ibn 'Abd Allah (d. 632). This universalist perspective is further reflected in the broad meaning assigned to the term *Muslim*: "one who submits/surren-ders to God." Such a broad definition has been applied to all those who have made a genuine affirmation of their faith in the one Divine Being and thus have professed "true submission to Him." This is the meaning of the Arabic verbal noun *al-Islam*, the name given to this primordial religion of all those who submitted to God through time. In this basic, non-denominational sense, all prophets and righteous believers are Muslims (for example, Qur'an 2:136).[1] Nature, created by God and submissive to Him, is also described as *muslim* in the Qur'an (3:83).

There is also the more circumscribed sense of "Muslim" and "Islam," which dates from the start of the prophetic mission of Muhammad at a spe-cific point in history. The Qur'an uses these terms in both these senses. We will, however, commence our narrative in the seventh century of the Com-mon Era from the time when Islam as a specific religious-historical phenom-enon and movement began, and not, like the famous pre-modern historian al-Tabari (d. 923), from the time of Adam. We do this while recognizing the simultaneously broad and circumscribed meanings of "Muslim" and "Islam," which remain germane to the Qur'anic self-understanding of the universality of its message and implicit in our use of these terms, particularly for the early period.

This is a book about certain key events, ideas, and trends in early Islam and how they came together in the formative period. Other than the Prophet Muhammad himself, it also focuses on key personalities around and after the Prophet who have left their indelible mark on the religious, social, and intellectual history of Islam and who are valorized by later generations for their unique contributions to the evolution of this history. These personalities are historical figures to be sure, but in the way that their memory and legacy have been partially and creatively reconfigured by posterity, they are also to an extent, mythical and "iconic" characters who have fulfilled and continue to fulfil a deeply emotive and symbolic role through the generations. Their influence on the thinking of Muslims in the contemporary period cannot be overestimated. Such is the role of al-salaf al-salih ("the Pious Forbears," salaf in short), with whom I have conflated the "First Muslims."

There are competing definitions of the Pious Forbears. The application of this nomenclature is sometimes restricted to the generation of the Companions only, sometimes to the generations of the Companions and the Successors together, and more broadly, to the three generations of the Companions, Successors, and the Successors to the Successors. We have opted for the third, more inclusive definition, mainly because it would allow us to survey a broader span of historical time and assess the contributions of key figures from the third generation as well, whose influence has been seminal for the subsequent development of Islamic thought and practice. We are thus focusing on the period from the early life of Muhammad to the death of the last Successor to the Successors, roughly between 570–855 CE. This broad swath of time for three generations is derived from the traditional dating given in the Arabic sources.

In roughly the first half of the book, we broadly sketch the rise of Islam and the development of the Islamic polity in order to provide a firm historical backdrop to contemporary discussions about the salaf and their milieu. In our later chapters, we explore the construction of the concept of al-salaf al-salih and its continuing relevance in contemporary reformist/modernist and Islamist discourses on diverse topics, such as political authority, the extent of the religious law, the nature of jihad, and the roles of women. How certain key figures, ideas, and events are selectively appropriated by these groups in the contemporary period to legitimize and authenticate their positions on these various issues will be discussed.

THE CHALLENGE OF WRITING SUCH A BOOK

It is a challenge to write a book on this topic in the contemporary period. As a consequence of the various ideological and geopolitical enterprises in which Islam as a perceived essence gets implicated today, writing a book even on the early pre-modern history of Islam may be perceived as a political act. How one chooses to understand and interpret the primary sources is regarded by some as taking an ideologically motivated stand, according to lines already drawn in the sand. Lest this depiction of events comes across as a bit melodramatic, I will proceed to delineate in brief recent pitched battles that have been waged on the question of the reliability of the sources regarding early Islam and, therefore, the historicity of the information available to us.

In the late 1970s, John Wansbrough from the University of London published two books[2] in which he provocatively advanced the thesis that the entire corpus of the traditional Arabic sources was to be rejected as ahistorical and to be regarded as essentially fabricated to reflect certain ideological and historical processes occurring through the eighth century of the Common Era. Among these sources he included the Qur'an, which he claimed, was compiled in its final form only around the beginning of the ninth century in the context of a sectarian monotheistic milieu primarily in Iraq. Therefore, Wansbrough argued in turgid prose, it has very little to do, if anything, with first/seventh century Arabia which was a later retrojection. Wansbrough's controversial study led to the subsequent publication of a number of books impugning the classical Islamic tradition.

Perhaps the most sensationalist of these was *Hagarism*, the brainchild of the authors Michael Cook and Patricia Crone, published in 1977. The authors sought to "debunk" the traditional accounts of the rise of Islam by using Syriac Christian sources, which offer a rather idiosyncratic account of the rise of Islam in the seventh century supposedly from a Jewish Messianic sect called the "Hagarenes" (in its Anglicized form). Cook and Crone understood the term "Hagarene" to be a reference to Muslims and found it significant that Muslims are not named as such in these works. Arguing from silence, they maintained that this was evidence that Islam and Muslims as we now know them to be could not have existed in this early period. As Neal Robinson has pointed out, the fact that Muslims were exclusively referred to as "Muhammadans" and "Saracens" in European languages until roughly the seventeenth century does not mean that this self-designation among Muslims did not exist before this period.[3] Remarkably, Cook and Crone chose to regard the tendentious Syriac material, whose authenticity has been doubted by scholars, as more reliable than the Arabic sources for recreating the formative period of Islam. Mischievously, they stated that their objective in writing the book was to cater to a fellow "infidel" audience.[4]

Other revisionist works by both academically trained scholars and amateurs impelled by various motives[5] were subsequently published in an attempt to establish that traditional accounts of the rise and consolidation of Islam were founded almost entirely on romantic myths and a complex web of fabrications. The polemical and provocative prose which characterizes much of this revisionist literature has generated the suspicion, not unreasonably, that some of its authors are less than wholly motivated by disinterested scholarship. In any case, none of these revisionists has provided irrefutable evidence for casting doubt on the overall reliability of the early Islamic material at our disposal. The criticism they level at their opponents – that much of their position rests on circular reasoning and is based on tenuous and circumstantial evidence at best, sifted to fit their assumptions – can be redirected at them and with better cause.

The more scholarly of these works in their time generated pointed debate in the Western academy, as might be expected. Scholars who took issue with, for example, Wansbrough's sweeping conclusions, pointed to their highly speculative nature, unsubstantiated by actual documentation.[6] Wansbrough's command of Arabic in critical areas has been shown to be shaky, leading to untenable conclusions. For example, he attempts implausibly to extract the meaning of "a surviving remnant" in the biblical sense from the Qur'anic term baqiyyat. Establishing this meaning is critical to Wansbrough's revisionist thesis which posits that Muslim scholars were influenced by the biblical election theory in their presumed sectarian milieu in eighth-century Iraq, which becomes reflected in the Qur'anic text. However, as Fazlur Rahman has remarked, the term baqiyyat in its Qur'anic context clearly means "good deeds that survive the doer" (cf. Qur'an 18:46; 19:76) and has nothing to do with "a surviving remnant," as maintained by Wansbrough. Other lexemes from the same root adduced by Wansbrough in the same vein are shown by Rahman to have no bearing on the concept of a "surviving remnant."[7] Such an idea, in any case, is completely antithetical to the Qur'anic world-view which talks of human salvation and success in this and the next world not in terms of divine election and membership in a privileged community but in terms of personal piety and individual striving (cf. Qur'an 7:128; 21:105; 33:27, etc.). This will also become apparent in our ensuing discussion regarding the nature and organization of the early Muslim polity.

Newly discovered manuscripts and published works since the late 1970s and 80s, which was the period of floruit for this particular genre of works, have rendered many of the revisionists' premises obsolete.[8] Qur'an manuscripts that have been dated by a number of scholars to the first century of Islam (seventh-century CE) were fairly recently discovered at the Grand Mosque in San'a, Yemen.[9] A number of exegetical works from the Umayyad and early 'Abbasid periods are now available in both manuscript and published forms, attesting to an already vibrant genre of Qur'an commentary (tafsir) by the late seventh century.[10] The earliest published exegetical work available to us now is that of Mujahid ibn Jabr (d. 722).[11] As more early sources have become available and better methodologies of interpreting these texts have developed, the more they have tended to confirm the broad historical contours of the information regarding early Islam known to us from traditional sources.[12] These recent developments have quite effectively served to undermine the radical revisionist thesis expounded by Wansbrough and his cohorts.

THE APPROACH AND METHODOLOGY OF THIS WORK

In its basic orientation and methodology, this book will reconstruct the era of the first three generations of Muslims by using primarily the classical Arabic sources which relate accounts of their lives and thought: biographical works, historical narratives and chronicles, Qur'an commentaries, heresiographical works, and adab (literary-humanistic or belle-lettristic) works, as well as relevant secondary literature. The foundational and normative religious texts – Qur'an and hadith – are, of course, essential sources for this project of reconstruction. The Qur'an as a document contemporaneous with the first generation of Muslims provided the inspiration for the overall moral, ethical, and organizational cast of the early polity, as I have shown in an earlier study.[13] As our following discussion will show, it played a seminal role in shaping a distinctive Muslim communal and historical consciousness from the very beginning which would remain an indelible feature of the polity through the vicissitudes of time. Specific Qur'anic vocabulary launched a specific discourse of piety and, consequently, a certain politics of piety, as will become apparent in subsequent chapters.

For skeptics who would challenge such conclusions, we would offer the following arguments. In addition to extra-Qur'anic textual documentation indicated above, there is considerable internal Qur'anic evidence which points to its provenance in the first/seventh century. The Qur'anic text itself is the best proof for establishing its contemporaneity (both as an oral and written text) with the first generation of Muslims and its central scriptural and inspirational function in this period. For example, a specific kind of Qur'anic vocabulary informs descriptions of the nature and organization of the early Islamic community which would not have been meaningful at a later date. Thus early Islamic discourse on legitimate leadership focused on two Qur'anically-derived concepts: "precedence" or "priority" (sabiqa; less frequently qadam) and "excellence" or "virtue" (fadl/fadila) (cf. Qur'an 9:20; 9:100; 56:10–12; 57:10). The debate predicated on these two concepts was conducted with much passion between the proto-Sunnis and the proto-Shi'a, since it essentially pitted the qualifications of the first caliph Abu Bakr, supported by the former, against those of the fourth caliph 'Ali, supported by the latter. The concept of sabiqa was particularly relevant to the status of Muslims in the first generation, and to a lesser extent, the second, since greater social and moral precedence was accorded to those who had converted to Islam early, emigrated to Medina in the first waves, and participated in the early battles with the Prophet.[14]

By the third century of Islam (ninth-century CE), sabiqa defined as such would no longer have an immediate, contemporary relevance for the faithful but would continue to be invoked in the recollection of these early debates by Muslims in this period. It would stretch one's credulity to suggest that the narratives recording these debates were created ex nihilo as late as the second or third centuries of Islam, cast in terms that could have been meaningful primarily in the milieu of the first generation of Muslims. Rather, one must more sensibly conclude that these concepts must have existed contemporaneously with the earliest Muslims.

Our sources often show that certain social attitudes and legal rulings prevalent after the second/eighth century had veered away from Qur'anic perspectives on these issues. These are important additional considerations in establishing the early codification of the Qur'an. For example, apostasy accompanied by treasonous acts toward the state (ridda/irtidad), was deemed punishable by death by most legal scholars by the late second/eighth century, yet the Qur'an does not mention such a penalty (or any other penalty) for apostasy. Apostasy is not a punishable offense in this world, according to the Qur'an; its judgment is deferred to God in the next world (Qur'an 2:217; 3:86–91; 4:137; 9:67;16:106). Similarly, lapidation for adultery was sanctioned by the legal scholars of this time, although not supported by any Qur'anic verse (cf. Qur'an 24:2). Furthermore, in their recounting of the creation of Adam and Eve, Qur'an commentators in this period tended to place the blame on Adam's wife for the "Fall," in accordance with the Creation account in the Bible. In the Qur'an, however, Adam gets singled out for blame or blamed equally with his wife (cf. Qur'an 7:11–26; 20:115–24). It is also worthy of note that the word *shahid* is used in the Qur'an only to refer to a "legal" or "eye-witness", but by the late eighth century the word was commonly used to refer to "a martyr," as we know from extra-Qur'anic literature. If the Qur'an was indeed the product of a later period, as the revisionists maintain, then its text should have reflected these attitudes and positions prevalent by the early ninth century among scholars, presumably the same scholars who, according to the Wansbroughian thesis, were busy putting the finishing touches on a final scriptural recension. The fact that it does not is powerful internal Qur'anic evidence for its codification in a much earlier period, as the sources consistently maintain.

By the late eighth/early ninth century, dust had begun to settle on the intense debates regarding the caliphate/imamate between the Sunnis and the Shi'a. In many ways, this issue by this period had become the overwhelming concern of Sunni theologians and political thinkers. If the Qur'an were still an open canon at this stage, as alleged by the revisionists, it would have been very easy for Sunni scholars as final arbiters of the text to interpolate into it "verses" that would have clearly settled the case in favor of Abu Bakr and 'Umar in particular. That this obviously did not happen is another robust reason to question the revisionist position.

Furthermore, the accounts concerning the collection of the Qur'an emphasize the role of a woman, Hafsa, the daughter of 'Umar ibn al-Khattab and the wife of the Prophet, in preserving an early form of the text committed to her safekeeping by her father. This manuscript is said to have formed the basis for the 'Uthmanic recension. By the ninth century, women had begun to recede to the sidelines of society. Earlier Near Eastern and Byzantine notions of female propriety and seclusion began to gain ground in Islamic societies by this time and the jurists of this period codified many of these changed perceptions of women's legal and social rights into law, sometimes in downright contradiction of the circumstances that had prevailed in the first century of Islam.[15] It is difficult to imagine these accounts which accord such a central role in preserving the word of God to a woman, however pious and prominent, being manufactured from whole cloth in the ninth century when women were beginning to be relegated to the margins of communal life.

Lastly, the sheer enormity of the task that would have been involved, the herculean degree of collusion that would have been required of various groups, and the massive wall of conspiratorial silence that would have had to be consequently maintained in forging a scriptural text at this late date and maintaining the myth of its early provenance underscore the implausible aspects of this revisionist thesis at the level of basic common sense and credibility. These colluding conspiratorial scholars, of course, could not have stopped here. They would have had to manufacture out of whole cloth, according to this revisionist theory, a voluminous corpus of ancillary literature that would project back into the past the labor of their activities, complete with names of first-century figures, detailed historical backgrounds, a literature of reception of the sacred text, its variant readings and praise for its excellences, etc. etc. – as actually exist! These allegations are all the more fantastical when we consider that the Islamic scholarly tradition on the whole is often quite exceptionally frank in recording dissenting opinions, emanating from various groups and factions in the early period, on various theological and doctrinal matters and practices. Al-Tabari's massive Qur'an commentary and Abu Da'ud's *Kitab al-Masahif* ("The Book of Qur'an Copies") may be considered prime examples of such works. Yet, there is not a whiff of such acts of wholesale forgery taking place in all the variegated reports amassed by these and other authors concerning the collection and interpretation of the Qur'an. Accusations of such suspicious activities cannot be found even among "unfriendly" camps such as the Shi'a, who could be logically expected to exploit such accounts, since their platform would stand to benefit from their propagation. Except for a few extremist Shi'i factions which alleged that 'Uthman's editorial committee had left out some key verses which presumably established 'Ali's claim to the imamate after the Prophet's death, the mainstream Shi'a accept the date and canonical status of the 'Uthmanic codex.

These examples should suffice to show the improbable and idiosyncratic nature of a number of the conclusions arrived at by the revisionists. From a purely heuristic point of view, titillating conspiracy theories often serve to spice up academic debates and force a more critical assessment of certain assumptions or beliefs taken for granted. This has certainly happened. The field has also moved ahead since the 1970s and, as mentioned earlier, newer sources have come to light which have rendered untenable the more outlandish views of the rejectionists.

With regard to the traditional historical and biographical sources, my view of their utility can be summed up as follows. I have basically approached them as the repository of valuable information regarding the early development of the Islamic community, which on careful, judicious scrutiny, yields a comprehensive and realistic account to a considerable extent of the early period. To be sure, the written recording of this information by the eighth and ninth centuries of the Common Era involved the conscious sifting and reworking of earlier oral and written material at the hands of the chroniclers and historians, as is inevitable in such a process. Parts of this recorded information represent straightforward, factual reporting while other parts tendentiously slant the facts and their interpretations to privilege the views of one faction over another. Yet other parts may represent fanciful and embroidered recreations or even fabrications of certain events. The various parts need to be assessed against one another; all have a tale to tell. Taken together and read with a discerning eye, the composite whole gives us a very good idea of the broad historical contours of the development of the Muslim polity in the first three centuries of Islam and of the issues which exercised the minds and imagination of the early Muslims. There is no reason to prevent us from regarding this corpus of material as less than a largely reliable reflection and reconstruction of actual events in their own time as well as their later perception, unless categorically proven to the contrary. This has not happened – despite the assertions of the minority rejectionist camp, which has based its contrarian position on its own rather tendentious reading of the sources and unsubstantiated speculations. The majority of careful and responsible scholars have not found this camp's position unassailably convincing and the scholarly consensus remains that the traditional historical, biographical, and prosopographical works together constitute an invaluable and indispensable source for the study of the formative period of Islam.[16] On this pragmatic note, our project of reconstruction and reappraisal now continues.

The Rise of Islam
and Life of the
Prophet Muhammad

In roughly 610 CE, an approximately forty-year-old man by the name of Muhammad ibn 'Abd Allah began receiving divine revelations in a cave in the mountains overlooking the ancient city of Mecca in the Arabian peninsula. Thus, the sources report, began the prophetic mission of Muhammad, the last in a long line of prophets sent by the one God (Ar. Allah) through time for the guidance of humankind. The emissary, through whom the Prophet received his communications from the divine sphere, commanded him to "Recite/read in the name of your Lord!" (Qur'an 96:1). Extra-Qur'anic tradition names this heavenly messenger Gabriel, the angel entrusted with imparting God's message to His specially chosen apostles on earth. The first word spoken to Muhammad, in Arabic *Iqra'* ("Recite/Read!"), foreshadowed the name *al-Qur'an* given to his collected pronouncements, translated as "the Recitation" and "the Reading."

From all accounts, Muhammad was an unpretentious and self-effacing young man who was given to introspection and long periods of meditation before his call to prophethood. Orphaned before birth and brought up in modest circumstances by his widowed mother, Amina, and after her death by his uncle, Abu Talib, he developed great compassion for those who were similarly economically and socially disadvantaged. Modern scholars have commented on the influence of Muhammad's personal and social circumstances upon his prophetic career.[1] There is no doubt that these early experiences predisposed him to a certain affinity for the downtrodden and the disadvantaged. The Qur'an itself underscores how God's mercy protected him during his orphaned childhood and rescued him from waywardness (Qur'an 93), on account of which he is exhorted to give thanks to his Creator and to be kind to those who are less fortunate. Considerable portions of the Qur'anic text must be read in this manner in the context of the Prophet's life.

Muhammad's early piety and upright character are well documented in the biographical literature. He is said to have earned the title *al-Amin* ("the Trustworthy") on account of his personal integrity and honesty. He formed an alliance, known as *Hilf al-Fudul* ("Alliance of the Virtuous"), with a group of like-minded young men, which required them to come to the aid of those who needed an extra helping hand, such as widows, orphans, slaves, the poor, and the elderly. Even after his call to prophethood Muhammad would fondly remember his membership in this alliance and is said to have remarked that were it to be revived in the Islamic period, he would gladly join it again.[2]

His honesty impressed a wealthy widow by the name of Khadija bint Khuwaylid for whom he worked as a merchant, and she proposed marriage to him. At the age of twenty-five, Muhammad married Khadija, who was about fifteen years his senior. The marriage produced three daughters, and two sons who died in their infancy, and conferred relative prosperity on Muhammad, allowing him to spend more time in seclusion and meditation. Khadija proved to be a devoted soul-mate who provided comfort and valuable counsel throughout their twenty-five-year, monogamous marriage. Although Muhammad would go on to marry other women after her death, the sources make clear that he never forgot her and did not cease to speak affectionately of her.[3]

The young Muhammad, the biographers tell us, was pained by the widespread immorality and social malaise that he saw around him. The sources paint this immediate pre-Islamic period, known in Arabic as *al-Jahiliyya*, as a period of social and moral decline. *Al-Jahiliyya* is commonly translated as "the Age of Ignorance;" ignorance, that is, of the word of God. Scholarly studies have uncovered another layer of meaning which is illuminating of Arab tribal values before Islam. In the pre-Islamic repertoire of virtues and vices, the noun *jahl*, from the same root as *jahiliyya*, was often contraposed to the noun *hilm*. *Hilm* was a prized trait in the well-bred, refined individual and particularly in the leader of the tribe. It is difficult to adequately translate *hilm* by a single English equivalent. The Arabic word refers to a combination of forti-tude, self-control, clemency, and urbanity of disposition, among other qual-ities. *Jahl*, as its antonym, indicates a certain recklessness of behavior and boorishness of disposition. Therefore, it is pertinent to understand the desig-nation *al-Jahiliyya* as also referring to an age of recklessness and disregard for certain moral, spiritual and social values revered by Muslims and other right-eous peoples.[4]

The Qur'an does not suggest that its constellation of values represents a sharp rupture from all *Jahili* values. Rather, it retains and promotes certain values held to be consonant with its world-view, transforms others, and cat-egorically rejects those that are in direct contravention of its own.[5] Thus, as mentioned, Muhammad in the Islamic era continued to speak highly of the *Hilf al-Fudul* because of the values of generosity, hospitality, chivalry and compassion for the poor and the helpless that this pact upheld, values that also fit very well within the Islamic ethical schema.

At first, the Prophet Muhammad preached quietly among relatives, friends, and acquaintances. The first to accept Islam at his behest was, as is universally acknowledged, his wife, Khadija. Among other early converts were his cousin and later son-in-law, 'Ali ibn Abi Talib, his close friend and later father-in-law, Abu Bakr, his freedman and adopted son Zayd ibn Haritha, and others. The Qur'an's clear and powerful message of egalitari-anism and social justice particularly appealed to those who were on the periphery of society. Thus younger people, women, and those from less influential tribes and non-Arab backgrounds were especially attracted to Islam. As the number of converts grew, the Prophet received the divine command to proclaim Islam publicly.

Out in the open, Muslims now became vulnerable to rank hostility from the pagan Meccans and persecution by them. An economic boycott imposed on the Muslims by the Quraysh (the Prophet's tribe) caused unbearable financial and social hardships for the former. To escape these hardships, a small band of Muslims was encouraged by the Prophet to escape to Abyssinia (present-day Ethiopia) whose ruler was the Christian Negus. The Negus' kindness toward the refugees would forever earn him and Christian Abyssinia a special place in the hearts and imagination of Muslims.

A brighter glimmer of hope appeared in roughly the year 620 CE when a small delegation of men and women arrived in Mecca from the neighboring city of Yathrib seeking an audience with the Prophet. News of Muhammad's preaching had reached them and they expressed their receptivity toward this new religious dispensation. Upon meeting the Prophet, they embraced Islam at his hands and swore to defend their new religion in what became known as the Pledge of 'Aqaba in 621. They also invited the Prophet to take up residence among them. During the following two years, Meccan Muslims began to migrate to Yathrib in small waves.

It was during this period shortly before the Migration that Muhammad is reported to have made his night journey to Jerusalem and from there ascended to the heavens. This event is referred to in Arabic as al-Mi'raj ("the ascension") in the hadith and biographical literature and is only obliquely referred to in the Qur'an (53:16–18). When the Prophet spoke of his nocturnal journey the day after the event, some expressed incredulity at his statement, but Abu Bakr is said to have believed in him without hesitation, thereby earning the epithet al-Siddiq ("the Truthful"). This mystical, otherworldly experience would fire the literary imagination of Muslims in the later period. A specific literary genre providing wondrous details about the Prophet's celestial steed, his ascent through the various levels of heaven, and encounter with the prophets of earlier times came into being.[6]

In 622, the Prophet finally received divine permission to migrate himself to Yathrib, which upon his arrival was re-named Madinat al-nabi ("the City of the Prophet"), Medina for short. Two Companions in particular, Abu Bakr and 'Ali, played a critical role in the hijra ("migration"), for which henceforth they would be gratefully inscribed in the collective memory of the polity. On the night of Muhammad's departure, loyal 'Ali slept in the Prophet's bed as his decoy and fooled the pagan Meccans into thinking he had not yet left for Medina. Accompanying Muhammad on his perilous journey toward Medina was his stalwart friend Abu Bakr, who sojourned with him in a cave outside Mecca for two nights to avoid detection by the Meccans in pursuit of them, an event widely believed to be referred to in Qur'an 9:40. Years later, 'Umar ibn al-Khattab, the second caliph, would recognize the cosmic significance of the hijra and declare 622 to be the first year of the new Islamic era.

THE CONSTITUTION OF MEDINA

After moving to Medina, Muhammad drew up a document which detailed the relations primarily between the Muhajirun (Migrant Muslims from

Mecca), the Ansar (lit. "helpers;" sc. the Medinan Muslims), and the Jews of Medina. The articles of this document, known in Arabic as *Sahifat al-Madina* (lit. "the Document of Medina," or, as is more commonly translated into English, as "the Constitution of Medina"), have been preserved in an early biography of the Prophet composed by Ibn Ishaq (d. 767), available to us in the redaction made by his student Ibn Hisham (d. 833). This document is generally accepted by modern scholars as authentic and largely believed to have been drawn up sometime before the Battle of Badr in 624. Among the reasons adduced for its authenticity are its archaic language and the use of terminology, such as "believers" (*al-mu'minun*) rather than "Muslims" that is more common in the early Medinan period. As Montgomery Watt has stated, "No later falsifier, writing under the Umayyads or 'Abbasids, would have included non-Muslims in the ummah, would have retained the articles against Quraysh, and would have given Muhammad so insignificant a place."[7]

In his preface to the terms of the treaty, Ibn Ishaq states that "the Messenger of God (peace and blessings be upon him) wrote a covenant between the Migrant Meccan Muslims and the Medinan Helpers, and included the Jews in it and concluded a pact with them. He guaranteed for them [sc. the Jews] their religion and their property, and conferred on them specific rights and duties."[8] The historical significance of the Constitution is considerable, since it gives us a very clear idea of the nature of the polity and of inter-faith relations envisaged in this early period. Some of the salient articles of this treaty are reproduced below:

> In the name of God, the Merciful, the Compassionate!
>
> This is a writing of Muhammad the Prophet between the believers and Muslims of Quraysh and Yathrib and those who follow them and are attached to them and who strive militarily (*jahada*) with them. They are a single community (*umma*) distinct from other people ... The God-fearing believers are against whoever of them acts wrongfully or seeks an act that is unjust or treacherous or hostile or corrupt among the believers; their hands are all against him, even if he is the son of one of them ... Whosoever of the Jews follows us has the (same) help and support ..., so long as they are not wronged [by him] and he does not help [others] against them.
>
> The peace (*silm*) of the believers is one; no believer makes peace apart from another believer, where there is fighting in the way of God, except in so far as equality and justice between them (is maintained) ... Wherever there is anything

about which you differ, it is to be referred to God and to Muhammad (peace be upon him). The Jews bear expenses along with the believers so long as they continue at war. The Jews of Banu 'Awf are a community along with the believers. To the Jews their religion (*din*) and to the Muslims their religion. (This applies) both to their clients and to themselves, with the exception of anyone who has done wrong or acted treacherously; he brings evil only on himself and on his household. For the Jews of Banu al-Najjar the like of what is for the Jews of Banu 'Awf. For the Jews of Banu al-Harith, the like ... For the Jews of Banu Sa'ida, the like ... For the Jews of Banu Jusham, the like ... For the Jews of Banu 'l-Aws, the like ...

It is for the Jews to bear their expenses and for the Muslims to bear their expenses. Between them, there is help (*nasr*) against whoever wars against the people of this document. Between them is sincere friendship, mutual counsel (*nash wa-nasiha*), and honorable dealing, not treachery. A man is not guilty of treachery through the (act of) his confederate. There is help for (or, help is to be given to) the person wronged ...

Whenever among the people of this document there occurs any incident (disturbance) or quarrel from which disaster for it (the people) is to be feared, it is to be referred to God and to Muhammad, the Messenger of God (peace and blessings be upon him). God is the most scrupulous and truest (fulfiller) of what is in this document.[9]

These salient articles point to six noteworthy features: (1) the military *jihad* in this early period is conceived of as a defensive enterprise in which not only the Muslims (referred to mostly as "believers") engage in but all those who are attached to them and the Prophet, and expressly includes the Jews; (2) the "single community" (*umma wahida*) is a multi-tribal and multi-faith community comprised of the Migrant Muslims, the Medinan Muslims, and the Jews, membership in which is predicated on honorable behavior, mutual cooperation, especially in matters of armed defense, and the avoidance of treachery; (3) the Jews and their clients are allowed to continue to practice their religion unmolested ("to the Jews their religion") as long as they, like the other parties, continue to uphold the terms of the agreement; (4) Jewish–Muslim relations in particular are to be based on honorable dealings with one another, sincere friendship and mutual counsel (*nash wa-nasihah*), and not treachery; (5) Kinship, the basis for individual membership within a tribe, is replaced with religious faith and personal righteous behavior as the bases for inclusion of the individual within the multi-faith *umma*; (6) and, finally,

Muhammad's claim to be God's apostle and thus to be acting in His name as the arbiter of the community is clearly established.

In recent times, there has been renewed attention paid to this highly important document by modern Muslims as an early testament to the pluralist connotations of the term *umma* and to its actual realization in the earliest years of the Muslim community. In its deployment of the term *umma*, the Constitution of Medina clearly reflects Qur'anic understandings of this term. It should be pointed out that the Qur'an uses the term *umma* not only in reference to the community of Muslims but to the communities of Jews and Christians as well, and specifically to refer to the righteous contingent within distinctive religious communities. Thus righteous Muslims constitute an *umma wasatan* ("a middle community;" Qur'an 2:143), while righteous Jews and Christians constitute an *umma muqtasida* ("a balanced community;" 5:66) and *umma qa'ima* ("an upright community;" Qur'an 3:113). The Constitution's emphasis on righteousness and upright behavior as constituting the principal requirements for membership within the Medinan community is thus shaped by the Qur'anic perspective on *umma*.

At the same time, it must be noted, the Constitution also clearly shows the influence of the Arab tribal milieu and culture. Muhammad's newly assumed role as political leader of his community, in addition to his prophetic function, reflects the role of the tribal arbiter (*hakam*), who exercised a certain degree of political authority within his tribe. The style and language of the document also show similarity with those of traditional Bedouin pacts, as has been cogently demonstrated by R. B. Serjeant.[10]

WAR AND PEACE

In the roughly twelve years of the Prophet's Meccan phase, resistance to the Meccan establishment and defense against Meccan persecution was conducted through non-violent means: through peaceful propagation of the message of Islam, the manumission of slaves and other acts of charity, and emigration at first to Abyssinia for some and then to Medina. This situation would change dramatically after the *hijra* or migration to Medina.

About two years after the Prophet's migration to Medina, the situation very soon turned belligerent between the Muslims and the Quraysh. Muhammad received a revelation (Qur'an 22:39–40) permitting the

Muslims to resort to armed combat, although its precise date cannot be determined.[11] Occasional skirmishes that had started earlier in the year culminated in the Battle of Badr outside Mecca on circa 17th of Ramadan, March 2/13, 634. During this battle a small Muslim army of about 300 men fought and triumphed over a larger, more experienced Meccan army of almost 1,000 men. For the early Muslims, this was a powerful vindication of the truth of Muhammad's prophetic mission and the righteousness of their cause. Qur'an 8:17 is understood by the commentators to refer to this event, which corroborates this sense of direct, divine aid for the Muslims by affirming, "You did not slay them, but God slew them, and when you threw, it was not you but God Who threw."

The surviving Meccans retreated, smarting from this unexpected defeat, only to regroup and return the next year with a vastly larger army. They met the Muslim army at Uhud in 625. At first, the Muslims were gaining ground in this battle, but the tide turned against them when a large contingent of Muslim archers, sensing victory at hand, deserted their post in the hope of being able to collect their booty. The Meccan cavalry led by the redoubtable Khalid ibn al-Walid, who would later rise to fame as a stalwart warrior in the caliphal armies, saw its chance and swooped down on the Muslim flank and rear. In the resulting mêlée, over seventy Muslims, including Muhammad's uncle Hamza, were killed, and the Prophet himself was wounded. The remaining Muslim forces at the last minute rallied, causing the Meccans to quit fighting instead of pursuing their earlier partial victory.

In contrast to Badr, Uhud represented a major setback for the Muslims but not a total defeat. The sources point to this event as representing a great trial for the Muslims and an appropriate chastisement for those who had let their greed for material recompense get the better of them. Qur'an 3:166, which states: "What afflicted you on the day when the two hosts met was by the permission of God, and so that He may know the believers and the hypocrites," is understood to refer to this event.

The next major battle known as al-Khandaq took place in 627 and lasted for about two weeks. Meccan resolve to break the back of the Muslims had hardened and a vast army of about 10,000 men was amassed against them. The Jewish tribe of Banu Nadir played a considerable role in the formation of the Meccan confederacy. According to the biographical sources, the Banu Nadir by this time had been exiled to Khaybar from Medina by the Prophet for the following reasons: (1) for non-payment of their contribution to the blood-money that they owed to the tribe of Banu Amir ibn Sa'sa'a on account of existing tribal alliances and for specific events that had transpired earlier at Bi'r Ma'una; and (2) the Prophet's receipt of a divine revelation warning him of a plot against him by the Banu Nadir. Another Jewish tribe, the Banu Qaynuqa' had previously been expelled from Medina after several of its members put to death a Muslim man, who in defending the honor of a Muslim woman, as the sources report, had killed the Jewish man who had insulted and dishonored her. In the prelude to the Battle of al-Khandaq, the Banu Nadir openly came out against the Muslims and succeeded in goading the Banu Ghatafan tribe to join the Meccan confederacy by promising them half the date harvest of Khaybar, on the assumption that they would regain their former lands if the Muslims were defeated. A third Jewish tribe, the Banu Qurayza, publicly feigned neutrality while entering into secret intrigues with the Quraysh and the Banu Ghatafan against the Muslims. These actions of the Jewish tribes, it should be noted, were in violation of the terms of the Constitution of Medina, which had predicated the friendship and alliance between Muslims and Jews on honorable conduct towards one another, avoidance of treachery, and mutual assistance against outside aggression.

The Battle of Khandaq acquires its name from the "trench" (*khandaq* in Persian) that was dug around the city of Medina, an idea attributed to the Companion Salman al-Farisi who knew it as a defensive strategy from his native Persia. The pagan Meccans tried vainly to cross the trench for two weeks but finally gave up. Their large confederacy dissolved and the Meccan troops retreated toward Mecca.

Muhammad now is said to have moved swiftly against the perfidious Banu Qurayza and demanded their unconditional surrender. The Prophet realized the threat they posed and decided that their fate should be determined by a member of one of their confederate tribes, to which plan the Jews acquiesced and all present agreed to abide by the decision. As Ibn Ishaq reports, Sa'd ibn Mu'adh was picked as the judge from the tribe of Aws, which was allied with the Qurayza. Sa'd decreed that all the men of Banu Qurayza should be put to death and the women and children sold into slavery, according to Old Testament decree, which sentence was duly carried out.[12]

A digressionary postscript is necessary here. There has been an unfortunate tendency in our time to see reflected in these early violent encounters the genesis of current Jewish–Arab hostilities in the Middle East, the implication being that these two peoples are destined to be at loggerheads with one another. It is important to remember, however, that these Jewish tribes were punished on account of specific acts of treachery which threatened the safety of the Muslim community, and not on account of their being Jews per se. One may contrapose to the incident involving the Banu Qurayza another report occurring in biographical sources regarding a Jewish woman from Khaybar. She brought the Prophet poisoned meat, which he tasted but did not swallow when he realized it had been poisoned. His companion, Bishr ibn Bara', however, swallowed a morsel of the deadly meat, fell grievously ill, and died soon thereafter. The woman was apprehended and brought to the Prophet who asked her why she had carried out this criminal act. When she replied that she had done so to avenge the defeat of her tribe, Muhammad pardoned her.[13] Admirably, this report has not been exploited for possibly fomenting anti-Jewish sentiment. The actions of one Jewish woman were not generalized to other members of her ethno-religious group. It is also worth remembering that Jews in the pre-modern Islamic world were better integrated into their host societies and more humanely treated there than in Christendom in general, something that could not have happened if Jews as a collectivity were perceived to be ontologically morally deficient by Muslims, as they generally were in pre-modern Europe.[14]

THE TREATY OF AL-HUDAYBIYYA

In 628, Muhammad decided to set out with about 1,400 to 1,600 of his followers to perform the pilgrimage ('umra) at Mecca. The Meccans interpreted this as a belligerent move and dispatched 200 cavalrymen to intercept them. The Prophet learned of this plan and encamped at a place called al-Hudaybiyya just outside the sanctuary of Mecca. The Meccans sent emissaries to the Muslims who conveyed to the latter that they would not be permitted to enter the city that year to perform the pilgrimage. Negotiations ensued between the two sides and finally a peace treaty, known in Arabic as al-sulh or al-hudna,[15] was agreed on by the two sides which guaranteed the cessation of war for ten years. Some of the provisions of the treaty of al-Hudaybiyya were unfavorable to the Muslim side, such as the one which stipulated that if an individual from Quraysh were to come over to the Muslims without permission from his guardian, he was to be sent back to his people, whereas a Muslim defector to the Quraysh would not be sent back. The Prophet later made an exception for Qurayshi women who, upon embracing Islam, escaped to join the Muslims in Medina. He refused to send them back, recognizing the exceptionally delicate situation they would find themselves in if dispatched back to their Meccan relatives.[16]

According to the terms of the treaty, permission was given to the Muslims to perform the pilgrimage the following year. While the negotiations were underway, the Muslims swore a pledge to Muhammad known as "the Pledge of Satisfaction" (Bay'at al-ridwan), sometimes also referred to as the *Pledge of the Tree* (Bay'at al-shajara) on account of having stood under a tree while making the pledge. This pledge figures prominently in accounts of the life of the Prophet and his Companions. Some sources regard it as establishing the greater moral precedence of the Companions who were present at this event over those who were not, since the pledge was regarded as a test of faith for the Muslims in these sorely trying circumstances. Thus the Qur'an commentator Muhammad ibn Jarir al-Tabari (d. 923) reports in his exegetical work that the phrases al-Muhajirun al-awwalun ("the First Migrants") and al-sabiqun al-awwalun ("the First of Those Who Preceded"), referred to in Qur'an 9:100, were understood by several authorities to refer in particular to those Muslims who took the pledge of al-Ridwan.[17] This high estimation of those who took the pledge under the tree is further reflected in a *hadith* in which the Prophet states, "Not one of those who pledged their allegiance under the tree will enter the fire."[18]

The Treaty of al-Hudaybiyya has also received due attention as an important example of the Prophet's willingness to resort to diplomacy and peacemaking with his non-Muslim adversaries, even under conditions that were largely unfavorable to the Muslims. Ibn Hisham reports that despite the Meccan arbitrator Suhayl ibn 'Amr's provocative behavior during the negotiations and the initial objections of a number of the Companions (including 'Umar) to the terms of the treaty, the Prophet exercised self-restraint and eventually persuaded all to come around. Qur'an 48:26 which states, "Then God caused His tranquil grace (sakinatahu) to descend upon His messenger and the faithful and made them firmly adhere to words of piety, for they were worthy and deserving of it," is understood to refer to the events leading up to the treaty and points to the facilitation of the peacemaking efforts on the part of the Muslims through the medium of divine grace.[19]

THE FALL OF MECCA

Within two years, however, in 630, the stipulations of the treaty were violated when members of the Du'il tribe affiliated with the leading members of
Quraysh, especially the tribe of Makhzum, attacked and inflicted losses on
the tribe of Khuza'a who had allied themselves with the Prophet. The
Prophet reacted decisively to this turn of events. He mobilized an army of
about 10,000 men and set out toward Mecca, encamping on the way at Marr
al-Zahran near the city. The Quraysh by now had become quite demoralized.
They had watched the ranks of the Muslims swell over the years, with tribe
after tribe giving their allegiance to the Prophet. Aware that they had violated
the terms of the treaty, the Qurayshi elite no longer wished to put up a resistance. They dispatched Abu Sufyan, a leader of the Banu Umayya who would
later play an important role in Islamic history, to the Muslim camp to declare
their submission to Muhammad. The Prophet accepted this offer from the
Quraysh and declared a general amnesty for all those inside Mecca who
would surrender without resistance.

Within a few days, Muhammad, along with his followers, entered the city
peacefully, quoting from Qur'an 17:81, "The truth has come and falsehood
has vanished. Indeed, falsehood must vanish." This signal event is referred to
in the sources as *al-Fath* or more fully *Fathat Makka*, literally "the Opening" or
"the Opening of Mecca." In a dramatic assertion of the establishment of the
new, monotheistic religious order, the Ka'ba was cleansed of the 300 plus
idols said to have been housed within it. The early biographers al-Waqidi
(d. 822) and al-Azraqi (fl. early ninth century) report that an icon of the
Virgin Mary with the Christ child in her arms and a painting of the patriarch
Abraham as a very old man were spared.[20] Whatever may be the probative
value of this report, its circulation points to the Muslim conviction that
Islam represented the continuation and fulfilment of the Judeo–Christian
tradition rather than a rupture from it.

Very few acts of reprisal took place. On the contrary, the Prophet's
clemency toward those who had earlier shown implacable hostility toward
him or his family and toward Islam in general is frequently recounted and
eulogized in the literature. Muhammad took his cue from the words spoken
by Joseph to his errant brothers, "There shall be no reproach this day. May
God forgive you, for He is the most merciful of the merciful" (Qur'an
12:92). Hind, the wife of Abu Sufyan, who had caused the death of Hamza,

the Prophet's uncle, at the Battle of Badr, was pardoned,[21] as was Habbar ibn al-Aswad, whose pursuit of the Prophet's daughter Zaynab, while attempting to escape from Mecca to Medina, had caused her to have a miscarriage.

Until his death a mere two years later in Medina whence he had retired after remaining for only about twenty days in Mecca, Muhammad remained preoccupied with consolidating his position in the rest of Arabia. The year 630–31 is known in the sources as the year of deputations when various Arab tribes sent delegations to Medina to profess their acceptance of Islam or, at the very least, to signal their acknowledgment of the Prophet's political authority. There was also a delegation of sixty men from the Christians of Najran which was received kindly by the Prophet and allowed to pray in the mosque at Medina over the protests of some. They Christians also concluded a pact with Muhammad, according to which they were granted full protection by Muslims of their churches and their possessions in return for the payment of taxes.[22]

In these last years of his life, Muhammad is also said to have sent invitations to various "countries and kings of the Arabs and non-Arabs."[23] Muslim scholars have understood this act to underscore the universalist nature of Islam and the duty to propagate the faith among non-Muslims, the parallel being drawn with the disciples of Jesus traveling to various parts of the world to proclaim the Gospel.[24] Among the recipients of these missives were the rulers of Byzantium, Alexandria, and Persia. According to the early biographer Ibn Sa'd (d. 845), the Persian emperor Chosroes was enraged by this missive while the two Christian rulers, the Byzantine emperor Heraclius and the Alexandrian governor Muqawqis, received it graciously, recognizing within it a message of religious kinship worthy of at least respect.[25] Heraclius' and Muqawqis' attitude, as depicted in the Islamic sources, confirmed a shared genealogy and world-view between Christianity and Islam and appears to point to an early optimistic belief that Christianity would prove to be an ally, not a rival, in a common religious mission to supplant polytheism with a belief in the one God.

FAREWELL PILGRIMAGE

In 632, the Prophet Muhammad set out to perform the pilgrimage (hajj) in Mecca. It was the final pilgrimage of his life. The sermon he gave at the conclusion of the sacred rites is much cited by Muslims, pre-modern and modern, as an encapsulation of the basic religious ideals and ethical orientation of Islam. A major part of this address is reproduced below:

> O People, listen to me attentively, for I do not know whether after this year I will be among you again. Therefore listen to what I am saying to you very carefully and convey these words to those who could not be present here today.
>
> O People, just as you regard this month, this day, this city as Sacred, so regard the life and property of every Muslim as a sacred trust. Return the goods entrusted to you to their rightful owners. Hurt no one so that no one may hurt you. Remember that you will indeed meet your Lord, and that He will indeed reckon your deeds. God has forbidden you to take usury, therefore all interest obligation shall henceforth be waived. Your capital, however, is yours to keep. You will neither inflict nor suffer any inequity ...
>
> Beware of Satan, for the safety of your religion. He has lost all hope that he will ever be able to lead you astray in big things, so beware of following him in small things.
>
> O People, it is true that you have certain rights with regard to your women, but they also have rights over you. Remember that you have taken them as your wives only as a trust from God and with His permission ...
>
> O People, listen to me in earnest, worship God, say your five daily prayers, fast during the month of Ramadan, and give [a portion of] your wealth in obligatory alms (*zakat*). Perform Hajj if you are able to.
>
> All mankind is from Adam and Eve, an Arab has no superiority over a non-Arab nor a non-Arab any superiority over an Arab; also a white person has no superiority over a black person nor a black person over a white person except through piety and good deeds. Learn that every Muslim is a brother to every Muslim and that the Muslims constitute one fraternity. Nothing shall be legitimate for a Muslim which belongs to a fellow Muslim unless it was given freely and willingly. Do not, therefore, do injustice to yourselves.
>
> Remember, one day you will appear before God and give an accounting of your deeds. So beware, do not stray from the path of righteousness after I am gone. O People, no prophet or apostle will come after me and no new faith will be born. Reason well, therefore, O People, and understand words which I convey to you. I leave behind me two things, the Qur'an and my example, the Sunna, and if you follow these you will never go astray.
>
> All those who listen to me shall pass on my words to others and those to others again; and may the last ones understand my words better than those who listen

to me directly. Be my witness, O God, that I have conveyed your message to your people.

At the conclusion of his farewell speech, the following revelations came to the Prophet, widely regarded as the final verse of the Qur'an:

> ... This day have I perfected your religion for you, completed My favor upon you, and have chosen for you Islam as your religion. (Qur'an 5:3)[26]

Here, Islam may be understood in the universal Qur'anic sense as referring to the primordial monotheistic religion of submission to the one God or in a narrow, confessional sense, which became the predominant understanding.[27]

On his way back to Medina, some Sunni and practically all Shi'i sources report that the Prophet stopped at a place called Ghadir Khumm (the pool of Khumm) where he declared to those gathered there with him "Of whomever I am the *mawla*, 'Ali is his *mawla* too." The Arabic word *mawla* is deliberately left untranslated here since it is the source of divergent interpretations of this prophetic utterance. This word may be variously interpreted as "master," "patron," "friend," "client," and "protégé" among others. The Shi'a consistently interpret *mawla* as occurs in this report as "master" and "patron" and has adoped this *hadith* as one of their principal proof-texts affirming the Prophet's designation of 'Ali as his successor. The Sunni sources which relate this *hadith* understand it as a general acknowledgment on the Prophet's part of his friendship and close relationship with 'Ali and do not read any further significance into it, especially on account of the ambiguity of the critical word *mawla*. Since major authorities like al-Bukhari, Muslim, and Ibn Sa'd do not record this *hadith*, its general reliability is also doubted by Sunni authorities.[28]

Shortly after returning from the pilgrimage, Muhammad contracted an illness from which he would not recover. He had a premonition of his death from one of the last revelations vouchsafed to him in Qur'an 110:1–3, which states, "When God's help and victory come, and you see people embrace God's faith in multitudes, give glory to your Lord and seek His pardon; for He is ever disposed to mercy." His prophetic mission was divinely proclaimed in this verse to have achieved success and nearing its end. During the last few days of his illness, the Prophet appointed Abu Bakr to lead the congregational prayers, an event recorded in all the authoritative Sunni sources. In view of the succession crisis which soon erupted after Muhammad's death, this event took on a signal significance for the proto-Sunnis who read into it the Prophet's endorsement of Abu Bakr as the most qualified to lead the Muslim polity after him. Some

Shi'i sources refer to this event but dismiss it as insignificant without any implications for the caliphate or portray Abu Bakr's appointment as the prayer leader as having occurred without the Prophet's permission or knowledge.[29]

On Monday, June 8, 632, the Prophet Muhammad breathed his last in his home in Medina. With the passing away of the "Seal of the Prophets" (Qur'an 33:40), the age of prophets and prophecy had forever come to a close for Muslims.

REMEMBERING THE PROPHET, THE BELOVED OF GOD

For believing Muslims, the Prophet is the moral exemplar for all time and the best of humankind. The Qur'an (33:21) declares him to be *uswa hasana*, a "beautiful model," who was sent "as a mercy to the worlds" (21:107). God and His Angels invoke blessings upon Muhammad (33:56), and he possessed a noble nature (68:4). Muslims confer on him the epithets *al-Mustafa* ("the Chosen One") and *Habib Allah* ("the beloved of God"), among other honorifics. The sum total of the Prophet's normative speech and actions, collectively known as the *sunna* ("way;" also "custom," "practices") represents the realization of Qur'anic ideals and injunctions and is the second source of law after the Qur'an. When 'A'isha, the Prophet's beloved wife, was asked about his character, she replied simply that his character was the Qur'an.[30]

Later biographical works, like the famous biography of Ibn Hisham (d. 833), tend to cloak the Prophet in an aura of almost supernatural mystique and eclipse to a degree the very human and historical Muhammad. Such a development is not unexpected; with distance, prominent personalities become larger-than-life in the collective imaginary. This is at once a testimony to the love and reverence in which these exceptional individuals are held and to the creative ways in which succeeding generations can tailor the representation of their character and their deeds as befitting their own distinctive milieux. One modern author has described this process in relation to the Prophet thus, "In the course of time, then, short Koranic remarks [regarding the Prophet] were elaborated and spun out into long tales and wondrous legends, which slowly illuminated the outlines of the historical Muhammad with an array of color."[31]

The Qur'an and the *hadith* literature to a certain extent, however, remain important correctives to this aggrandized image of the Prophet. For example, the Qur'an emphasizes Muhammad's mortality (Qur'an 21:34; 39:30) and reprimands him on one occasion for slighting a poor, blind man (80:1–4). The Qur'an (28:56) reminds the Prophet that "You cannot guide on the right path whom you want for it is God who guides" and that he is "no more than a messenger" (Qur'an 3:144). It stresses his dependency on God's will, for "Indeed if We wanted We could take away what We have sent down upon you and then you would not be able to find a protector against us" (17:88). Various *hadiths* from both standard and non-standard compilations detail Muhammad's daily conduct in the domestic sphere, in the mosque, and elsewhere. The vignettes afforded are often folksy and undoctored, yielding the portrait of a man who was at once inspired and charismatic yet vulnerable and down-to-earth. A number of *hadiths* relate that the Prophet occasionally made mistakes in decisions concerning mundane matters, in which he had no particular expertise. In one well-known report concerning date farming, when Muhammad became aware of the consequences of a faulty decision on his part, he remarked to some of the Companions, "I am only human. If I ask you to do something concerning religion, then accept that, but if I ask you to do something on the basis of my personal opinion (*ra'y*), then [remember], I am only human."[32]

The love harbored by Muslims for their very human and idealized Prophet remains undeniable and palpable to this day. Such devotion to the Prophet has inspired a literary genre in Islamic lands known as *dala'il al-nubuwwa* ("proofs of prophethood") and *shama'il* ("characteristics [of the Prophet]") which praise, for example, Muhammad's external and internal beauty and nobility of character. One particularly evocative passage from a well-known *shama'il* work composed by Qadi 'Iyad (d. 1150) runs as follows:

> God has elevated the dignity of His Prophet and granted him virtues, beautiful qualities and special prerogatives. He has praised his high dignity so overwhelmingly that neither tongue nor pen are sufficient [to describe him]. In His book, He has clearly and openly demonstrated his high rank and praised him for his qualities of character and his noble habits. He asks His servants to attach themselves to him and to follow him obediently. It is God – great is His Majesty! – who grants honor and grace, who purifies and refines. He that lauds and praises and grants a perfect recompense ... He places before our eyes his noble nature, perfected and sublime in every respect. He grants him perfect virtue, praiseworthy qualities, noble habits and numerous preferences. He supports his message with radiant miracles, clear proofs, and apparent signs.[33]

Other passages in the *shama'il* praise Muhammad's specific attributes, such as his fortitude in the face of tribulations, the gentleness of his disposition, his humility, love of poverty, and aversion to ostentatiousness, which are to be emulated by later generations of believers. Many Muslims in the modern period emphasize in particular the message of social justice and gender egalitarianism that they discover in Muhammad's preaching and conduct, a message which has a special resonance in our contemporary world.[34] Some Muslims, like the Sufis, have declared the Prophet to be "The Perfect Man" (*al-insan al-kamil*).[35] During celebrations of his birthday (*mawlid al-nabi*), an observance that began fairly late, a famous poem known as the "Mantle Ode," composed by the thirteenth-century Berber poet al-Busiri (d. 1294), is often recited. The opening lines of the poem pay homage to the Prophet's perfection:

> He is the one whose interior and exterior were made perfect,
> Then the Creator of men chose him as a beloved friend.
> Far removed [is he] from having any partner in his good qualities,
> For in him the essence of goodness is undivided.[36]

One imagines the Prophet himself would have disclaimed the honorific of "the Perfect Man," for perfection belongs to God alone. Later theologians would also ascribe infallibility to him and the other prophets. These trends, although perfectly understandable and perhaps even inevitable through the passage of time, tend to mask the earlier, more accessible Muhammad who is more of a realistic role model for mere mortals than the later, highly idealized Muhammad. But the "array of color" that progressively cloaked the historical persona of the prophet of Islam brings into sharp relief the loyalty and deep affection that his memory continues to inspire among the Muslim faithful.

In the post-Prophetic era, the first generation of Muslims inherited the formidable task of continuing to consolidate the Islamic polity and preserve and disseminate the apostolic message vouchsafed to them. We now turn to an account of the Prophet's close associates and followers, the *Sahaba* or the Companions, who were especially charged with carrying out this task.

The Issue of Succession to
the Prophet

It is accepted by the majority of Muslims that the Prophet left no specific instructions for the selection of his successor nor did he so designate any specific Companion. This has become the axiomatic position of the Sunnis (*ahl al-sunna*; broadly glossed as "people who adhere to the custom of the Prophet"), who today comprise about 85–90 per cent of the world's approximately 1.3 billion Muslims. The rest of the Muslims belong to the Shiʿa, short for *shiʿat ʿAli* ("the partisans of ʿAli"), who came over time to subscribe to the position that Muhammad had designated ʿAli ibn Abi Talib, his cousin and son-in-law, to be his immediate successor on the basis of blood-kinship. According to the Shiʿa, ʿAli, furthermore, was wrongfully prevented from assuming the caliphate by the majority of the Prophet's Companions. This difference of view over the issue of succession became the primary distinction between the two principal denominations of Islam, based at first on a political disagreement which would acquire theological dimensions in the course of time.

Sunni sources overwhelmingly maintain that the Companions were driven by the exigencies of the situation to hastily select a successor to the Prophet. The situation was dire indeed in the immediate aftermath of his death. Several Arab tribes in south and central Arabia had risen up in revolt against the government in Medina, assuming that their loyalty to the government had lapsed on the death of the Prophet. ʿUmar, later to be recognized as the principal architect in many ways of the Islamic polity after the death of Muhammad, hastily called together an assembly of the prominent Muhajirun (Meccan Migrants) and Ansar (Medinan Helpers) at a portico (*saqifa*) in Medina. This critical event henceforth became known as the incident of the Saqifa. According to most accounts, one prominent Migrant – 'Ali – was missing at this conclave. The usual explanation given for 'Ali's absence was that he was occupied with compiling a written copy (*mushaf*) of the Qur'an and, as a blood-relative of the Prophet, was also detained by the arrangements for his funeral. However, 'Ali is said to have had his share of supporters at the meeting, who advanced on his behalf his claim to the office of the caliph on the basis of his moral excellences.[1]

During this event, some of the Ansar voiced the suggestion that the Muslims should select one leader (*amir*, which may also be understood as "counselor") from among them and another from among the Muhajirun. 'Umar is said to have reacted strongly against this suggestion, saying, "Two swords in one scabbard, that will never do!" Then he took Abu Bakr by the hand and asked the crowd to ponder the "verses of the cave" (*ayat al-ghar*, Qur'an 4:90), understood by Sunnis to refer to Abu Bakr and his sojourning in the cave with the Prophet on their way to Medina in 622. 'Umar asked:

> To whom do these three [verses] refer? "When he said to his companion" – who was his companion? "When the two were in the cave" – who were the two? "Indeed God is with us" – with whom?[2]

'Umar then gave his allegiance to Abu Bakr and advised the assembled people to do the same, upon which "the people proclaimed their allegiance in a most seemly and decorous manner."[3]

Abu Bakr's inaugural address as the first caliph must rank as one of the most important speeches in the annals of Islamic history. The famous historian and exegete al-Tabari (d. 923) in his magisterial universal history records a transcript of this address made toward the end of the Saqifa episode when Abu Bakr got up to address the Ansar in the mosque at Medina, who had at first opposed his nomination as the caliph. This address presents in microcosm the main issues at stake in this period and the principal criteria invoked to rank the qualifications of the potential caliphal candidates. Abu Bakr commences by reminding the Medinan Helpers that God had bestowed special distinction upon the early Meccan Migrants on account of the fact that they had been the first to believe in the Prophet's mission, to place their faith in him, and offer him consolation while patiently bearing the afflictions visited on them as a consequence of their fidelity. Furthermore,

> they are the first to worship God on earth and to place their faith in Him and His messenger. They are his [the Messenger's] closest associates and his kinfolk and are the most entitled to this matter [sc. the caliphate] after him. Only the wrong-doer opposes them in that. O gathering of the Ansar, [you are] those whose excellence in religion cannot be denied or whose great precedence in Islam cannot be denied. It pleased God to make you helpers of His religion and His Messenger. He made his [the Messenger's] emigration to you and from among you are the majority of his wives and his Companions. After the first emigrants, there is no one else of your status in our estimation. Thus we are the rulers (al-umara') and you are the assistants (al-wuzara'). We do not fail to consult you with regard to political matters and we do not adjudicate matters without you.[4]

An early ninth-century source, the *Risalat al-'Uthmaniyya* ("The Treatise of the 'Uthmaniyya"), gives a variant account of this address. This work, composed by the celebrated ninth-century belle-lettrist 'Amr ibn Bahr al-Jahiz (d. 869), records the views of an early faction called the 'Uthmaniyya on the caliphate. The views of this group had a considerable bearing on the formation of the classic Sunni position on this topic. In the version preserved in this work, Abu Bakr counsels the Medinan Muslims thus:

> "You must be Godfearing, for piety is the most intelligent practice and immorality is the most foolish. Indeed I am a follower, not an innovator: if I perform well, then help me, and if I should deviate, correct me. ... O gathering of Helpers, if this matter [sc. the caliphate] is deserved on account of inherited merit and attained on account of kinship, then the Quraysh is more noble than you on account of inherited merit and more closely related than you [to the Prophet]. However, since it is deserved on account of moral excellence in religion, then those who are foremost in precedence from among the Emigrants are placed ahead of you in the entire Qur'an as being more worthy of it compared to you."[5]

Both versions of the address foreground the Qur'anic attribute of precedence or priority which confers moral excellence on the individual. In the case of the caliphal candidate, greater precedence conferred greater moral excellence on him and established his greater right to the office. In al-Jahiz's version, the pre-Islamic valorization of inherited merit (*hasab*) in determining the moral and social standing of the individual is clearly decried in favor of the new Qur'anic valuation of the individual based on his or her moral excellences and track record of service to Islam. There is strong evidence that al-Jahiz wrote his *Risalat al-'Uthmaniyya* before 820 CE. This early treatise thus provides valuable evidence that a discourse on leadership based on the Qur'anic paradigm of precedence and moral excellence was already clearly formulated before the ninth century.

'Umar's use of Qur'anic reference (4:90) to Abu Bakr's sojourning in the cave with the Prophet in the midst of great danger, which confirmed Abu Bakr's exceptional fealty and closeness to the Prophet and consequently his stronger credentials for the office of the caliph is stressed in several sources. Thus al-Jahiz discusses in his *Treatise* how the "verse of the cave" was invoked as a proof-text in this early discourse on leadership to underscore Abu Bakr's personal courage and loyalty to the Prophet in the service of Islam.[6] Qur'anic attestation of this type was understood to provide irrefutable testimony for Abu Bakr's unparalleled precedence among the Companions, and thus his greater qualification for the caliphate.

EARLY TENSION BETWEEN KINSHIP AND INDIVIDUAL MORAL EXCELLENCE

The disagreement between the supporters of Abu Bakr and 'Ali is conventionally regarded as being based on the incompatibility of the criterion of kinship with that of personal moral excellence. It is part of received wisdom to maintain that 'Ali's earliest supporters pressed his claim to the caliphate by emphasizing his blood-kinship with the Prophet and his prior designation as Muhammad's successor. Yet a careful examination of the available diverse sources allows us to question this conventional narrative.

For instance several, especially Shi'i, sources maintain that when Abu Bakr entered the mosque at Medina after having been appointed caliph, twelve men from among the Meccan Migrants rose up one after another to proclaim the excellences of 'Ali, thereby affirming his greater right to the caliphate.[7] According to the Mutazili pro-'Alid scholar, Ibn Abi 'l-Hadid (d. 1257), the supporters of 'Ali were the first to put into circulation reports that praised his unique virtues immediately after the death of the Prophet. In response, Abu Bakr's partisans, who are sometimes named in the early sources as the Bakriyya,[8] are said to have generated reports of their own which advanced the merits of their candidate. Ibn Abi 'l-Hadid further makes the trenchant observation that the existence of this discourse based on excellences and precedences proves that the Prophet could not have designated anyone, for such a designation would have rendered unnecessary these debates on the merits of Abu Bakr and 'Ali, as recorded even in Shi'i sources.[9]

A careful scrutiny of the sources leads us to believe that contrary to what became the standard position of the Shi'a in the later period, the early supporters of 'Ali, in tandem with the early supporters of Abu Bakr, stressed the greater excellences and precedence of 'Ali in the debate over who should assume leadership of the polity rather than his blood-kinship with Muhammad. An emphasis on kinship at this early stage would, after all, have flown in the face of the Qur'anic espousal of individual merit and personal piety in establishing a person's moral and social standing and would have been rightly perceived as a throwback to the Jahili period. In the pre-Islamic period, the key terms *nasab* ("lineage") and *hasab* ("inherited merit") determined the individual's status in tribal society.[10] *Hasab* in particular connoted not so much the individual's personal accomplishments but rather the sum-total of achievements attributed to the ancestors of the individual, the individual serving as a repository of these collective achievements.[11] Stated so baldly, this concept runs counter to the Qur'anic emphasis on merit (*al-fadl*), which individuals earn only on account of their personal deeds and accomplishments. The Qur'anic view, after all, had deliberately challenged the older, pre-Islamic notions of both kinship and inherited merit, notions which were to survive, however, into the Islamic period. Pious Islamic ideals of egalitarianism and pre-Islamic notions of hierarchical privilege would remain at loggerheads for much of the formative period of Islam. The influence of ancient Greek and Persian thought with their emphasis on hierarchy and social differentiation would eventually leave its mark on the Islamic polity starting in the ninth century and attenuate to a considerable extent this early egalitarian thrust.[12]

In his political treatise, the previously mentioned al-Jahiz eloquently underscores this tension between the accrual of excellence on account of blood relationship to the Prophet and the attainment of excellence through individual exertion and performance of meritorious deeds. He points to the error of the first position, which fosters objectionable pride in one's lineage, contrary to the Islamic spirit of egalitarianism. Thus, the man who is a blood relative may see this fact alone, he maintains, as "absolving him from the requisites of knowledge and deed." Shiʻi insistence on regarding kinship as the indisputable basis for the most excellent leadership runs counter to divine injunctions such as "To humans belong only what they strive for" (Qurʼan 53:37–39), asserts al-Jahiz.[13]

Significantly, some early Shiʻi reports preserve for us as well the tension between the religious egalitarianism advocated by the Qurʼan and the notion of inherited merit (hasab) on account of kinship with the Prophet. One early report from the eighth Shiʻi Imam (religious leader) ʻAli al-Rida (d. 818) states that the Prophet counseled his associates, "Come to me with your individual works and not with your kinships or collective [tribal] accomplishments," in exegesis of the verse, "When the trumpet is blown, there will be no kinships and you will not ask one another" (Qurʼan, 23:101).[14]

The early Shiʻi exegete, ʻAli ibn Ibrahim al-Qummi (d. after 919), also maintained that Qurʼan 23:101 took issue with those who took pride in their pedigrees.[15] He quotes the sixth Imam Jaʻfar al-Sadiq (d. 765), in exegesis of this verse, who affirms that no one will advance on the Day of Judgment except by their deeds. Al-Qummi affirms that this understanding is further in accordance with the following prophetic statement:

> O people! Arabic is not a father or grandfather but rather a spoken tongue. Who-ever speaks in it is an Arab except that [all of] you are the children of Adam and Adam is of dust. By God, an Abyssinian slave who obeys God is better than a Qurayshi chieftain who disobeys God. Indeed the most honorable among you is the most righteous among you.[16]

These trends are corroborative of our contention that the earliest partisans of ʻAli (or at least a significant part of them) are not to be regarded as legitimists, that is, advocates of succession to the Prophet on the basis of blood-kinship. These early partisans appear to have genuinely believed that ʻAli was the bet-ter candidate in terms of his track record of service to Islam and personal qualities, on account of which he should have been recognized as the most excellent member of the polity and thus entitled to its leadership. This would be in accordance with the Qurʼanic vision of the righteous inheriting the earth, as in Qurʼan 24:55, which states, "God has promised those among you who believe and perform righteous deeds to inherit the earth …"[17] Some of the early supporters of ʻAli went on to accept Abu Bakr as the practical choice of the community, like the Zaydis with their acceptance of the imamate of the less excellent candidate (*mafdul*), while continuing to revere 'Ali for his exceptional personal qualities.

The proto-Shi'a appear to have adhered to such Qur'an-based egalitarian views through the early Umayyad period.[18] Kinship became the cornerstone of Shi'i doctrine sometime later during the Umayyad period since the Umayyads had based their own political legitimacy on kinship to the Prophet. The 'Alids had to respond to these claims in a deliberate appeal to pre-Islamic tribal values. Their insistence on kinship as establishing the legitimacy of political and religious authority would thus become particularly strident in response to similar Umayyad claims and eventually become incorporated as part of fundamental Shi'i doctrine.[19] How broad was the appeal of kinship initially is not easy to determine due to the paucity of early Shi'i sources at our disposal.

There is indication that such a claim was regarded with suspicion by some as being an idea of foreign importation and alien to indigenous Arab notions of appointing leaders. One report states that such an accusation was made against the Persian Companion Salman al-Farisi, whose ethnic heritage is supposed to have predisposed him to blood-succession. The well-known Shi'i scholar Abu Ja'far al-Tusi (d. 1067) reports that Salman had been accused by his contemporaries of advocating the adoption of the Persian custom of dynastic rule or succession, regarded as an alien concept by Arab Muslims.[20] Even in the pre-Islamic period, although lineage determined the Arab's overall identity and inter-tribal relations, the internal tribal organization was informed by more or less an egalitarian spirit. Political authority within an individual tribe tended to be decentralized and may be described as being more democratic-consultative rather than authoritarian in its orientation. Islam reinforced this basic tendency in the early period.

The growing importance of kinship becomes patently clear, however, in the later literature of excellences (*manaqib*) on 'Ali, which records reports testifying to his merits. Qur'anically inspired notions of egalitarianism progressively yielded space (but never completely acquiesced) to the old Arab notions of *hasab* ("inherited merit") and *nasab* ("lineage"). The resurgence of these two notions would shape the later Shi'i valorization of 'Ali's blood-kinship with the Prophet, which established his unparalleled claim to the caliphate/imamate. This development was in accordance with the overall societal trend after the eighth century toward increasing Arabization on the one hand, and, on the other, the adoption to a considerable extent of Persian and Greek concepts of social hierarchy, as previously mentioned.

WHY DID THE PROPHET NOT INDICATE A SUCCESSOR?

The above question is frequently posed in discussions concerning succession to the Prophet. Sunni sources uniformly affirm that Muhammad did not name a successor for himself; some early pro-'Alid sources appear to concur. Classic Shi'i sources from after the eighth century, however, resolutely maintain that the Prophet had explicitly designated 'Ali as his successor.[21] Speculation on why Muhammad did not indicate a successor, as the Sunni majoritarian position affirms, has led a few modern scholars to suggest that early Islam was primarily an apocalyptic movement and that the Prophet and his followers expected the world to end in their lifetimes.[22] This argument is hardly convincing. The early Meccan chapters of the Qur'an do warn of an impending Day of Judgment and their powerful imagery often conveys a sense of great urgency. But the Medinan chapters go on to provide broad moral guidelines and specific injunctions for leading an orderly social existence and building a cohesive community of believers, with much of the eschatological urgency considerably mitigated.

We would suggest, rather, that the succession issue was not a matter of Qur'anic concern nor broached by the Prophet before his death because matters concerning political rule and administration were not considered to be within the purview of divine revelation and/or prophetic counsel. Political administration was a temporal matter and could be devised, changed, and launched according to the dictates of human deliberation and public utility. The Qur'an clearly establishes the need to maintain law and order on earth, contain chaos and prevent "corruption on earth" (for e.g., Qur'an 2:11, 27, 205; 7:56, 85; 8:73; 11:116, etc.). Moral values were expected to be upheld in both the public and private spheres; there was no artificial demarcation between these two spheres in the modern post-industrial Habermasian sense. Beyond offering broad moral and ethical guidelines for proper political conduct, no particular mode of governance was mandated, however, in Qur'anic prescriptions. Our following discussion of the era of the Rightly-Guided Caliphs and their legacy establishes their flexible and experimental, often very personal, approach to political governance, which was a consequence of the lack of a presumed religiously mandated "blueprint" for a specific form of "Islamic government." This is a topic to which we will return in the concluding chapters.

The Age of the Rightly-Guided Caliphs

ABU BAKR, THE FIRST CALIPH

Although Abu Bakr ruled for only two years (632–34), his tenure as caliph was decisive for the community, suddenly bereft of its prophet and leader. Insurrection had broken out in parts of Arabia, led in some cases by false prophets such as Musaylima from the tribe of Banu Hanifa and Tulayha from the tribe of Banu Asad. These tribes refused to pay allegiance to the new government in Medina, assuming that their fealty to it, conceived more in political rather than religious terms, had lapsed with the death of the Prophet. Consequently, they withheld the payment of *zakat*, the obligatory alms which is one of the five main pillars of duties binding upon the believer. Abu Bakr was resolutely determined to quell these insurrections. With Medina, Mecca, and Ta'if solidly aligned with him, he moved quickly to bring the rebel tribes to heel in what became known as the *ridda* wars. *Ridda* here does not refer to apostasy, as has been unfortunately translated in a number of English-language works, but rather to political rebellion. In fact, these rebel tribes had not renounced their allegiance to Islam. Instead they had declared that with the death of the Prophet, their allegiance to Medina had also ceased since their agreement was with Muhammad himself and represented a personal and exclusively political compact.

In response to the refusal of the rebellious tribes to pay their *zakat* to Medina, Abu Bakr stated firmly that even if only the hobble of a young camel were withheld in payment of zakat, he would fight those dissenters. The Muhajirun and the Ansar protested this decision, saying that the Prophet had announced that the utterance of the basic creedal statement (shahada), "There is no god but God," alone made the lives and property of the believer inviolate.[1] Abu Bakr said, however, that the hadith continued with "illa bi-haqqiha" ("except for what is due upon it").[2] All then acknowledged, according to the sources, that Abu Bakr had spoken the truth. Our ninth-century polymath al-Jahiz comments that Abu Bakr thereby taught the people what they did not know and steered them toward the correct understanding of the Prophet's statement.[3] Knowledge, after all, was an essential ingredient in the repertoire of virtues possessed by the worthy successor to the Prophet; in fact, "his strongest natural trait should be his intellect ('aql)," asserts al-Jahiz.[4] The sources report that Abu Bakr was regarded as the most knowledgeable among the Companions particularly concerning genealogy of the Arab tribes and that he was "the most quoted concerning their virtues and their vices."[5] This was but one aspect of Abu Bakr's practical knowledge that stood the Muslims in good stead during this extremely critical period.[6]

Within a year of the Prophet's death, the rebellious tribes were dealt a crushing defeat under the leadership of Khalid ibn al-Walid, the indomitable military commander during and after the Prophet's time. A significant contingent of Abu Bakr's forces was comprised of the ahl al-qurra', usually translated as the "Qur'an reciters"/"readers," but whose exact identity continues to be debated.[7] The most important victory was won at the Battle of 'Aqraba in 633 against the powerful Banu Hanifa and its false prophet, Musaylima. Soon thereafter practically all of Arabia was brought under the control of Medina. For this remarkable feat in achieving unity in such a short period of time, Abu Bakr has been gratefully lionized in the collective memory of the polity. Thus, a laudatory report is recorded by al-Khazin al-Baghdadi (d. 1341), author of a well-regarded Qur'an commentary, which relates that there was no one more excellent than Abu Bakr born after the Prophet, and that in preserving the unity of the community Abu Bakr had even attained the position of "a prophet from among the prophets."[8]

During Abu Bakr's tenure as caliph the campaigns of conquest began that would within a few decades extend the borders of the Islamic realms to an unimagined extent. These campaigns began in the wake of the ridda wars, which had caused a great deal of disruption of trade in the Arabian peninsula, and new sources of income had to be found at their end. Khalid ibn al-Walid's great success at 'Aqraba also caused him to cast a covetous eye toward the neighboring rich Sassanian territories, where Arab tribesmen since before the advent of Islam had been conducting raids. The sources suggest that Abu Bakr may not have been fully aware or fully approving of Khalid's decision to make excursions into neighboring Sassanian territory, but once underway he appears to have acquiesced in it. Abu Bakr also allowed forays into Byzantine territories, especially in southern Palestine, under the command of the seasoned Qurayshi chieftains 'Amr ibn al-'As and Yazid ibn Abi Sufyan. On both the Sassanian and Palestinian fronts, he forbade the inclusion of the former *ridda* tribesmen who had risen in revolt against Medina in the army.[9] The Arab army in Palestine, once joined by Khalid and his forces recalled from Iraq, decisively routed the Byzantine army at the Battle of Ajnadayn in 634, shortly after Abu Bakr's death.

As the first of the Rightly-Guided Caliphs, Abu Bakr is much lauded in the sources for his simple and abstemious lifestyle, his legendary generosity, and unwavering devotion to Muhammad, whose father-in-law he became when 'A'isha, his daughter, married the Prophet. At first Abu Bakr lived in a modest house in Sunh, a suburb of Medina, but then moved into the town itself for the sake of convenience. Under Abu Bakr the collection of the Qur'anic verses is said to have begun, prompted by 'Umar who was alarmed by the death of a large number of Qur'an reciters during the *ridda* wars. This preliminary effort to put together a written compilation of Qur'anic verses was entrusted to Zayd ibn Thabit, the Prophet's secretary. This early collection was then given to 'Umar after the death of Abu Bakr.[9]

Abu Bakr's official title was *Khalifat Rasul Allah* ("the Successor to the Messenger of God"), signifying his status as the only direct successor to Muhammad.[10] Among the honorifics conferred upon him were *al-Siddiq*, "the Truthful," and *al-'Atiq*, "the Manumitter," the former because he had readily believed Muhammad's account of his nocturnal journey to the Heavens and the latter on account of the large number of slaves he had set free in Mecca. Before his conversion, Abu Bakr had been a very wealthy merchant. On becoming Muslim, he is said to have given away most of his wealth valued at 40,000 dirhams in charity before the Migration. The Prophet expressed fulsome admiration for such generosity by remarking, "The most gracious of people toward me with regard to his wealth and his companionship is Abu Bakr …"[11]

Historical and *hadith* works praise Abu Bakr for his sojourning in the cave with Muhammad for three days as his faithful companion on their perilous journey from Mecca to Medina. Even early pro-'Alid authors such as 'Abd al-Razzaq al-San'ani (d. 827) included *hadiths* praising Abu Bakr for his role in this critical event.[12] The Companion Sa'id ibn al-Musayyab quoted the Prophet as saying, "If I were to choose an intimate friend (*khalil*) I would have chosen Abu Bakr as an intimate friend ..."[13] Some Sunni scholars stress that the Arabic term *khalil* is used only in reference to Abu Bakr from among the Companions, underscoring the unusually close bonds of friendship between Abu Bakr and Muhammad as exemplified in the "cave episode." The four-teenth-century Mamluk scholar Ibn Taymiyya (d. 1328) commented that the cave verse established the exceptional nature of Abu Bakr's companionship (*suhba*) and proved his unparalleled superiority over the other Companions on account of the role he played during the *hijra*.[14]

During his last illness leading to his death in 634, he was nursed by his daughter 'A'isha. As requested by Abu Bakr himself, he was laid to rest in 'A'isha's apartment close to where the Prophet lay buried.

'UMAR IBN AL-KHATTAB, THE SECOND CALIPH

Before his death, Abu Bakr had designated 'Umar as his successor, a decision which apparently met with little resistance from the larger community. There was good reason for this general acceptance. According to the criteria of precedence and excellence, 'Umar ranked very high indeed due to his record of early and prodigious service to Islam and its prophet. 'Umar's immediate goals as caliph included the consolidation of gains made by his pre-decessor and to build on them. This he proceeded to do with great resolution and considerable brilliance, transforming the fledgling polity that he inher-ited very nearly into a major world power upon his death ten years later.

Some Western scholars have expressed the opinion that 'Umar was to early Islam what St. Paul of Tarsus was to early Christianity. The analogy is not misplaced. Both went through dramatic conversions which turned them from persecutors of their later co-religionists into avid practitioners of their new faith. Both men left an indelible, personal stamp on the nature of their faith communities in the formative period and charted a course for them that proved to be practically irreversible. Both had strong, assertive personalities and instituted measures that were not always well-liked during their life-times. One author's assessment of Paul's overall legacy would hold *mutatis mutandis* for 'Umar's as well: "He brought intellectual stiffening to the church – oaken ribs of closely reasoned thought to strengthen the Fisherman's barque against the storms ahead."[15]

'Umar, above all, was a bold innovator and a pragmatic, yet grand, visionary. His reign in particular is upheld as paradigmatic by later generations for a number of important reasons. Primary among these reasons is the general consensus among the majority of Muslims that 'Umar best exemplified and implemented the moral, social, and political objectives envisioned by the Qur'an for the post-prophetic Muslim polity. This evaluation of 'Umar and his far-sighted policies is captured in a statement attributed to the Prophet, "If God had wished that there be a prophet after me, it would have been 'Umar."[16]

The second caliph rose to prominence within the fledgling Muslim community in Mecca immediately after his dramatic conversion in circa 618. Before his conversion, 'Umar had been one of the most implacable enemies of Muhammad and his mission. He was devoted to the pagan cult centered on the Ka'ba and blamed Muhammad for dividing the loyalties of the Quraysh by questioning their ancient religion. As the sources relate, things came to a head when he was informed one day that his sister Fatima and her husband had secretly converted to Islam. In fury, he headed for their home, where he heard them reciting Qur'anic passages under the instruction of a poor Muslim friend named Khabbab. On hearing his irate voice at the door, Khabbab hid from 'Umar. The latter entered and extracted an admission from his sister and her husband that they had indeed become followers of Muhammad. Upon hearing this 'Umar struck his brother-in-law. When his sister sprang up to defend him, he struck her as well and drew blood, at the sight of which he was stricken with remorse. Sensing the change in his mood, Fatima urged 'Umar to read the Qur'anic chapter she had been reciting, which he proceeded to do after having washed himself. Ibn Hisham describes what happened next:

> And when he had read a passage he said: "How beautiful and how noble are these words!" When Khabbab heard this he came out from his hiding-place and said: "'Umar, I have hope that God hath chosen thee through the prayer of His Prophet, whom yesterday I heard pray: 'O God, strengthen Islam with Abu l-Hakam the son of Hisham or with 'Umar the son of Khattab!'" "O Khabbab," said 'Umar, "Where will Muhammad now be, that I may go to him and enter Islam?"[17]

'Umar then departed for the Prophet's residence and declared his intention to become a Muslim. "God is Most Great," exclaimed the Prophet, in such a way that every man and woman in the house knew that 'Umar had entered Islam, and they all rejoiced.[18]

The fortunes of early Islam did change to a measurable degree after 'Umar's "defection" to the Muslim side. As the Prophet had predicted, Muslims were emboldened by the addition of such a strong individual to their camp, which enabled them to more publicly bear witness to their faith. 'Umar's reputation as a formidable defender of Islam and the Prophet would be proved over and over again in the course of Muhammad's lifetime. 'Umar would also acquire a not undeserved reputation, particularly in contrast to the mild-mannered and avuncular Abu Bakr, for being rather stern and fear-inspiring in his demeanor. Muhammad is said to have once light-heartedly remarked that "even Satan flees from 'Umar!"[19] A combination of these traits, however, on the whole, stood him and the community in good stead in the difficult days following the Prophet's death.

'Umar and his establishment of the diwan

One of the major innovations undertaken by 'Umar during his tenure as caliph was the institution of the state register of pensions known as the *diwan* (a loan-word from Persian), in order to effectively and equitably disburse the increasing revenues pouring into the state treasury. It is well known that when this official register of pensions was first established by 'Umar in ca. 634, the precedence (Ar. *sabiqa*) of each Muslim became an important criterion in determining the amount of stipend he or she would be awarded. Those who were among the earliest converts to Islam and had fought in the early battles of Islam were given larger stipends.[20] Although the *diwan* was organized according to tribal affiliation, it was the principle of precedence which determined the overall function of the *diwan*.[21]

Kinship to Muhammad, by marriage and blood, was also a point of consideration in the allotment of stipends, but in conjunction with precedence. Thus the Prophet's wives, who were awarded generous pensions,[22] are counted among the early converts to Islam from among the Migrants and the Helpers and, therefore, in themselves and through their closeness to Muhammad, possessed both precedence and moral excellence. The Andalusian scholar Ibn Hazm (d. 1064) underscores this most forcefully when he states that after all the prophets, the wives of the Prophet are the most excellent of people, placing them even before Abu Bakr in rank.[23] Reports which suggest that blood-kinship in itself was a priority in the setting up of the *diwan* are definitely spurious and must be regarded as having originated later with the gradual forefronting of kinship among both the Sunnis and the Shi'a. Of this ilk are the reports which state that al-'Abbas, the uncle of the Prophet, a notoriously late convert to Islam, headed the register of pensions.[24]

There is evidence of early resistance to 'Umar's official recognition of precedence in this manner, considered to be tantamount to showing "preference" for some Companions over others and thus militating against the Qur'anic notion of the complete equality of all believers. An early author, Abu 'Ubayd al-Qasim ibn Sallam (d. 839), states that both Abu Bakr and 'Ali believed in complete equality in the disbursement of pensions while 'Umar subscribed to a preferential system "based on precedences and indispensable service to Islam."[25] Abu 'Ubayd further reports that Abu Bakr declined to rank people in terms of their excellences, demurring that "their excellences were known to God" and that the system of pensions was better served by the principle of egalitarianism.[26] Another very early authority, Abu Yusuf (d. 798) adds that when 'Umar assumed the caliphate, he refused to place those who had fought against the Prophet on the same level as those who had fought with him, and, therefore, awarded larger stipends to "the people of precedences and priority."[27]

In his discussion of the *diwan*, the well-known fifteenth-century historian al-Maqrizi (d. 1442) gives us an idea of how its underlying principle became a matter of debate among the early Muslims. The conflicting reports he records regarding the establishment of the *diwan* encode for us the competing views through the generations on what constituted precedence and moral excellence.[28] According to one report, when the secretaries of Quraysh (*kuttab Quraysh*), who included 'Aqil ibn Abi Talib (a younger brother of the fourth caliph 'Ali), were queried as to how the *diwan* should be set up, they responded, "Write down the names of people according to their ranks." They began with the Banu Hashim (the Prophet's clan), after which followed the sons of Abu Bakr and his kin (*qawmuhu*), then 'Umar and his kin; after which they wrote down the names of the tribes. When 'Umar was presented with this list, he rejected it, and suggested instead that they begin with the kin of the Prophet, proceeding from the closest relative to the most distant "until you place 'Umar where God Himself has placed him." At that, al-'Abbas, who as the closest blood-relative of the Prophet, would have headed the list, is said to have expressed his gratitude to 'Umar.[29] We may justifiably detect a pro-kinship, pro-'Abbasid flavor in this report.

But according to another report from Ibn 'Abbas, al-Maqrizi relates, 'Umar sought the counsel of the people after the conquest of the Sawad (in Iraq) and Syria on how the spoils were to be distributed. Both 'Ali and 'Umar concurred that the division should occur according to the Qur'anic ruling which stipulated that one-fifth (khums) of it "belonged to God and His Prophet"(to be distributed among close of kin, orphans, and the poor). On the basis of another Qur'anic verse, they determined that the remaining four-fifths should be distributed first among the Meccan Migrants, then the Medinan Helpers, then those who followed them and supported them.[30] This arrangement reflects adherence to the principle of precedence strictly on the basis of religious merit rather than of kinship to the Prophet.

The fourteenth-century Mamluk scholar Ibn Taymiyya in his discussion of 'Umar's diwan indicates the difference of juridical opinion concerning its validity. It is known, he says, that Abu Bakr showed no preference in the distribution of stipends and neither did 'Ali; 'Uthman, however, followed in 'Umar's footsteps. Among the eponymous founders of the Sunni madhahib (schools of law which came into existence by the tenth century), Abu Hanifa and al-Shafi'i were in favor of equal distribution of stipends while Malik recommended a system of preference.[31] In vindication of 'Umar, Ibn Taymiyya proceeds to demonstrate, however, that Muhammad himself had set in motion a preferential system for awarding stipends based on the merit and rigor of service rendered to the community. Thus, on the basis of reports contained in the two sound hadith compilations of al-Bukhari and Muslim, he shows that the Prophet was in the habit of apportioning three times the share of one foot-soldier to a cavalryman.[32] Ibn Taymiyya further affirms that the basis of the system of stipends was egalitarianism but, on occasion, the showing of preferential treatment in the interests of the greater benefit of society was held to be perfectly licit. Furthermore, 'Umar did not set up the diwan capriciously nor did he award stipends arbitrarily or out of favoritism but only on the basis of religious merit. His own son and daughter, for example, were awarded smaller pensions compared to those who surpassed them in excellences.[33]

We have engaged in this discussion of the diwan to indicate that the manner in which 'Umar was perceived to have set up the register of pensions had an important bearing on the organization of the Muslim polity and the conception of legitimate leadership. The Qur'anic espousal of precedence and moral excellence as a principal mode of socio-political organization was at loggerheads with the pre-Islamic valorization of kinship. The tension between the two in the early period and the subsequent dilution of the principle of precedence in the later period are reflected in the conflicting reports we have regarding the establishment of the *diwan*. The discussion in the sources regarding the underlying principles of the *diwan* reflects in microcosm the larger debate about how the polity should be constituted and the specific moral and socio-political order it should reflect. Though this specific register of pensions would not survive much past the early Umayyad period as far as we can tell, 'Umar's implementation of these basic Qur'anic principles in the establishment of the *diwan* would have considerable implications for the crystallization of a specific communal and historical consciousness.

'Umar's legal and religious activities

The most important epithet applied to 'Umar ibn al-Khattab is *al-Faruq*, roughly, "one who distinguishes between right and wrong." This epithet is commonly understood to point to his role as a prolific interpreter of the evolving religious law (*al-Shari'a*) and his generally recognized status as the caliph who left the strongest imprint on the shape and course of the early polity in many important aspects. 'Umar appears to have been called at first *Khalifat Abi Bakr* ("the Successor to Abu Bakr") since it would have been cumbersome to address him as *Khalifat Khalifat Rasul Allah* "Successor of the Successor of the Messenger of God"). Then he adopted the title *Amir al-Mu'minin* ("Counsellor/Leader of the Faithful"), which henceforth became the title of the legitimate ruler of the polity after him.[34] The Arabic word *amir* emphasizes the role of the leader primarily as a counsellor, which is fitting for the caliph's position in this period as "first among equals." The ninth-century Byzantine historian, Theophanes, appropriately translated the title *Amir al-Mu'minin* into Greek as *protosymbolous*, or "first counsellor.[35] The title *Khalifat Allah* ("deputy of God") is said to have been rejected by both Abu Bakr and 'Umar as presumptuous and over-weening, implying the arrogation of an absolutist religious authority that no Muslim ruler had the right to claim. When a man once addressed 'Umar as "O Deputy of God," the annoyed caliph exclaimed, "May God prove you wrong!"[36]

'Umar's knowledge of legal and religious matters finds generous mention in Sunni sources, specifically in the praise (*manaqib*) literature which documents the personal excellences and accomplishments of the Companions in particular. According to one report, fourteen people used to make legal pronouncements (*fatawa*; sing. *fatwa*) during the lifetime of the Prophet, among whom were the first four caliphs.[37] Many reports point to 'Umar's judicial decisions, particularly in the complex matter of inheritance shares. Ibn Taymiyya states, for example, that 'Umar's decision in favor of granting the grandfather a share in inheritance and to accord him a status higher than a paternal uncle was met with widespread approval.[38] 'Umar is said to have punctiliously carried out the prescribed penalties (*hudud*; sing. *hadd*) for theft, illicit sexual relations, and public drunkenness when the required evidence to establish such misconduct was available and certain societal conditions prevailed. At the same time, it should be pointed out, there are *hadiths* in the standard compilations which point to a great reluctance on 'Umar's part to impose the *hadd* penalties on even self-confessed perpetrators.[39] His punctiliousness seems to have been mitigated by leniency in extenuating circumstances. When the "Year of the Ash" occurred during his reign, which is the name given to a year of severe famine and drought in 683, 'Umar declared the punishment for theft to be effectively suspended, since the state first had to be capable of maintaining a certain level of subsistence for all its subjects before it could impose this penalty.[40]

Among other civil and legal acts, 'Umar established the Islamic (*hijri*) calendar dating the beginning of the Islamic era to the Prophet's migration in 622. He abolished the practice of temporary (*mut'a*) marriage, a pre-Islamic custom that had continued to be practiced sporadically during the Prophet's time. He established the office of the judge (*qadi*), designated official *mu'adhdhins* ("callers to prayer"), and appointed professional reciters of the Qur'an for men and women.[41]

The sources point to intensive engagement of the early Muslims at this time with the Qur'an, both as an oral and written text. As mentioned earlier, the preliminary collection of the Qur'an made by Zayd ibn Thabit under Abu Bakr is said to have remained in 'Umar's possession and entrusted to his daughter Hafsa, the widow of the Prophet, for safekeeping after 'Umar's death.[42] The Qur'an would not be codified in its final form until the time of the third caliph 'Uthman's time in circa 651. Before its final codification, the sources inform us, the Companions often discussed among themselves the correct reading and, therefore, the correct interpretation of key Qur'anic verses. One such verse was Qur'an 9:100 whose parsing and exegesis potentially had significant implications for the organization of the polity. 'Umar played a prominent role in determining the preferred reading of this verse. The exegete al-Tabari reports that 'Umar used to read Qur'an 9:100 with certain declensional endings which yielded the meaning, "God is satisfied with the first of those who preceded from among the Migrants as well as with the Medinan Helpers and those who follow them in charity."

However, Zayd ibn Thabit parsed the verse differently in 'Umar's presence which yielded the meaning, "God is satisfied with the first of those who preceded from among the Migrants and from among the Medinan Helpers and from among those who follow them in charity." Wishing to ascertain the correct reading, 'Umar sent for Ubayy ibn Ka'b who was acknowledged to be highly proficient in reciting the Qur'an and who had his own copy of the Qur'an.[43] When Ubayy confirmed the reading of Zayd, 'Umar readily acceded saying, "Then we shall follow Ubayy."[44] The implications of the two variant readings are telling: 'Umar's reading restricts "the first of those who preceded" to the Muhajirun while Zayd's and Ubayy's reading, which is the commonly accepted one, broadens it to include the Ansar and the righteous believers in general.

This episode, along with others similar to it, suggests that the religious authority of the caliph to the extent that it existed in this early period was no greater than that of any other Companion who was equally knowledgeable of the Qur'an and the *sunna* and who felt free to challenge the caliph if he or she disagreed with their interpretations and application of the legal precepts (see further below). It would be more accurate to describe the authority possessed by the caliphs in this early period as "epistemic authority,"[45] that is, authority predicated on their knowledge of matters, religious and mundane, rather than on religious charisma or any kind of supernatural election.

Military conquests

'Umar continued the territorial expansion of the realm of Islam already begun under his predecessor. He saw that it was to the greater benefit of the community to fully integrate the former rebel tribes of the *ridda* wars and harness their energies in the continuing expansion of the borders of Islam.

Whereas Abu Bakr had registered his disapproval of the rebels by refusing them any role in the Sassanian and Byzantine expeditions, 'Umar specifically requested Abu 'Ubayd al-Thaqafi, whom he had appointed commander on the Sassanian front, to recruit all the tribesmen he could muster regardless of their affiliation during the *ridda* uprisings. The relative lack of resistance in the Sassanian territories and the spectacular victory at Ajnadayn appeared to convince 'Umar and the community at large that the territorial gains resulting from these expeditions would plausibly offset the loss of revenue from the disrupted trade. Fortified by the increasing numbers of ex-*ridda* tribesmen, Arab armies in Iraq inflicted a crushing defeat on the Sassanian forces at the Battle of Qadisiyya in 637 and on the Byzantines in Syria at the Battle of the Yarmuk in the same year. Between 640 and 642 'Amr ibn al-'As gained control of Egypt, with the defeat of the Byzantines there occurring in 645.

As distant lands came within the orbit of Muslim control, 'Umar established garrison cities (*amsar*) in Fustat (Egypt), Basra and Kufa in Iraq. These conquests have been named "Openings" (*futuh*) in the Arabic sources. Chafing under Byzantine persecution, the natives of these regions in most cases appear to have welcomed their new Arab rulers. The ninth-century Muslim historian al-Baladhuri reports that Christians and Jews in the Syrian city of Homs pleaded with Muslim soldiers to remain when the Byzantine emperor Heraclius threatened to launch an offensive against it. When the Byzantine army was defeated, the Muslim soldiers were said to have been welcomed back with much jubilation.[46] It would be tempting to see in this account a reflection of the Muslim historian's wish to cast these conquests in a favorable light, except that we also have attestations of similar sentiments from Jewish and Christian sources.

Nestorian Christians in Syria and Mesopotamia, like the Egyptian Copts, were Monophysite Christians, and therefore considered to be heretics by the Byzantine church which had adopted the Diophysite position as its official creed. As a consequence, these Eastern Christians were subjected to heavy taxes and other discriminatory measures under Byzantine rule. Switching to Muslim rule resulted in lighter taxes and a general non-interference in the religious affairs of both Christians and Jews in this period. The general sense of relief among Jews at having been delivered from the Byzantines is expressed in a Jewish apocalyptic work, in which a rabbi is comforted by an angel in the following words:

Do not fear, Ben Yohay; the Creator, blessed be He, has only brought the Kingdom of Ishmael in order to save you from this wickedness (i.e. Byzantium) ...
The Holy One, blessed be He, will raise up for them a Prophet according to His
will, and conquer the land for them, and they will come and restore it ...[47]

Similar sentiments are expressed by Michael the Elder, Jacobite Patriarch of
Antioch, in the late twelfth century, when he made known his gratitude for
the end of Byzantine rule thus:

This is why the God of vengeance, who alone is all-powerful, and changes the
empire of mortals as He will, giving it to whomsoever He will, and uplifting the
humble – beholding the wickedness of the Romans who, throughout their
dominions, cruelly plundered our churches and our monasteries and con-
demned us without pity – brought from the region of the south the sons of
Ishmael, to deliver us through them from the hands of the Romans.[48]

The inhabitants of the newly conquered areas remained mostly non-Muslim
under Muslim rule for at least two centuries. On payment of a head-tax
(*jizya*), the indigenous peoples were usually left to their own devices and
allowed to live in relatively autonomous communities. This trend should not
appear surprising to us: the desire to proselytize and convert the local peoples
appear to have been singularly lacking in these early military campaigns.
Some of the sources suggest that the pressure of over-population in the Arabian peninsula combined with internal economic problems led to the desire
of many Arab tribes to seek new realms in which to settle down, a process
that had already begun in the sixth century before the rise of Islam. The pre-
Islamic tribal practice of conducting raids (*ghazw*) on the territory and property of rival tribes for the collection of booty was well-entrenched and these
early conquests appear to have evolved out of them. Later historians, such as
al-Tabari (d. 923), however, would foreground religious motivations and
see the hand of providence fortuitously paving the way for the spread of
Muslim rule through these conquests.[49]

Relations with women

'Umar was criticized for his authoritarian manner at times in his inter-
actions with particularly the women around him. He tried to interfere in
the Prophet's household when he perceived that the situation was somewhat lax there. The sources report that he attempted to convince

Muhammad to impose certain restrictions on the movements of his wives; his importunate demands is listed as one of the occasions of revelation for the "*hijab* verse" (Qur'an 33:53). It should be pointed out that *hijab* in this case does not refer to personal attire, as does the word in modern usage, but to a curtain or some other kind of a barrier.[50] The verse states,

> O believers, do not enter the Prophet's house until permission is given you for a meal, without waiting for its time. But when you are invited, enter, and when you have eaten, disperse, without seeking familiar talk. This used to annoy the Prophet but he is ashamed before you. But God is not ashamed of what is right. And if you ask them [the women] for anything, then ask them from behind a *hijab* (curtain). That is more pure for your hearts and theirs.

According to one cause or occasion recorded by the exegetes to explain the revelation of this verse, 'Umar urged the Prophet to shelter his wives from public view on account of the fact that good and bad people entered his house. 'Umar's entreaty appears to have been spiritedly opposed by Muhammad's wives, particularly by the aristocratic Umm Salama. But 'Umar's vigilance was perceived by later exegetes as being "for the good of the Prophet's wives," since the wisdom of his advice appeared to be confirmed by the revelation of 33:53.[51]

And vigilant he was, but one must not be hasty to assign misogynist impulses to such vigilance. It was 'Umar, after all, who had entrusted the Qur'an manuscript in his possession, which formed the basis for the final redaction of the Qur'anic text, to the safekeeping of his daughter, Hafsa, rather than to that of one of his sons. During his caliphate, he appointed a woman, Shifa' bint 'Abd Allah, as the inspector of markets in Medina, a position roughly equivalent to that of a city mayor. It was also 'Umar who humbly and publicly accepted an older woman's legal opinion as valid over his own. According to this account, 'Umar once attempted to impose a ceiling on the value of the gift (*mahr*) to be made to the bride by the groom, which was met with lively resistance. When 'Umar made an announcement to this effect in the mosque at Medina, he was chastised by an older woman who accused him of taking back from women "what God and His apostle had given them." The chastened caliph admitted his mistake in public by saying, "'Umar is wrong and a woman is right."[52] This anecdote shows that he was not above taking criticism from women when it was well-deserved (a trait not universally found among men).

Although less than diplomatic on occasion in reprimanding people in general when they did not measure up to certain standards he held dear, and generally more feared than loved by his people, the Sunni consensus remains that 'Umar was an upstanding man of exceptional integrity who ultimately wished to promote only the welfare of the Muslim community, even if that entailed risking the displeasure of some. His steely resoluteness and moral consistency are lauded as particularly commendable qualities during a highly sensitive and fractious time, providing firm and inspired leadership for the still fragile polity. Such an attitude is encoded in the statement attributed to the Prophet, in which he remarks, "The truth after me is with 'Umar, wherever he may be."[53]

Relations with the People of the Book

When it comes to the earliest generation of Muslims, we should take care to read our sources critically and particularly compare earlier and later biographical accounts of their lives. Attitudes and certain acts which needed to be legitimized in the later period were sometimes attributed backwards in time to the Companions.[54]

Nowhere is this perhaps more obvious than in the case of 'Umar. A critical reading of the sources permits the construction of two different 'Umars, particularly when it comes to his relations with the *ahl al-kitab* ("the People of the Book" or "scriptuaries"). They are the Jews and Christians, also known in Arabic as *ahl al-dhimma* ("the Protected People;" sing. *dhimmi*). One 'Umar is tolerant and highly magnanimous toward them while the other shows condescension toward them and attempts to place certain restrictions on their religious practices. The latter image is often predicated on a document called the Pact of 'Umar in which the Christians of Syria, in exchange for safe conduct (*aman*) from 'Umar, allegedly agreed to observe certain discriminatory practices, such as refraining from building new places of worship for themselves, from dressing like Muslims, and publicly displaying their religious symbols.[55] Modern scholars have regarded this document with considerable skepticism for good reason. The Pact of 'Umar is not mentioned by any early scholar before roughly the ninth century. As a document, the pact encodes sentiments toward non-Muslims that were more prevalent in the later 'Abbasid era than during roughly the first two centuries of Islam and appears to show the influence of medieval Christian European laws concerning the status of Jews.[56] The attribution of less tolerant attitudes to 'Umar, a tower-ing paradigmatic figure of piety and integrity whose practices were of normative value, justified such attitudes for some and made them potentially enforceable by later authorities.[57]

Contrast the tone and stipulations of the Pact of 'Umar, as indicated above, with the agreement drawn up by the second caliph upon the surren-der of Jerusalem in 638, the terms of which read:

> In the Name of God, the Merciful, the Compassionate. This is the security which 'Umar, the servant of God, the commander of the faithful, grants to the people of Ilya.[58] He grants to all, whether sick or sound, security for their lives, their possessions, their churches and their crosses, and for all that concerns their reli-gion. Their churches shall not be changed into dwelling places, nor destroyed, neither shall they nor their appurtenances be in any way diminished, nor the crosses of the inhabitants nor anything of their possessions, nor shall any restric-tion be placed upon them in the matter of their faith, nor shall any one of them be harmed.[59]

A practically identical agreement was drawn up with the inhabitants of Ludd in Palestine. These accounts are recorded by the ninth-century historian al-Tabari in his widely consulted universal history.[60] It is further reported that 'Umar visited the holy places in Jerusalem in the company of the Patri-arch of the city. When the time for prayer came, the Patriarch graciously invited the caliph to offer his prayers in the Church of the Resurrection. 'Umar declined, saying that if he were to do that, later Muslims might wrongfully claim the church as their own place of worship.[61] Anecdotes such as this and others recorded by early historians reinforce the tolerant and magnanimous image of the second caliph.

Under 'Umar, state funds were often disbursed for the maintenance of poor Jews and Christians. Adult able-bodied male scripturaries were required to pay a head-tax called the *jizya* in return for state protection, military or otherwise, of their rights. Women, minors, the infirm, old, destitute and religious personages, like monks, were normally exempted from its remittance. According to some early sources, the infirm, the old, and the destitute among the scripturaries were additionally able to receive pensions from the state treasury as wards of the state, whose maintenance was consequently a basic, humane responsibility of Muslim rulers.[62]

Eighth-century authorities such as Abu Yusuf Ya'qub ibn Ibrahim (d. 798) have left us detailed accounts of early Islamic fiscal systems. Abu Yusuf reports that 'Umar recognized two categories of poor and desperate people who qualified for state support: the *fuqara'* who were Muslims, and the *masakin* who were the People of the Book residing in Islamic realms.[63] Both received provisions from the public treasury for their maintenance. In this connection, Abu Yusuf relates a touching anecdote about 'Umar, who once encountered an old, blind Jewish man begging for alms and brought him to his home out of pity. He offered the destitute man a modest sum of money from his own funds as alms and upon inquiry discovered that the latter had been paying taxes to the state. A shocked 'Umar proclaimed this to be an injustice and ordered the state treasury to immediately desist and to treat him instead as one of the impoverished scriptuaries entitled to state maintenance.[64] In this early pre-modern system of state welfare, poor residents of Islamic lands, irrespective of religion, could expect to be entitled to a portion of the government's *zakat*-revenues.

'Umar's practice allowed later jurists to conclude that non-Muslims, like Muslims, had certain claims on the Islamic state for their basic welfare and sustenance in accordance with the Qur'anic verse (9:60) which states: "Verily the obligatory alms (*sadaqat*)[65] are for the poor (*al-fuqara'*), the destitute (*al-masakin*), those who collect the alms/taxes, those whose hearts are to be reconciled, to ransom (slaves and prisoners of war), for those in debt, those who are engaged in the path of God, and for the wayfarer – a duty imposed by God."[66] "Those whose hearts are to be reconciled" referred primarily to new Muslim converts and non-Muslims, whose continuing goodwill should be cultivated by Muslims and whose socio-economic welfare were of concern to the state. According to the principle of *ta'lif al-qulub* ("reconciliation of hearts") engendered by Qur'an 9:60, the non-Muslim poor would appear to be doubly advantaged in being needy and belonging to the category of "those whose hearts are to be reconciled."

Comparison of the documentary evidence available to us clearly establishes that the early sources knew primarily of a compassionate and tolerant 'Umar in his treatment of the People of the Book, which was meant to set a valuable precedent for succeeding generations. Certain stipulations of the Pact of 'Umar forbade the building of new churches. But archaeological evidence shows that new churches continued to be built in Palestine under the Rashidun caliphs and under their early successors and that monastic life continued to thrive through the late seventh and early eighth centuries.[67] Muslim rule in this period proved to be particularly favorable for the Jews as well, especially in comparison with the preceding Byzantine period. Jews were allowed to return to Jerusalem under 'Umar and they came to form a sizeable community under his early successors, not only in Palestine but in Iraq as well.[68] However, the vicissitudes of political circumstances would allow for less benign attitudes to surface among later Muslims on occasion, which sometimes became reflected in discriminatory administrative policies, as evidenced in the so-called Pact of 'Umar. Regrettably, 'Umar's historical persona had to be rewritten to a certain extent in the later period by some authorities to accommodate and validate these lamentable transformations through time.

'Umar's assassination and the electoral council (al-shura)

In 644, 'Umar was attacked by a Persian Christian slave named Abu Lu'lu'a and died after three days from the serious wounds inflicted on him. Abu Lu'lu'a had apparently acted out of vehement nationalist sentiment, seeking to avenge the pride of his fellow Persians bristling under the Arab conquest. During the three days while he hovered between life and death, 'Umar made arrangements for the elections of his successor. He appointed a six-man advisory council called the *shura*, consisting of the following members, prominent Companions who were all candidates themselves for the caliphal office: 'Abd al-Rahman ibn Awf, al-Zubayr b. al-'Awamm, Talha b. 'Ubayd Allah, Sa'd b. Abi Waqqas, 'Uthman, and 'Ali. 'Umar left trenchant instructions for the selection of the finalist; by a process of elimination, only 'Uthman and 'Ali remained at the end. They were both asked if they would follow "the *sunna* of the Prophet and the *sira*s of their two predecessors," that is, Abu Bakr and 'Umar.[69] Worthy of note is the semantic and technical equivalence of the terms *sunna* and *sira* in this early report, both referring broadly to "custom" and "practices."[70] 'Uthman agreed to this condition but 'Ali did not, declining the office by saying that he preferred to chart his own course. This paved the way for 'Uthman to assume the caliphate. 'Ali's independence would not ultimately prevent him from becoming the fourth caliph. But, according to these accounts, it was clearly perceived at this time that the third caliph should continue to build on the achievements and practices (*sira*) of Abu Bakr and 'Umar, which in turn was assumed to reflect the practices (*sunna*) of the Prophet, in order to establish the polity on an even more firm footing.

This process of electing a successor to the caliph through an advisory council established by 'Umar has become idealized by pro-democracy advocates today. Whether traditionalist, modernist/reformist, or Islamist in orientation, Muslims in the contemporary period venerate the *shura* as the example par excellence of Islam's inherent democratic impulse, allowed to blossom in the past in a formal, quasi-institutional way, and setting a powerful precedent for generations of Muslims to follow. In fact, the longing for consultative government based on the Qur'anic principle of *shura* (cf. Qur'an 3:158–59 and 42:38) remained a persistent theme in the later literature. As dynastic rule became the norm after the death of 'Ali in 661, invocation of *shura* as a desirable and even mandated social and political practice became a way of registering disapproval of a political culture that had progressively grown more authoritarian by the 'Abbasid period. Qur'an commentaries and certain genres of ethical and humanistic literature (*adab*) continued to extol the merits of consultation in various spheres – particularly the bureaucratic, military, and political – throughout the pre-modern period.

Representing a fairly common perspective on the *shura*, the Qur'an commentator Muhammad al-Qurtubi (d. 1273), in his exegesis of Qur'an 3:158–59, records that, "It is the obligation of the rulers to consult the scholars on matters unknown to them and in religious matters not clear to them. [They should] consult the leaders of the army in matters having to do with war, and leaders of the people in administrative issues, as well as teachers, ministers, and governors in matters that have to do with the welfare of the country and its development."[71] In the twelfth century, the Andalusian scholar and exegete Ibn 'Atiyya (d. 1146) was of the opinion that consultation was one of the pillars of the religious law and of judicial activity and "whoever did not consult with the people of knowledge and religion should be subject to removal [sc. from public office]."[72]

The point to be made from these and similar accounts is that non-consultative, dynastic rule came to be regarded in most circles as un-Islamic, representing a betrayal of the early Islamic ideal of collective decision-making. To this day, therefore, the concept of *shura* resonates strongly with a significant cross-section of Muslims, which they understand as leading the way, in accordance with Qur'anic precept, to just and consultative power-sharing in contrast to arbitrary despotism (*istibdad*). In the contemporary period, liberal and reformist Muslims tend to conflate *shura* with modern notions of democracy, while the radical right-wing resolutely refuses to concede any reflection of the latter in the former. The latter's refusal to concede any parallelism between the two concepts is a "logical" consequence of its rigid notion of "divine sovereignty," a topic we will discuss in chapters 9 and 10.

The End of Rightly-Guided Leadership

The six-man electoral council set up by 'Umar finally selected 'Uthman ibn 'Affan, a prominent member of the Umayyad clan within the tribe of Quraysh. From all accounts 'Uthman was a pious, self-effacing man despite his wealthy, privileged background, who embraced Islam early and emigrated first to Abyssinia and then to Medina, all of which established his precedence in Islam. After becoming Muslim, he was first married to Ruqayya, a daughter of the Prophet; upon her death, he married Umm Kulthum, another daughter of Muhammad. For this distinction, he earned the honorific *Dhu al-Nurayn* ("He of the Two Lights"). 'Uthman is said to have been physically handsome, elegant and dapper in appearance.[1] As an Umayyad, 'Uthman was related to men like Abu Sufyan and his shrewd son, Mu'awiya, who had been implacable foes of Islam until the very day Mecca fell to the Muslims in 630. These relatives would ultimately play a role in 'Uthman's downfall. In usurping the reins of power, the Umayyads would be vilified by later generations for their worldly ambition and lukewarm adherence at best to Islam. But we are getting a little ahead of ourselves here. First we move on to a discussion of 'Uthman's eventful tenure as the third Rightly-Guided caliph.

POLITICAL ADMINISTRATION

The sources tend to divide 'Uthman's tenure (644–56) as caliph into six good years in the beginning and six bad years in the end.[2] Under 'Uthman, new frontiers were opened up in North Africa through carefully planned expeditions and the rest of the Sassanian empire fell to Muslim control. Increased revenues began to pour into Iraq and Egypt, the sites for the launching of these expeditions, and ultimately into Medina which was entitled to one-fifth (*khums*) of the shares. 'Uthman was concerned with asserting his control over the provinces which had seen fresh new waves of tribesmen immigrating from the Arabian peninsula. Part of his policy was to appoint relatives from his own clan as governors. In Kufa, he appointed a cousin, al-Walid ibn 'Uqba, who was later replaced by another cousin, Sa'id ibn al-'As. In Syria, yet another cousin of his, the above-mentioned Mu'awiya, son of Abu Sufyan, was already installed as governor. Such appointments made 'Uthman vulnerable to charges of nepotism and of disregarding the Qur'anic principles of precedence and moral excellence in making political appointments. Thus, an early poem accused 'Uthman of having violated the established *sunna* of the Prophet, which at his investiture he had promised to follow.[3]

'Uthman moreover decided to assert Medinan control over the *qurra'*, the Qur'an reciters, many of whom had settled in the rich lands of the Sawad in Iraq. The *qurra'*, who in other sources are equated with the *ahl al-Qur'an* ("people of the Qur'an"), were from Mecca and had impeccable Islamic credentials. They were not Johnny-come-latelies to Islam like most of 'Uthman's Umayyad relatives, and many of the Reciters had fought in the *ridda* wars against the rebellious southern and central Arabian tribes. The Reciters were highly displeased with 'Uthman's attempts to bring them more firmly into the Medinan orbit and to control the disbursement of the revenues from the Sawad lands. They also resented the appointment of Sa'id ibn al-'As, 'Uthman's cousin, and eventually forcibly deposed him and appointed Abu Musa al-Ash'ari as their governor, who possessed the requisite Islamic precedence.

THE COLLECTION OF THE QUR'AN

The achievement that 'Uthman is forever remembered for and which proved to be a decisive milestone in the consolidation of the Muslim polity as a religious, scripture-based community was the final recension of the Qur'an, completed around 651 CE, as the sources overwhelmingly report. 'Uthman appointed an editorial committee headed by Zayd ibn Thabit to collate the various textual versions already in existence and cull disparate verses and sections committed to memory by various Companions in order to produce a final canonical edition. The sources list various reasons why 'Uthman felt impelled to do this during his caliphate. In the various battles fought in the early years, and particularly during the *ridda* wars, a number of the Companions who had memorized the Qur'an perished, raising the concern that eventually the oral transmission of the Qur'an would cease and thus significant parts of the Qur'an would be lost. There were also a number of variant readings that had developed and some prominent Companions, such as 'Ali ibn Abi Talib, Ibn Mas'ud, and Ibn 'Abbas, are said to have had their own personal copies, known as *mushaf*s. The 'Uthmanic codex (*al-mushaf al-'uthmani*) was meant to supersede all other extant manuscripts, since it was feared that variant versions would lead to sectarian divisiveness, as had happened among earlier religious communities. Once the text was finalized, 'Uthman ordered that variant copies be destroyed and a copy of the canonical text be sent to all the major garrison cities.[4]

Later sources have recognized the wisdom and foresight inherent in 'Uthman's decision to impose uniformity on the Qur'anic text and produce a standard *textus receptus* when he did, forestalling a probable increase in variant readings with time and future acrimonious disputes over textual variations that would very likely have ensued.[5] Although the content of the canon was now forever determined, the unpointed and unvowelled text still permitted relatively minor differences in pronunciation and understanding of some verses. Up to seven (sometimes ten) variant readings (*al-qira'at*) of the text are recognized till today as equally authoritative.[6] The Qur'anic text progressively acquired diacritics and vowel marks in the course of the first century. Some sources attribute the addition of these features to the Umayyad governor of Basra, al-Hajjaj (d. 714), a former schoolteacher.[7]

But there were also others who criticized 'Uthman for having produced a canonical Qur'anic text. They seem to have regarded this act as an undue arrogation on his part of a religious authority that did not properly belong to the office of the caliph.[8] This criticism seems at least partly anachronistic because it is doubtful that at this early stage there was any clear conception of how caliphal or imamic authority should be defined. According to the early historical accounts at our disposal, the three caliphs devised rules of political conduct as they went along, reacting to the exigencies of their particular circumstances as they occurred. But they were also more than political stewards of their community. Because of their standing as some of the closest Companions of the Prophet, they saw themselves entitled to interpret the Qur'an as the occasion arose and cite *hadiths* from the Prophet to elucidate some finer point of law or justify some course of activity. We are reminded of Abu Bakr who justified the launching of the *ridda* wars by correctly interpreting the *hadith* regarding the conditions which ensure the inviolability of Muslim life and property. Many among the populace were willing to concede to the caliphs this interpretive authority on account of their moral and social standing. Others who were equally qualified, notably Ibn Mas'ud and Ibn 'Abbas, participated in this hermeneutic activity as well and were not hesitant to make known their points of view when different from the caliph's.

TOWARD FRAGMENTATION OF THE COMMUNITY

Because of his bid to exercise greater control over the provinces, particularly Iraq and Egypt, 'Uthman earned the ire of the settlers there who increasingly resisted his policies. In the last year of his reign, a few hundred embittered tribesmen from Iraq and Egypt arrived in Medina to present their grievances before 'Uthman. Negotiations and debates were held for almost fifty days with the caliph practically under siege in his own house. His supporters had abandoned him and 'Uthman had to fend for himself. The protracted and heated negotiations appeared to be leading nowhere. Sometime in June, 656, while 'Uthman sat reciting the Qur'an in the mosque at Medina, a cabal of angry Egyptians burst in on the caliph and assassinated him. His blood is said to have spilled onto the pages of the sacred text and his wife, Na'ila bint al-Furafisa, was wounded while trying to protect him. The third caliphate ended with 'Uthman's secret burial in the middle of the same night.

A critical point had now been reached in the unfolding history of Islam which was to have far reaching consequences for the early community of Muslims. Muslims had killed their own legitimate leader and the cauldron of communal dissent had finally boiled over.

THE CALIPHATE OF 'ALI IBN ABI TALIB

In the aftermath of the shocking events that had transpired, 'Ali ibn Abi Talib emerged as the clear front-runner to succeed 'Uthman. The sources suggest that he was understandably initially reluctant to assume leadership in the difficult circumstances that had ensued. But as he seemed to be the obvious choice on account of his greater precedence and moral excellence vis-à-vis the rest of the Companions, he was eventually prevailed upon to acquiesce.

'Ali's credentials for the office were impeccable at this juncture in history. Both Sunni and Shi'i sources maintain that he was the first male to accept Islam at the tender age of about nine years. He was Muhammad's cousin, the son of Abu Talib, the Prophet's kindly uncle who protected him during the worst trials of his life. 'Ali married Fatima, Muhammad's daughter; the marriage produced the two famous grandsons, al-Hasan and al-Husayn. 'Ali's devotion to the Prophet is best evidenced during the *hijra* when he acted as Muhammad's decoy in Mecca while the Prophet slipped out under the cover of night, and accompanied by Abu Bakr, took off for Medina. Just as Abu Bakr is praised for his courage in the cave with the Prophet, 'Ali is eulogized in the literature for this singular act of bravery. One Shi'i author praises this event as "more wondrous than Isma'il's submission to possible death at his father Abraham's hands."[9]

The situation in 656 was quite different from that in 632 immediately after the Prophet's death. 'Ali at that time was a young man in his early thirties and thus perceived as too inexperienced to assume the mantle of leadership. His youth, constantly contrasted to Abu Bakr's mature age, was widely regarded then as an impediment to his candidacy for the office of the caliph.[10] But now a mature man himself in his fifties, 'Ali had emerged as the most eligible successor to 'Uthman.

During his caliphate, 'Ali reversed the policy of his immediate two predecessors in regard to the *diwan*. In contrast to 'Umar and 'Uthman, 'Ali decreed that henceforth all those entitled to stipends from the state would draw equal amounts, regardless of whether they were early or latecomers to Islam, and whether they had participated in the *ridda* or not. This reflected 'Ali's egalitarian interpretation of the Qur'anic principle of precedence (*sabiqa*) and its applicability in the present circumstances. It was also a shrewd political move on his part. His policy of disbursing stipends without showing preferential treatment caused people of diverse backgrounds to rally around him, especially from those groups who had to defer to the Meccan Migrants according to the standards invoked by the principle of precedence. Thus Medinan Helpers, former *ridda* rebels rehabilitated during the battles of conquest, and latecomers to Islam in general did not feel discriminated against in the disbursement of state revenues. 'Ali wisely realized that the time for a preferential distribution of stipends was past to allow the polity to heal from the recent wounds inflicted on it in the course of political dissension and strife.[11]

However, the powerful centripetal forces unleashed by 'Uthman's assassination indicated that the healing of wounds was not about to happen any time soon. Almost immediately trouble began brewing in connection with the murder of 'Ali's predecessor, instigated by a group of people who wished to see 'Uthman's death avenged. Heading this group were the two prominent Companions Talha and al-Zubayr, supported by 'A'isha, the Prophet's widow and Abu Bakr's daughter. They, however, overestimated the support that would be available to them. On their way to meet 'Ali's army, the three conspirators saw their anticipated reinforcements in Basra and Kufa fail to materialize. 'Ali, on the other hand, drew the enthusiastic support of the Helpers in Medina. The two opposing forces met outside Basra in what became known as the Battle of the Camel on December 4, 656, which ended with a resounding victory for 'Ali and his supporters. Talha and Zubayr were killed and a chastened 'A'isha sent back to Medina with the proper decorum due to the Prophet's widow.

THE FIRST CIVIL WAR

'Ali returned to Basra after the Battle of the Camel and set about putting communal affairs in order. He did not move back to Medina, preferring to move his base from there to Kufa in Iraq, which became his new capital. It is not clear from the sources whether this was intended as a permanent transfer of his capital from Medina to Kufa, but it is clear he wished to establish firmer control over Iraq. He also turned his attention to Egypt where the situation still remained unstable. 'Ali's appointed governor there was accepted by the Egyptians. Things were quite different in Syria, though, where 'Uthman's first cousin, Mu'awiya, remained governor and continued to press for 'Uthman's assassins to be brought to justice. Mu'awiya refused to give allegiance to 'Ali until the latter had properly investigated the death of his cousin. 'Ali refused to accede to Mu'awiya's demand and events moved speedily toward war.

'Ali mustered enough Iraqi tribesmen to his side to put a coalition of troops together and met Mu'awiya and his Syrian forces at a place called Siffin in Iraq in 657. Hostilities did not break out right away and there were attempts to negotiate some kind of a deal for about three months. Battle finally commenced, but no sooner had it begun than the Syrian troops are said to have hoisted copies of the Qur'an on their swords and petitioned for arbitration. 'Ali acceded to this petition. 'Amr ibn al-'As was selected to represent the Syrians while Abu Musa al-Ash'ari, despite 'Ali's objections, was designated to be the Iraqi representative. The Qur'an reciters appear to have had a disproportionately strong role to play in the selection of these representatives who were perceived to be advocates of their position. The arbitration led nowhere. And then in a curious and fateful move, a significant number of the Reciters seceded from 'Ali's army, claiming that the arbitration was unwarranted and that arbitration was the prerogative of God alone. Their slogan was "Judgment/arbitration belongs to God alone" (*La hukm illa lillah*; cf. Qur'an 12:67), which they appear to have understood to mean that an issue as momentous as political leadership could be determined only by direct divine intercession (it is not clear what form they might have expected this to take). They also considered 'Ali to have forfeited his right to the caliphate by agreeing to human arbitration. This group of Qur'an reciters became known as the Khawarij (lit. "those who go out," "seceders;" sing. Khariji).

'Ali realized their potential to do considerable harm to the community and pursued the Khawarij to a place called Nahrawan. There, 'Ali persuaded some of them to abandon the rest of the Khawarij and return to Kufa. As for those who refused to turn back, 'Ali and his army met them at the Battle of Nahrawan in 658 and inflicted a decisive defeat on them, decimating their numbers and causing the survivors to flee into the countryside. From their temporary strongholds in parts of the countryside, the Khawarij continued to cause much havoc and dissension on account of their fanatical certitude that only they were the true believers. They maintained that the rest of the Muslims, whom they regarded as having lapsed from Islam by their yardstick, were to be fought till the bitter end. After 'Ali, they would remain a thorn in the side of various administrations for about two generations when they were finally vanquished.

After Nahrawan, 'Ali returned to his headquarters at Kufa and waited for the results of the arbitration which was dragging its feet. No firm decision resulted from this process which lasted for about a year. In any case, 'Ali's standing as caliph and thus his political authority had been irreparably damaged in the aftermath of the battle of Siffin. His decision to accept arbitration was widely regarded as an abdication of caliphal authority and the situation continued to deteriorate. With relatively few supporters rallying to his side, 'Ali was gradually losing his hold over the tribesmen in Iraq and his attempts to forge a new coalition of forces loyal to him were largely ineffective. In 661, 'Ali was assassinated by 'Abd al-Rahman ibn Muljam, a Khariji who held a personal grudge against the caliph. 'Ali was either 58 or 63 years old at the time of his death, according to different accounts, and was buried in Kufa.

In the aftermath of 'Ali's death, Mu'awiya, the governor of Syria, swiftly moved in to take control of the situation and declared himself to be the new caliph. There was scarcely anyone to put up any resistance. Al-Hasan, 'Ali's eldest son, attempted a show of opposition but was quickly neutralized by Mu'awiya who, according to some of the sources, offered him a handsome settlement and exiled him to Medina. Pro-'Alid sources report, however, that al-Hasan persisted in his resistance and was poisoned by the Umayyad caliph. In any case, Mu'awiya was now quite the undisputed ruler of all he surveyed. The era of the Rightly-Guided Caliphs had come to an inauspicious end.

THE LEGACY OF THE ERA OF THE RIGHTLY-GUIDED CALIPHS

The thirty years which constitute the era of "the Rightly-Guided Caliphs" (al-Khulafa' al-Rashidun) have become enshrined in the collective memory of the Muslim polity as a golden, paradigmatic age. The prescriptions, policies, and practices of the four caliphs as remembered and recorded by succeeding generations became normative precedents for the majority of Muslims so that it is possible to speak of the normative practice of the Companions of Muhammad (sunnat ashab Muhammad), which complements the normative prophetic practice (sunnat al-nabi). The Rightly-Guided Caliphs are an integral and, after the Prophet, the most significant component of al-Salaf al-Salih, the Pious Forbears, a powerful emotive concept that would expand in the view of many to include the next two generations of Muslims, the Successors and the Successors to the Successors as well.

It is not clear precisely when the term *al-Khulafa' al-Rashidun* gained currency. Very likely, the concept began to crystallize at some point during the Umayyad period when, against the backdrop of what appeared to be a deliberate reversion to pre-Islamic values, nostalgia for the age of the Prophet and his Companions must have become pronounced. The famous *hadith* in which the Prophet states, "The caliphate after me will last thirty years," gained broad circulation at this time. Abu Hanifa (d. 767) and Ahmad ibn Hanbal (d. 855) are credited with being the earliest scholars to recognize the chronological order of the four Rashidun caliphs and to have imparted a certain degree of theological significance to this order. Ibn Hanbal would affirm that this chronological order was in fact a reflection of the four caliphs' merits relative to one another.[12] In other words, the actual historical chronological order of the four caliphs was deemed to reflect an a priori hierarchical ordering of their precedence and moral excellence as well. It is interesting to note that Ibn Hanbal uses the compound term *al-Rashidin al-Mahdiyyin* (these substantives are synonyms, approximately meaning "the Truly Guided") to refer to the first four caliphs.[13]

There are reports, however, which indicate that 'Ali was initially excluded from the roster of the Rightly-Guided Caliphs by the proto-Sunnis in the late seventh century while a consensus was crystallizing around the legitimacy of the first three caliphs in their historic order. The foremost compiler of Sunni *hadith*, al-Bukhari (d. 870) records a report from 'Abd Allah Ibn 'Umar (d. 693), the son of 'Umar, the second caliph, in which he says, "We used to show a preference for [certain] people during the time of the Prophet, peace and blessings be upon him. We would show preference for Abu Bakr, then 'Umar ibn al-Khattab, then 'Uthman ibn 'Affan, may God be pleased with them."[14] Another well-known compiler of *hadith*, Abu Da'ud al-Sijistani (d. 888) records a version of the above report, in which the following remark is appended, "Then we left aside the Companions of the Prophet, peace and blessings be upon him, and we would not compare them [on the basis of their merits]."[15]

The sentiments expressed in such reports reflect an early hard-line pro-'Uthman stance adopted by "the partisans of 'Uthman" (*shi'at 'Uthman*, also known as the 'Uthmaniyya) from the seventh century, who appear to have rejected out of hand 'Ali's claim to the caliphate. The partisans of 'Uthman reportedly sprung up after the murder of the third caliph in 656 and were particularly active in Egypt.[16] They believed that 'Uthman was decidedly superior to 'Ali in terms of his qualifications for the caliphate, and that 'Ali was not even qualified to become the fourth caliph. Some of the Mu'tazila (often referred to as the "Rationalists" in English) were counted among the 'Uthmaniyya.[17]

Our sources also indicate that this hard-line 'Uthmani stance softened over time and eventually came to include 'Ali as one of the Rightly-Guided Caliphs. By the late eighth century, the 'Uthmaniyya were rather more inclined to stress the greater excellence of 'Uthman over 'Ali in contradistinction to the 'Alids who believed that 'Ali was more excellent than 'Uthman.[18] This later 'Uthmaniyya is often regarded as the prototype of the Sunnis who were fully formed more or less by the mid-to-late ninth century. Before the final, "orthodox" Sunni point of view on the caliphate would be articulated, however, the positions of 'Uthman and 'Ali in this hierarchy continued to vacillate for some time. There are reports which indicate that in the ninth century considerable confusion still reigned over the issue of ranking 'Uthman and 'Ali vis-à-vis one another and that the moral consequences of preferring one over the other had not been fully worked out.[19]

Issues concerning legitimate political and religious authority had become highly divisive for the community in this period. Concerned about the fragmentation of the community, a group known as the Murji'a made its appearance. The earliest Murji'a (lit. "those who defer or postpone") in the eighth century were so-called because they wished to "postpone" the decision regarding the status of 'Uthman and 'Ali as believers. The main tenets of the Murji'a evidenced a concern for the unity of the Muslim polity and an unconditional and absolute approval of Abu Bakr and 'Umar.[20] It is apparent that the larger Muslim community was greatly influenced by this Murji'i position, which strove above all to contain dissension within the umma that had erupted particularly after the murder of 'Uthman. The Murji'a also believed, in contradistinction to the Khawarij, that the individual Muslim who proclaimed his or her belief in the one God and the prophetic mission of Muhammad (that is, affirmed the basic creedal statement of Islam) remained a Muslim, regardless of the commission of even grave sins, thereby holding out the hope and promise of moral rehabilitation in this world and of forgiveness in the next. A sinning Muslim was liable for punishment for a specific criminal act but could not be labeled an unbeliever by his co-religionists. This position known in Arabic as irja' ("deferral/suspension of judgment") was the exact opposite of takfir ("accusation of unbelief") as practiced by the Khawarij.

The specific Qur'anic proof-text (9:106) invoked to sanction this position (and from which the Murji'a get their name) is as follows: "There are those who are deferred (*murjawna*) to God's commandment — and He may chastise them or turn towards them (sc. in mercy)." The verse was interpreted by the Murji'a (and those inclined to agree with them) to refer to God's exclusive prerogative in judging human faith and the moral valence of one's conduct and to restrict human interventionist judgment in this regard. This liberal attitude was key in shaping the final inclusive doctrinal position of the majoritarian Sunni Muslim community. Its full appellation — *ahl al-sunna wa-'l-jama'a* ("the people of prophetic custom" [sc. those who follow the practices of Muhammad] "and of communal solidarity") — underscores their basic accommodationist outlook which strove to contain dissension as much as possible in order to preserve the unity of the Muslim community.

It appears that by the mid-ninth century, a less hard-line 'Uthmani position that was willing to include 'Ali as one of the Rightly-Guided Caliphs and a considerably watered-down 'Alid position that was willing to settle for third place for 'Ali were fast finding niches for themselves within the broad platform of the Sunnis-in-the-making. Membership within the *ahl al-sunna* began to broaden at this juncture in history to include all those who accepted the caliphate of the four Rashidun caliphs, with Abu Bakr and 'Umar inevitably ranked as first and second in order of excellence while some compromise was allowed (and even expected) in the ranking of 'Uthman and 'Ali relative to one another. The eleventh-century scholar 'Abd al-Qahir al-Baghdadi (d. 1037) indicates as much when he describes the Sunnis as those who showed preference for Abu Bakr, 'Umar and those who were after him, even though they differed with regard to the respective merits of 'Ali and 'Uthman.[21]

A clear and more detailed hierarchy of merit for the Companions of the Prophet had emerged by the late tenth to early eleventh century. This is apparent in the following statement made by al-Baghdadi:

> The *ahl al-sunna* are universally agreed that the most excellent of men after the Messenger of God, peace and blessings be upon him, are Abu Bakr, then 'Umar, then 'Uthman, then 'Ali, then the rest of the ten [sc. the ten Companions assured of heaven by the Prophet],[22] then the rest of the people of Badr, then the rest of the people of Uhud, then the rest of the people of allegiance (*ahl al-bay'a*),[23] then the rest of the Companions.[24]

Once this consensus regarding the legitimacy of the first four caliphs had emerged after the ninth century, the memory of the earlier ambivalence toward the third and the fourth Rashidun caliphs became progressively dim and even obliterated. This development is indicated in a number of laudatory reports recorded in late Sunni *hadith* works, which maintain that the historical chronological order of the succession of the Rashidun caliphs was divinely pre-ordained. Thus a report recorded in a thirteenth-century source states that on the night of his ascension to the heavens, the Prophet saw written on the divine throne the following: "There is no god but God and Muhammad is the Messenger of God; Abu Bakr is the Veracious One, 'Umar, the Distinguisher of Truth, 'Uthman, the Martyr, and 'Ali, the Approved One."[25] This report encodes the consensus of the Sunni Muslims from after the ninth century that there could have been no more morally excellent leaders for their community than the Rightly-Guided Caliphs and that such a fortunate state of affairs could not but have been providentially decreed.

The Age of the Companions

So far we have concentrated on the four Rightly-Guided Caliphs as the most prominent among the Prophet's Companions and on the seminal role tradition ascribes to them in shaping the contours of the early Muslim community and in laying the bases of religious, legal, and political thought. But other Companions also left an indelible stamp on the growth of the community in remarkable and distinctive ways. The Companions as a collectivity were eulogized by the early biographer Ibn Sa'd (d. 845) in the following manner:

> All the Companions of the Messenger of God, peace and blessings be upon him, were models to be emulated, whose actions are remembered, whose opinions were consulted, and who voiced their opinions. Those who were the most prominent among the Companions of the Messenger of God, peace and blessings be upon him, listened to *hadith*s and transmitted them.[1]

As this statement points out, particularly significant is the role of the best known Companions in the preservation of the memory of the Prophet, his actions and particularly his speech – that is to say, their role in the formation of the *sunna*, the second most important source of law after the Qur'an, of which the primary component is Muhammad's recorded speech known as *hadith* (literally, "statement," "speech"). A Companion's narration of a statement attributed to the Prophet is crucial for establishing at least the probable veracity of its content.

Typically, a *hadith* consists of two parts: (1) *isnad*, which refers to the chain of transmission, containing the names of the *hadith*'s narrators; and (2) *matn*, which refers to the text of the *hadith*. If the *isnad* lacks the name of the Companion who would have heard and related the statement directly from the Prophet, the *hadith* is called *mursal* or "suspended" and its probative value as a legal proof-text is considerably diminished. The best kind of a *hadith* is what is termed *sahih*, which means "sound." Such a *hadith* has an uninterrupted chain of transmitters, and each transmitter in the chain is deemed to possess personal moral probity and a highly retentive memory. In addition, the transmitters must have been known individuals whose biographical details provide reasonable certitude that they were alive at their purported time of transmission activity and would have also met the next transmitter in line.

The next best kind of *hadith* is *hasan* or "good." In terms of its reliability as a proof-text, it is slightly below that of a "sound" one and is so ranked on account of minor flaws known to exist in the character or general reputation of one or more of the transmitters in the *isnad*. Other *hadith*s that do not meet these stringent criteria of reliability are termed *da'if* or "weak." Among the deficiencies of a weak *hadith* may be a chain of transmission which consists of one or more narrators who are widely regarded as dishonest, or deemed to have possessed a faulty memory, or regarding whom not enough biographical details are known. They are generally not considered to be reliable proof-texts in legal or doctrinal matters. Missing links in the chain of transmission also diminish a *hadith*'s reliability and consequently its value as a proof-text. There are also *hadith*s that are regarded as outright fabrications (*mawdu'at*), both on account of their faulty *isnad*s and spurious content, which may display political and/or doctrinal bias.

On account of the importance of *hadith* transmission in the development of the religious sciences after the Qur'an and the indispensable role of the Companions in this activity, interest in recording the details of the lives of the Companions emerged fairly early. The oldest, written biographical work known to us is the afore-mentioned Ibn Sa'd's *Kitab al-tabaqat al-kubra* ("The Book of the Great Generations"). It is a veritable treasure trove of information on the formative period. Biographical works written specifically for the assessment of the reliability of *hadith* transmitters are termed *rijal* (lit. "men"). This term is a misnomer since the *rijal* literature contains entries on women transmitters as well, typically set apart as a special section.

In order to more sharply delineate the contribution of the Companions (other than the Rightly-Guided Caliphs) to the religious and intellectual history of Islam and to highlight their role as moral exemplars for succeeding generations of Muslims, we will now focus briefly on the lives of a number of these exceptional individuals. Some of them are more distinguished for their scholarship while others deserve special mention for their commendable piety and remarkable personal attributes and/or for their "iconic" status as individuals who embody the basic ideational changes wrought by Islam. Length considerations prevent us from discussing a great number of these remarkable individuals, whose leap of faith changed the course of world history.

IBN 'ABBAS (D. CA. 688): THE SAGE OF THE MUSLIM COMMUNITY

'Abd Allah Ibn al-'Abbas (or, more frequently, Ibn 'Abbas) is arguably the most important Companion after the four Rashidun caliphs. A cousin of the Prophet, he was born a Muslim three years before the migration to Medina. His mother had embraced Islam, but her husband and his father, al-'Abbas (eponym of the 'Abbasid dynasty), would not convert until much later.[2]

At a very young age, Ibn 'Abbas is depicted as showing an unusual aptitude for scholarship, in which he was aided by a highly retentive memory and a natural love for learning. He is particularly renowned in Qur'anic exegesis, which he claimed to have learned from the Prophet himself. An early report on the authority of the Companion 'Ikrima affirms that Ibn 'Abbas was more learned than 'Ali with regard to the Qur'an while 'Ali was more learned than Ibn 'Abbas with regard to verses of the Qur'an which referred to unidentified people or events (mubhamat).[3]

Ibn 'Abbas was deeply devoted to the Prophet, enjoying an exceptionally close relationship with the latter since his birth. Some sources present this relationship as almost an organic one, signified in the anecdote which relates that when his mother brought him as a newborn to Muhammad, the latter placed some of his saliva on the child's tongue. Other anecdotes show him faithfully emulating the Prophet in matters of worship and expressing his devotion to and humility before Muhammad. Once, when Ibn 'Abbas was with the Prophet, he meticulously followed Muhammad as he performed his ablutions. Then he stood behind the Prophet to pray but the latter gestured to him to stand beside him. Ibn 'Abbas failed to comply. When the prayer was over, Muhammad asked him why he had not stood beside him. Ibn 'Abbas replied that the Prophet was too great in his eyes to allow him to stand by the latter's side. Muhammad responded by praying, "O God, grant him wisdom!"[4]

Ibn ʿAbbas was only thirteen when the Prophet died and came into his own as a scholar during ʿUthman's reign, achieving much renown. He is said (perhaps somewhat hyperbolically) to have memorized about 1,660 hadiths, some of which were included by al-Bukhari and Muslim in their authoritative hadith compilations. He was appointed by ʿUthman as the leader of the pilgrimage in the year 656. After ʿUthman's assassination, Ibn ʿAbbas offered his services to ʿAli who appointed him governor of Basra. Accusations that Ibn ʿAbbas absconded with quite a bit of money from the state treasury of Basra remain a blot on his reputation, although some later historians attribute this act to his brother ʿUbayd Allah and present it as a case of mistaken identity.

Much harder to brush aside by ʿAbbasid historians was his apparent "defection" to the Umayyad side after ʿAli's assassination and after al-Hasan, ʿAli's elder son, had relinquished any claim to the caliphate. Although some historians relate that Ibn ʿAbbas protested, along with others, Muʿawiya's institution of dynastic rule by naming his son, Yazid, as his successor, he appears to have made his peace with it.[5]

Whatever his political proclivities, the sources universally extol Ibn ʿAbbas' erudition by conferring on him the epithets Hibr al-umma ("the sage of the Muslim community"), al-Bahr "the sea [of learning]"), and Tarjuman al-qurʾan ("the consummate interpreter of the Qurʾan"). Like two other prominent Companions, Ibn Masʿud and Ubayy ibn Kaʿb, he had his own copy of the Qurʾan (mushaf), which is said to have differed in the arrangement of its chapters in comparison with the ʿUthmanic text.[6]

With regard to hadith transmission, a substantial number of reports were circulated that were falsely attributed to him, the reason for which is obvious. As a prominent Companion and extremely learned scholar, a hadith putatively transmitted on Ibn ʿAbbas' authority was more likely to gain acceptance, regardless of its actual text. The late eighth-century jurist al-Shafiʿi (d. 820) reached the conclusion that fabrications in the name of Ibn ʿAbbas had been so widespread that only about a hundred reports attributed to him could be held to be reliable.[7]

Ibn ʿAbbas died quietly in Taʾif in the Arabian peninsula circa 688 (other death dates given). One later source glowingly assesses his overall standing among the Companions as follows: he was the inspired teacher and gifted instructor, the focus of pride, the full moon of the sages, the pole of the luminaries, the noble king, the gushing river and abundant spring [of knowledge], explicator of the Revelation and its lucid interpreter, sharp of sensibility, humble in attire, showing honor to his companions, and a generous host to his friends.[8]

IBN MAS'UD (D. 653): INTERPRETER OF THE WORD OF GOD

His full name was 'Abd Allah ibn Ghafil ibn Habib ibn Hudhayl, of humble Bedouin descent. On his father's side he was a *mawla*, that is a client or protégé, of the clan of Zuhra, a member of the tribe of Quraysh. Ibn Mas'ud embraced Islam very early, being among the first six or seven people to do so. His case illustrates the appeal of the new religion for those who, on account of humble birth and low social status, were assigned to the margins of a tribal kinship-based society, causing them to seek personal and social valorization within the egalitarianism promised by Islam. After his conversion, Ibn Mas'ud soon became very attached to Muhammad, becoming one of his closest associates and performed some domestic tasks for him.[9]

Based on the usual criteria invoked to establish a Companion's precedence and moral excellence, Ibn Mas'ud ranks very highly indeed. In addition to early acceptance of Islam, he emigrated first to Abyssinia and then to Medina and took part in the battles of Badr, Uhud, and Khandaq. He holds the distinction of having been the first to publicly recite the Qur'an in Mecca before the Migration to Medina. His excellences were recognized in the caliphal period when he was awarded a very high stipend – 6,000 dinars – from the public treasury.[10]

His constant companions in Medina were drawn from the ranks of the Medinan Helpers and the non-Arab converts or *mawali*, such as Salman al-Farisi from a Persian background. Given his own non-elite Bedouin background, such associations were natural for Ibn Mas'ud and would also explain why some of his strongest supporters tended to come from similar non-Qurayshi backgrounds.

As one of Muhammad's closest associates, Ibn Mas'ud was among those select Companions privy to the Qur'anic revelations as it was being received and recited by the Prophet. Like Ibn 'Abbas, Ibn Mas'ud was a recognized *qari'* (Qur'an reciter) during and after the Prophet's lifetime. He is also said to have had his own copy of the Qur'an and his variant readings, which were relatively minor, have been preserved for us by later authorities. Some sources relate that Ibn Mas'ud opposed 'Uthman's authorization of a single canonical text and resisted relinquishing his own copy of the Qur'an.[11] Part of this opposition, however, may be attributed to his political differences with 'Uthman and his general disaffection with the Qurayshi elite.

In the field of Qur'anic exegesis, Ibn Mas'ud plays a very prominent, if to a degree, controversial role. He was partial to allegorical interpretation (*ta'wil*) of Qur'anic verses and his fervent devotion to the Prophet and his family finds frequent reflection in his exegesis, causing him to be accused of harboring a pro-'Alid bias. The tenth-century celebrated exegete al-Tabari (d. 923) was strongly critical of him on account of these "questionable" inclinations. Ibn Mas'ud's exegesis, as might be expected, finds favor with the Shi'a in particular and he is one of their most frequently cited Sunni authorities in establishing the privileged position of the Prophet's family (*ahl al-bayt*).[12]

Ibn Mas'ud was, furthermore, a prolific transmitter of *hadith*, particularly of the eschatological and admonitory type, which emphasized constant self-vigilance in preparation for the next world and exhorted the cultivation of morals and good manners, and learning. Kufan traditionists of the next generation, such as the well-known Ibrahim al-Nakha'i and Ibn Mas'ud's own son, Abu 'Ubayda, circulated *hadith*s attributed to Ibn Mas'ud widely but which were scarcely reported by traditionists from other cities. Among the Sunni compilers of authoritative *hadith*, al-Tirmidhi includes a number of Ibn Mas'ud's reports. Like his exegesis, many of Ibn Mas'ud's *hadith*s also found favor with the Shi'a and, to a considerable degree, with the proponents of Sufism (*tasawwuf*), like al-Ghazali (d. 1111) in the eleventh century.

During the reign of Abu Bakr, Ibn Mas'ud took part in the battle of Yarmuk in 634 and after the conquest of Iraq was given some land there. He was present at the founding of the new Arab garrison town of Kufa. Even after his return shortly thereafter to Syria he continued to maintain strong links with the town and its people. In 642, he moved to Kufa to take up permanent residence and served there as lieutenant to his close friend 'Ammar ibn Yasir.

Ibn Mas'ud died in 653, very likely in Kufa, Iraq, where he was highly esteemed for his piety and learning, although some sources relate that he died in Medina. A short while before his death, Ibn Mas'ud had politically fallen out of favor with the Medinan establishment for his pietistic and populist sympathies. Such sympathies pitted him against the Qurayshi aristocrats who were being increasingly appointed to public offices under the third caliph 'Uthman. His tendency to speak "truth to power" eventually led to his political eclipse under 'Uthman. In the year 649, he publicly criticized al-Walid ibn 'Uqba, appointed governor of Kufa, for his blatant impiety and disregard for Islamic norms. The following year, Ibn Mas'ud had a falling out with the caliph himself, the exact reasons for which are not given in the sources, but for which he is said to have been punished in some manner.[13]

As we have indicated, Ibn Mas'ud gets mixed reviews in the sources on account of his strong religious and political beliefs which met with considerable sympathy in some quarters but were censured by others. His insistence on holding public officials accountable for their behavior, according to generally accepted moral standards, did not go over well with those who had obtained their positions mainly on the basis of their lineage. On the other hand, he was held in great esteem by particularly his Kufan supporters for the same reasons. The Kufans saw in him a champion for the rights of all those who felt betrayed by the resurgence under 'Uthman of the Qurayshi/Umayyad elite, who had been bitter foes of the Prophet and his family until the fall of Mecca. A significant number of these Qurayshis appeared to be still, at best, nominal or lukewarm Muslims.

The complex and contested image of Ibn Mas'ud that emerges from the variegated, sometimes tendentious, sources encapsulates for us some of the burning issues of his day, highlighting the politics of piety then underway pitting pious idealists who subscribed to Islamic egalitarianism against too-worldly rulers and administrators who had re-valorized pre-Islamic values of kinship-based privilege to a considerable extent. The ways in which the scholars of the later period assessed Ibn Mas'ud – the man and his imprint upon Islamic piety and scholarship – demonstrate for us the continued resonance of some of these issues with succeeding generations. They further illustrate for us how an authoritative (albeit controversial) figure from the first generation of Muslims could be invoked to mediate critical issues of the later period.

'A'ISHA BINT ABI BAKR (D. 678): THE BELOVED OF MUHAMMAD

'A'isha bint Abi Bakr is arguably the most famous woman of early Islam and also its most controversial. She was born circa 614 in Mecca to her famous parents, Abu Bakr ibn Abi Quhafa and Umm Ruman bint 'Umayr ibn 'Amir. 'A'isha is deemed to have been the nineteenth person to embrace Islam.

Her fame and status as one of the Mothers of the Believers (*Ummuhat al-Mu'minin*; a term applied to all the wives of the Prophet in Qur'an 33:6) derives of course from being associated with Muhammad himself: as his wife, lover, confidante, and friend. Nicknamed Humayra' ("little ruddy one") by the Prophet, Muhammad's deep and abiding love for his youngest and only virgin wife is touchingly portrayed in the sources. 'A'isha was clearly his soul-mate in many ways and, although by no means the only woman in his life, she was the best loved and most cherished in his household after his first wife Khadija's death. Her special position in Muhammad's life is signaled by her unique epithet *Habibat habib allah*, "the beloved of the beloved of God."[14] Among her other sobriquets were *Siddiqa bint al-siddiq*, derived from her father's common honorific *al-Siddiq* ("the Truthful"), and the *kunya* Umm 'Abd Allah ("mother of 'Abd Allah") on account of her very close relationship with her nephew 'Abd Allah ibn al-Zubayr, whom the childless 'A'isha came to look upon as her own "son."[15]

'A'isha entered Muhammad's home as his wife at a tender age; the range of years given is between six and nine. The marriage was not consummated until she reached puberty; again a range of years between nine and twelve is given in the sources,[16] reflecting the trend in this period not to keep accurate logs of such events and thus to guess at people's ages. Child marriage was not an uncommon practice in the Arabian peninsula at this time (as elsewhere), often being contracted for political purposes between leading families. Since 'A'isha was the daughter of Abu Bakr, one of Muhammad's closest Companions and trusted ally, this liaison carried significant political overtones.

Be that as it may, there developed genuine intimacy and strong devotion between 'A'isha and the Prophet. Evocative domestic vignettes preserved in the sources show her as being concerned with his physical well-being, cautioning him against staying out too long in the sun, helping with his personal grooming, and fussing over him when he fell sick. When 'A'isha once asked Muhammad how he would characterize his love for her, he replied, "Like a firm knot in a rope," meaning, as he explained, that it was always constant.[17]

Once, overcome by his love for her, Muhammad exclaimed before her, "O 'A'isha, may God reward you handsomely. I am not the source of joy to you that you are to me!"[18] Anas ibn Malik, a close Companion, eulogized their relationship thus, "The first love in Islam was the love of the Prophet, peace and blessings be upon him, for 'A'isha, may God Almighty be pleased with her."[19]

Secure in her husband's affection, 'A'isha took pride in claiming at least ten distinctions that were hers alone, as follows: (1) she was the only virgin wife of Muhammad; (2) both her parents were migrants to Medina; (3) God had proclaimed her innocence in the Qur'an; (4) Gabriel had revealed her likeness to Muhammad and had instructed him to marry her; (5) she had washed in the same vessel with the Prophet; (6) Muhammad had offered his prayers in her company; (7) she was the only wife in whose presence he received revelations; (8) the Prophet died in her arms; (9) he passed away on the night allotted to her; and (10) he was buried in her apartment.[20]

The third distinction is in connection with a critical incident in the life of the young 'A'isha and of the nascent community, which came to be known as *hadith al-ifk* ("the incident of the lie"). This incident occurred when the Prophet was returning from the campaign against the Banu Mustalik in 628. During one of the stops not far from Medina, 'A'isha wandered off by herself to search for a missing piece of jewelry, leaving the curtains of her camel litter closed. In the meantime, Muhammad gave the signal for departure and the litter-bearers made off without noticing her absence. When 'A'isha came back to the stop and discovered what had happened, she waited there for someone to escort her back. A young man by the name of Safwan ibn al-Mu'attal happened to arrive at the spot and brought her back to Medina mounted on his camel, which he led by the rein. 'A'isha's return to Medina alone in the company of a young man generated scandalous accusations among a number of influential people, chief among them being 'Abd Allah ibn Ubayy who was one of the Medinan *al-munafiqun*, the name given to lukewarm or nominal Muslims at best. Shortly thereafter, her name was cleared through verses revealed to Muhammad (Qur'an 24:11–17), which censured those who had spread the unsubstantiated accusations against her.[21] These verses became the basis for classical legal rulings on establishing proof of illicit sexual conduct. Qur'an 24:13 specifically enjoins that four eye-witnesses who witnessed the actual act of penetration be produced before a charge of adultery can be established, while Qur'an 24:4 threatens with caning those who slander (*qadhf*) chaste women without producing such witnesses. In a later period when her distress had become a dim memory, 'A'isha would take pride in the fact that she had been a "cause of revelation" and that God Himself had exonerated her in these verses.

'A'isha's lively temperament, obvious intelligence, and ready wit destined her to play a leading role in many of the activities in the Prophet's household during his lifetime and particularly in the stormy period after his death. Muhammad breathed his last in her arms when she was only about eighteen years old in 632. Deeply affected by the trauma of watching her beloved husband die, she accepted her fate as a childless widow and retired to her mosque apartment for a period of mourning.

It was after the murder of 'Uthman, the third caliph, in 656 when she assumed a public political role. 'A'isha publicly demanded that 'Ali, who had succeeded the slain caliph, find and bring the assassins to justice, which he was reluctant to do. 'A'isha, along with her staunchest two allies, Talha and Zubayr, launched the Battle of the Camel (so-called because of 'Askar, the camel she rode on) against 'Ali, in which her side lost. Talha and Zubayr were killed and 'A'isha was courteously escorted back to Medina by 'Ali.

'A'isha's role in the civil war after 'Uthman's death is much debated in the sources. Some historians criticize her decision to lead the Battle of the Camel as precipitous and unbecoming of a "Mother of the Believers," and of gentlewomen in general. Thus al-Tabari reports that 'Ai'sha's followers were dismissed by many as constituting "a faction headed by a woman."[22] Others have suggested that she was pressured and deceived by those around her, who exploited her less than amicable sentiments toward 'Ali.[23] Shi'i sources tend to vigorously reproach 'A'isha for her political campaign against 'Ali, their first rightful Imam. Most Sunni sources, however, portray her as filled with remorse toward the end of her life for her role in the Battle of the Camel, which grants her exculpation and allows her at the same time to set a cautionary example for future generations of women who might be contemplating a political career. This cautionary example appears to have become crystallized in a *hadith* in which Muhammad warns that no nation ruled by a woman would prosper. Although this report occurs in a number of authoritative collections, it is worthy of note that this solitary *hadith* (*khabar al-wahid*, sc. a report transmitted by very few narrators) was related by the Companion Abu Bakra who was known to be less than reliable in his transmissions and who had been caned by 'Umar, the second caliph, for some infraction.[24] The sentiment expressed in this report is also at odds with the Qur'anic verses (27:22–41) which speak favorably of the rule of the Queen of Sheba and with Muhammad's practice of taking political counsel from his wives. These observations collectively suggest political motivations in the circulation of this report, in all likelihood owing no small measure to 'A'isha's controversial leadership in the insurrection against 'Ali.[25]

The disastrous Battle of the Camel effectively ended 'A'isha's political influence but not her public role in general as a teacher and counsellor. She continued to be widely revered by her contemporaries for her learning and was frequently consulted by the senior Companions (akabir) for her exceptional knowledge of many matters, including that of inheritance shares (fara'id).[26] A full one-third of al-Bukhari's sound collection of hadiths is attributed to her and she issued many legal opinions (fatawa) on different topics. 'A'isha once corrected the prominent Companion 'Abd Allah ibn 'Umar's narration of a hadith which was accepted by the latter in silence.[27] She was also a respected exegete of the Qur'an and transmitted her exegesis to her student 'Urwa ibn al-Zubayr.[28] The pious successor 'Ata' ibn Abi Rabah glowingly described her as "the most perspicacious and learned among people and the best among them in her opinions."[29] She is also said to have excelled in poetry and in knowledge of medicine (al-tibb), in addition to law.[30] Remembering the Prophet's example and advice to her to shun the luxuries of this world, she maintained an abstemious lifestyle until her death, inclining to long periods of prayer and fasting.[31] She was exceptionally generous towards relatives and the poor in general and is said to have disbursed about 70,000 dirhams in charity.[32] Perhaps the highest praise ever paid to a Muslim woman (or perhaps any woman in a religious context) was Muhammad's general counsel to his Companions "to take half your religion from Humayra'," in affectionate reference to 'A'isha.[33]

'A'isha died in 678, when she was between 64 and 67 years of age during the reign of Mu'awiya, the first Umayyad caliph. Her funeral was attended by a large crowd of people who were among the most prominent Muslims of the time. Abu Hurayra, the governor of Medina at the time, led her funeral prayer and her beloved "son" 'Abd Allah ibn al-Zubayr and his brother 'Urwa ibn al-Zubayr, her faithful student, were among the relatives who attended to the burial rites. Her body was laid to rest in the famous cemetery of Baqi' in Medina.

'A'isha is said to have sought oblivion during her later years, wishing out loud that she could be completely forgotten (*mansiyyan*).[34] But such desired oblivion proved especially elusive after death. For many contemporary Muslims, women and men, 'A'isha is more of an iconic figure than ever, whose passionate and eventful life is invoked to challenge the master narratives which have eclipsed to a considerable degree women's contributions to the making of the Islamic tradition. Renewed focus on her life and achievements by contemporary, especially women, scholars is allowing her to emerge from the shadows to which time and prejudice on occasion have relegated her. Muslim feminists today underscore her prominent role in religious scholarship, her bold (if foolhardy) attempt to lead an army against 'Ali to redress a perceived political injustice, and the respect and admiration she commanded among her contemporaries on the strength of her own accomplishments, not solely because she was the most prominent widow of the Prophet, as embodying the gender-egalitarian spirit of the early period. Contrasted to the public social status of women in succeeding centuries, she has become an idealized symbol of the religious and social empowerment that Islam had promised women but which realpolitik considerably attenuated over the centuries.

UMM 'UMARA: VALIANT DEFENDER OF THE PROPHET

Although better known as Umm 'Umara, her actual name was Nusayba bint Ka'b. She was a celebrated woman Companion from the Banu Najjar in Medina, known for her courage and indomitable spirit. Ibn Sa'd devotes what amounts to three and a half pages in print to the recounting of her martial exploits. According to Ibn Sa'd, Umm 'Umara gave her allegiance to the Prophet very early before his migration to Medina and eventually witnessed several key events of early Islam: she was present at Uhud, al-Hudaybiyya, Khaybar, Hunayn, and al-Yamama (633–34). At Uhud, she was present with her husband Ghaziyya ibn 'Amr and her two sons. Ibn Sa'd tells us that the valiant Umm 'Umara had headed for Uhud with the intention of quenching the thirst of the combatants but soon found herself engaging in fighting against the enemy. In the course of the battle, she is said to have sustained twelve wounds to her body, inflicted either by a spear or a sword.[35]

Ibn Sa'd includes a detailed account from Umm 'Umara who confided the following details to a female companion Umm Sa'd, when the latter asked her what precisely had happened on that day. According to Umm 'Umara, she had gone out to the battlefield in the early part of the day, carrying her water-skin to feed the thirsty, and worked her way through the battlefield until she reached the Prophet. As the tide of the battle began to turn against the Muslims, she remained by the side of the Prophet and began to fight herself, defending the Prophet with a sword and a bow and an arrow, until she was grievously injured. Muhammad himself commented on Umm 'Umara's valor thus, "Indeed the position of Nusayba bint Ka'b today is higher than anyone else's."[36] She is also said to have lost a hand at al-Yamama during the battle fought against the false prophet Musaylima from the Banu Hanifa after the fall of Mecca in 630. She heard *hadith*s from the Prophet and transmitted from him. Among the *hadith*s she transmitted is the one in which Muhammad states, "The angels pray for those who fast until they are done (or eat their fill)." Umm 'Umara's stature remained high among the early Muslims after the Prophet's death; and it is said that Abu Bakr would frequently inquire about her after he became the caliph.[37] She married three times and bore three sons.

Umm 'Umara's valor on the battlefield and her public persona are often highlighted in modern studies of Muslim women from the first generation to set up a contrast to the more restricted lifestyles imposed on women in the High Middle Ages. We have thus not yet bade her a final farewell; we will encounter her again in chapters 9 and 10 when we discuss the appropriation of the Pious Forbears by the modernists and the Islamists and the pivotal role depictions of her life play in modern debates concerning gender.

BILAL IBN RABAH (D. CA. 641): THE VOICE OF ISLAM

Bilal ibn Rabah is famous for having been the first caller to prayer (*mu'adhdhin*), chosen for his strong and mellifluous voice. He was a slave from an Abyssinian (Ethiopian) background and was one of the early converts to Islam who openly proclaimed his conversion. On account of his public avowal of his new faith, he was persecuted severely by a pagan Meccan, Umayya ibn Khalaf. The biographical literature extols his exemplary steadfastness in the face of great provocation and describes him as "one of the helpless believers" (*al-mustad'afun*; cf. Qur'an 8:26) of the early period. It further describes evocatively how Bilal would cry out "One!" "One!" when asked to recant his newly discovered monotheism by his persecutors. His plight came to the attention of Abu Bakr, who purchased him and set him free. 'Umar ibn al-Khattab was wont to praising Abu Bakr for this act of manumission by saying, "Abu Bakr is our master and he liberated our master," here referring to Bilal.[38]

After his manumission, Bilal lived in Abu Bakr's house. He migrated to Medina with the Prophet and was paired as a brother to the Medinan Khath'ami Abu Ruwayha (other names also given). Shortly after the arrival in Medina, Muhammad consulted with his Companions on the best way to summon the faithful to prayer. Some proposed that a horn be sounded or a wooden clapper be used, as was common among the Eastern Christians. Finally, one Companion 'Abd Allah ibn Zayd related that he had a dream the night before in which someone called the Muslims to prayer from a rooftop. This idea found favor with the Prophet and with many of the other Companions. Bilal, on account of his strong and mellifluous voice, was appointed the mu'adhdhin by Muhammad. In a hadith, the Prophet praises Bilal thus, "What an excellent man is Bilal! For he is the leader of all the callers to prayer (sayyid al-mu'adhdhinin)."[39]

Bilal took part in most of the early military campaigns, including Badr, where he slew his former persecutor Umayya ibn Khalaf. He married an Arab woman from the tribe of Banu Zuhra. When Mecca fell to the Muslims in 630, Bilal is reported to have climbed to the top of the Ka'ba, after it had been cleansed of the idols, and gave a sonorous call to prayer, symbolizing the inauguration of a brand new era. Bilal also gave the heartbreaking call to prayer when the Prophet died and before he was buried. When he intoned, "I bear witness that Muhammad is the Messenger of God," the people gathered in the mosque are said to have dissolved uncontrollably into tears.[40]

During the time of 'Umar, the second caliph, Bilal was one of a handful of non-Arab Muslims who were granted pensions from the state treasury on account of their precedence and moral excellence. This group included the previously mentioned Salman al-Farisi and the Byzantine Greek Suhayb ibn Sinan al-Rumi. Bilal took part in the Syrian campaign under 'Umar. He died in roughly 641 (or slightly later) and was buried in or near Damascus (a few accounts say in Aleppo). He was roughly 60 years old.

Bilal's piety is highlighted in a hadith in which Muhammad relates that when he entered Paradise, he heard a sound in front of him and was surprised to discover that Bilal had preceded him there. When the Prophet inquired how Bilal had attained such a status, the latter replied that it was on account of his scrupulous attention to personal cleanliness and performance of supererogatory prayers.[41] This unexpected precedence granted to Bilal is meant to foreground his exceptional piety and implying (or holding out the possibility) that a believer could perhaps surpass even a prophet in status through supererogatory acts of worship. This report occurs in a Sufi biography and is transgressively suggestive of a mystical leveling of all good, holy people in the next world, transcending the constructed socio-political categories of this world.

Like Salman the Persian and Suhayb the Byzantine, Bilal, the non-Arab African convert, is invoked in many circles today to underscore the universalism of the Islamic message, which in its ideal implementation recognizes no difference among humans on the basis of ethnicity or race but only on the basis of piety. It is no wonder that the leading African-American Muslim newspaper between 1975–81 was called *The Bilalian News*.

CONCLUSION

These capsules of the lives of a few of the most prominent Companions (*Sahaba*) allow us to make the following observations. The early sources are often remarkably candid in documenting both the positive and negative traits of individual Companions, as we saw in the case of Ibn 'Abbas and Ibn Mas'ud, for example. One does not sense as yet the highly laudatory and sometimes exculpatory attitude that would develop among later Sunni scholars toward the majority, if not all, of the Companions. Some of the most critical comments regarding a number of the Companions occur in the *rijal* (biographical) literature and other works of *hadith* analysis which assess the moral probity and general reliability of *hadith* transmitters through several generations. Thus the ninth-century scholar Ibn Qutayba (d. 889) relates in regard to the prominent Companion Abu Hurayra, for example, that 'Umar, 'Uthman, 'A'isha and 'Ali rejected *hadith*s related by him as unreliable.[42]

Early biographical and *hadith* works are also distinctive in depicting many women Companions (*Sahabiyyat*) as deeply involved in community affairs and assuming prominent roles in defending the community against its enemies, in carrying out humanitarian activities, and in educating and counselling men and women. Compared with some late biographical works, Ibn

Sa'd's *al-Tabaqat* gives fulsome and admiring descriptions of many of the women Companions' achievements. As conceptions of women's public roles changed over time, so did the portrayals of the women Companions' lives to a certain extent in contemporary works. Thus 'A'isha's very public and almost embarrassingly aggressive persona by later standards had to be explained away or ameliorated by later male biographers in a bid to preserve her role as a first generation moral exemplum.[43] Reconstructions of the lives of some of the women Companions and their moral-political implications is a topic we will revisit in subsequent chapters.

The candid portrayals of Companions found in early authoritative sources did not impede, however, the progressive development over time of an image of the Companions as near-perfect individuals who exemplified the highest Islamic ideals in both their private and public conduct. With increasing temporal distance, as occurred with the Prophet, his followers too became larger-than-life figures for later generations, who through the vicissitudes of time tended to regard their collective past as a pristine, golden era, peopled by paragons of unfailing virtue and intellectual acumen. More than as individuals with unique gifts and aptitudes, the Companions in the later period were lionized as a collectivity, as we discern in the statement by Ibn Sa'd quoted above. Such a process would allow even someone like Mu'awiya, the first Umayyad caliph, who is excoriated in the early sources for instituting dynastic rule and for fomenting the first civil war, to be at least partially rehabilitated mainly on account of his ascription to the *Sahaba*.[44]

One of the main impetuses for this evolution was the growing dialectical exchanges between the Sunnis and the Shi'a in the making. The Shi'a would progress from an earlier neutral and ambivalent stance toward the *Sahaba* to outright denunciation of the majority of the Companions for having withheld from 'Ali what was assumed to be his pre-ordained right to become the caliph/*imam* after the Prophet's death. The Sunnis, in turn, formulated the collective moral excellence of the Companions, which was predicated primarily on their status as contemporaries of Muhammad and on any measure of proximity or access to him. Thus "companionship" (*suhba*) could be ascribed to someone who had known the Prophet intimately and interacted with him on a regular basis as well as to someone who had met him only once. The chronological excellence imputed to the first three generations of Muslims, and particularly to the first generation, with a gradual attrition in such moral excellence among succeeding generations with the passage of time, finds full expression in a statement attributed to the Prophet. In it he remarks: "The best of people are from my generation; then from the second [generation], then from the third. Then will come a group of people in whom there will be no good."[45]

It is worthy of note that the exculpatory attitude toward the Companions in general has intensified in some quarters in the modern period An indication of this is a monograph written in defense of Abu Hurayra in the 1970s.[46] But again, in other quarters, re-engagement with the earlier classical works has led to renewed criticism of a number of the *Sahaba* and their reported actions, particularly their putative role in the dissemination of spurious traditions. Contemporary dialectics between traditionalists and Islamists on the one hand and modernists and reformists on the other are to a large measure conducted in regard to the highly sensitive issue of the reliability of the *hadith* corpus as it now exists, with the former camp disinclined to revisit the issue, while the latter insists on its absolute necessity in order to winnow out problematic spurious reports even more stringently than the pre-modern scholars did. We will refer to these dialectics in our concluding chapters.

The Age of the Successors

The Age of the Companions is reckoned to have come to an end with the death of Anas ibn Malik (d. 710 or 713). Those who belong to the following generation are called "the Successors" (*al-Tabi'un*). The period of the Successors, beginning circa 713, came to an end in approximately 796 and was followed by the next generation, known as "the Successors to the Successors." This chapter will briefly deal with the Age of the Successors while the next chapter will deal with the Successors to the Successors. Both chapters will discuss the significance of these two generations in continuing to build on and expand the edifice of the religion and civilization of Islam.

THE HISTORICAL MILIEU

The Age of the Successors spans the heyday of the Umayyad period through its fall to the 'Abbasids, and extends into the early decades of the latter dynasty's rule. It was a highly eventful period marked by large scale territorial and political expansion and intellectual ferment, but also marred by communal dissension and strife. By the end of the Umayyad period, the boundaries of the Islamic world had extended to include all of North Africa and southern and central Spain (al-Andalus). Important forays had also been made into central Asia and northern India, setting the stage for future settlements of these areas.

These territorial expansions, which placed large numbers of non-Arabs and non-Muslims under Muslim rule, were followed by a process of

Arabization and, eventually at a much slower pace, of Islamization. Arabization, that is the replacement of the widely spoken languages of the Fertile Crescent (Aramaic and Greek) and of Egypt and North Africa (Coptic, Greek, and Berber) by Arabic, proceeded more rapidly than Islamization, that is, the conversion of the native peoples to Islam. In fact, until about the tenth century, the indigenous populations of these areas remained largely non-Muslim, although considerably Arabized by then. As the historian Richard Bulliet, among others, has shown, conversion was delayed several centuries among Christian, Zoroastrian, and Jewish communities[1] and belies the accusation still heard today that Muslims effected forced conversions of these peoples upon conquest. Bulliet observes that the "post-conquest world, at least through the first two centuries of Islam, was one of geographically dispersed, largely illiterate communities of Arab Muslims constituting the ruling stratum of a multilingual, multiethnic, overwhelmingly non-Muslim empire," and that between the late 630s when the conquests began and the end of the Umayyad period in 750, "fewer than ten percent of the non-Arab populace had converted."[2] Robert Schick in his analysis of the historical and archaeological evidence for the Christian communities in Palestine arrived at a similar conclusion.[3]

Persia was exceptional in having resisted the initial drive toward Arabization. Although Persian as a language of literature and high culture went into a decline for the first three centuries of Islam, it remained the spoken language of the majority of the Persians. Classical Arabic was adopted as the cultivated linguistic medium for theological and belle-lettristic works in most parts of the Islamic world. Thus al-Tabari, who, as his name suggests, was a non-Arab from Tabaristan (south of the Caspian Sea), wrote all his scholarly works in Arabic as did Ibn Sina (d. 1037), a Persian by birth from Balkh (now a part of modern Afghanistan). The Persian literary language enjoyed a revival in the tenth century, but now written in the Arabic script and considerably influenced by the introduction of an extensive Arabic vocabulary and literary forms. This revival was spurred by a resurgence of Persian nationalism and led to the composition of national epics in Persian, such as the famous *Shahnameh* ("The Book of Kings") of the poet Firdawsi (d. ca. 1020).

Most of the Successors lived the greater part of their lives under the Umayyads. The Umayyads in general have an unenviable reputation within the Islamic historical tradition, the reasons for which are understandable.

The Sufyanid branch of the Banu Umayya, which first assumed the caliphate based in Damascus after 'Ali's death in 661, was supremely unqualified for this office, according to the Islamic criteria of precedence and moral excellence. Abu Sufyan, Mu'awiya's father, had remained an implacable foe of Islam during the lifetime of the Prophet, as had been most of the members of the Banu Umayya, until the final fall of Mecca. The most notable exception to this general Umayyad proclivity was the third caliph 'Uthman ibn 'Affan, Mu'awiya's cousin, who had converted early and emigrated to both Abyssinia and Medina.

Mu'awiya's Islamic credentials were not much better than his father's. As late a convert to Islam as Abu Sufyan, he is particularly vilified in the later literature for introducing dynastic succession, derided in the sources as "kingship" (mulk), into the Islamic world when he nominated his son Yazid as his successor. Mu'awiya (ruled 661–80) is also censured for his role in instigating the civil war (fitna) after the murder of 'Uthman through his insistence on bringing the assassins to justice. All the Umayyad rulers, with the one notable exception of 'Umar ibn 'Abd al-'Aziz (on whom we focus below), are portrayed by later historians as impious tyrants who made a travesty of the highest ideals of Islam and irrevocably caused the fragmentation of the Muslim polity. They are accused of presumptuous arrogance in having adopted the title Khalifat Allah ("Deputy of God") in contradistinction to the Rashidun caliphs who spurned this title. As mentioned earlier, Abu Bakr had called himself Khalifat Rasul Allah ("Successor of the Messenger of God") and his successors were more commonly called Amir al-Mu'minin ("Counselor/ Commander of the Faithful"), the title first adopted by 'Umar.

Many of the Umayyad rulers appointed inept and opportunistic governors like Mughira ibn Shu'ba (d. 670) or ruthless ones like Ziyad ibn Abihi (d. 673) and his son 'Ubayd Allah (d. 684). Such choices did not endear them to the people. The Umayyads are further blamed for having resurrected the pre-Islamic Arab pride in noble lineage and tribal descent. The fiscal and administrative policies of the Umayyads were often discriminatory toward non-Arab converts (mawali; sing. mawla) to the extent that on occasion, Arab non-Muslims escaped without paying any taxes in comparison with non-Arab Muslims, who were sometimes taxed harshly.[4] The Umayyads emphasized their tribal kinship with the Prophet and considered this factor, in the absence of precedence in service to Islam, to legitimize their accession to the caliphate. All of this was viewed as a grave betrayal of the ideals of the prophetic and Rashidun eras and a throwback to the values and mind-set of the *Jahili* period. It is against this backdrop that we must view the gradual evolution of the legitimist claims of the proto-Shi'a during the Umayyad period. Such claims were a response to the Umayyad revaloriza-tion of kinship and represented a bid on the part of the proto-Shi'a to out-trump the Umayyad rhetoric by emphasizing 'Ali's closer blood-kinship to the Prophet.

One event in particular has forever tarred the reputation of the Umayyads in the general Muslim imaginary and has earned the undying hatred of the Shi'a in particular, galvanizing the latter's sense of themselves as a belea-guered community that was increasingly becoming distinct from the larger collectivity. In 680, under Yazid ibn Mu'awiya's rule, al-Husayn, the second son of 'Ali ibn Abi Talib, openly challenged Umayyad claims to the caliphate. Al-Husayn had withheld his allegiance from Yazid and was encouraged by his coterie of supporters in Kufa to engage the latter in battle. The Kufans promised valuable reinforcements for al-Husayn's army. Al-Husayn, with a small entourage of family members and close friends, accordingly set out from Mecca (whence he had fled from Medina) for Kufa. On the way, he and his entourage encamped at a site called Karbala' to the north of Kufa and were waylaid there by an Umayyad army which had learned of al-Husayn's itinerary. Fighting broke out between al-Husayn's small, rag-tag "army" and 'Ubayd Allah ibn Ziyad, the Umayyad commander, and his vastly superior forces. Al-Husayn and his loyal followers were slain almost to a man, although al-Husayn's young son, 'Ali ibn al-Husayn, is said to have survived the carnage and was spirited away by pro-'Alid supporters to be later recog-nized as their fourth Imam.

The tragic events at Karbala', as may be expected, hardly enhanced the popularity of the Umayyads among the general population and further con-firmed their image as unscrupulous wielders of political authority usurped from those more morally qualified to exercise it. Umayyad disdain for the *ahl al-bayt* ("the family of the Prophet"), a concept now slowly being fore-grounded, had become evident in the bloody reprisal they had visited on Muhammad's descendants. Al-Tabari relates that when al-Husayn's severed head was placed before 'Ubayd Allah, the Umayyad commander, the latter callously struck his lips with a stick. A man called Abu Barza al-Aslami protested in horror, "Raise your stick!" he said. "By God, I have seen the Messenger of God, peace and blessings be upon him, kiss those lips!"[5] The anecdote conveys to us 'Ubayd Allah's rather sadistic disposition and indicates that Islam sat very lightly upon him and his cohorts.

In the wake of al-Husayn's death, his supporters in Kufa expressed public remorse in not having come to his aid. They consequently became known as "the Penitents" (al-Tawwabun). The Penitents organized themselves into a band of militants and marched to Syria to challenge 'Abd al-Malik, Yazid's successor, and his considerably superior forces. The Umayyad army easily defeated them. The few survivors fled back toward Kufa and kept up their opposition to 'Abd al-Malik and his immediate successors.

A few years after the tragedy of Karbala', the Umayyads perpetrated another act which scandalized the pious and further blemished their image. During the counter-caliphate of 'Abd Allah ibn al-Zubayr (for more on whom, see below) in Mecca, the Umayyad army while bombarding the town set fire to the Ka'ba and caused considerable damage to it. Previously, they had laid siege to Medina and sacked it and forcefully extracted oaths of allegiance to Yazid from the Medinese residents. Muslim historians have pointed to these instances, along with the other acts mentioned above, as affirming the general proclivity of the Umayyads toward impiety and tyranny.

Against this general negative reputation of the Umayyads in the sources as briefly sketched above, some of the Umayyad rulers, however, are given their due for having imposed order on the polity after the first civil war (fitna). Mu'awiya, in particular, gets grudging admiration for his political finesse and adroitness in handling the delicate situation after 'Ali's death and for his personal qualities of clemency (hilm) and shrewd intelligence. Hilm, as we have had occasion to mention in the first chapter, was a highly prized trait in the pre-Islamic tribal leader and in the political leader of the Islamic period as well. It referred to a cluster of virtues which included clemency, self-restraint, and magnanimity. A report found in the manaqib literature on Abu Bakr, for example, describes him as the halim of Quraysh,[6] reflecting Islamic co-optation of pre-Islamic positive virtues. Like Mu'awiya, 'Abd al-Malik, the Umayyad caliph from the Marwanid branch of the family, also wins a measure of praise from later historians for having restored order and unity after the second civil war in 680 (for more on which, see below).

As we mentioned in the previous chapter, there developed a tendency among the Sunnis in the later period to speak well of the Companions in general, in large measure as a defensive reaction to Shi'i denunciation of the same. It is this tendency that has specifically rehabilitated Mu'awiya in Sunni historiography, since he had served as a secretary to the Prophet after the fall of Mecca and is counted among the Companions. In modern times, Syrian Arab nationalists have appropriated the Umayyads as a positive symbol of confident Arab rule and leadership.[7]

THE POLITICS OF PIETY AND THE SECOND CIVIL WAR

After al-Husayn's abortive uprising against the Umayyads, the second major 'Alid revolt was staged by a man called al-Mukhtar ibn Abi 'Ubayd al-Thaqafi in Kufa between 685–87.[8] At first, Mukhtar tried to forge an alliance with 'Abd Allah ibn al-Zubayr but was spurned by the latter. He then decided to champion the cause of the proto-Shi'a and called for vengeance for al-Husayn's blood, rallying the remaining Penitents and other partisan 'Alids, led by a man called Ibrahim al-Ashtar, as well as some of the *ashraf* or tribal notables of Kufa, to his cause. Al-Mukhtar launched his revolt in the name of Muhammad ibn al-Hanafiyya, a son of 'Ali by a woman whom 'Ali wed after Fatima's death. The ascription al-Hanafiyya stems from her affiliation with the tribe of Hanifa.

A highly important religious concept, particularly for the Shi'a, appears to have been born during al-Mukhtar's movement: that of the *Mahdi*, a messianic, divinely guided figure who heralds the inauguration of a just era. This is what al-Mukhtar declared Muhammad ibn al-Hanafiyya to be while proclaiming himself to be the Mahdi's *wazir* or "assistant." Other innovations are attributed to al-Mukhtar, some rather bizarre, such as the habit of having his followers carry an old chair belonging to 'Ali into battle and paraded around like the biblical Ark of the Covenant.[9] These ideas have been attributed to the large number of *mawali* (non-Arab converts) who were attracted to al-Mukhtar's movement (which also contained a significant proportion of Arabs) and who presumably injected these foreign non-Arab ideas into it. Jewish influence has also been suggested in the development of this messianic strain.[10] The *mawali* in particular comprised his corps of personal bodyguards led by Abu Amr Kaysan; thus al-Mukhtar's followers are often called al-Kaysaniyya.[11] Messianic ideas and cultic reverence for 'Ali and his relics are not attested before this time.

Led by Ibrahim ibn al-Ashtar, al-Mukhtar and his forces inflicted a decisive defeat on the Umayyad army in 686 near Mosul, killing its commander

'Ubayd Allah ibn Ziyad. The latter's death was seen in some quarters as a fitting retribution for his role in the carnage during the battle of Karbala'. A year later, al-Mukhtar himself was defeated by a coalition of Ibn al-Zubayr's forces in Basra and the Kufan notables who had abandoned him, very likely on account of his strong pro-*mawali* stance. Al-Mukhtar and about two hundred of his most dedicated followers fell in this battle.

However, al-Mukhtar's movement left a decisive imprint upon the organization of the successful 'Abbasid revolution about sixty-four years later. When Muhammad ibn al-Hanafiyya died, some of the Kaysaniyya declared his son Abu Hashim to be their legitimate Imam. Abu Hashim gives his name to the Hashimiyya movement, which played a crucial role in the launching and final execution of the 'Abbasid revolution, as we will discuss below.[12]

A major crisis erupted after the death of Yazid I in 683, when his son Mu'awiya the second became caliph. From all accounts Mu'awiya II was a sickly youth and never commanded much political authority. By now the Umayyads were largely regarded as illegitimate rulers, which bolstered the position of other Qurayshi claimants to the caliphate based in Medina with stronger Islamic credentials. One was al-Husayn, as we have already discussed, whose rebellion proved abortive but had long-lasting consequences. The other most important claimant was 'Abd Allah ibn al-Zubayr, the son of the prominent Companion al-Zubayr ibn al-'Awamm and Asma' bint Abi Bakr, daughter of the first caliph. Ibn al-Zubayr is said to have been the first Muslim child to be born in Medina after the *hijra*. He, like al-Husayn, was thus a much more traditionally sympathetic figure and on account of his precedence in Islam, a more credible candidate for the caliphate from the viewpoint of the piety-minded. After al-Husayn's rebellion was crushed decisively, Ibn al-Zubayr emerged as the strongest rival of the Umayyads.

The Khawarij, who were far from extinct at this time, had also kept up their opposition to the Umayyads, whom they regarded with pietistic antipathy as well. Yazid's reputed free-wheeling lifestyle which included a fondness for alcohol and singing-girls had scandalized the pious in general. But the Khawarij were particularly incensed by the Umayyad resuscitation of the pre-Islamic notion of 'asabiyya or sense of tribal solidarity. The Khawarij were known for their radical egalitarianism and opposition to anything that smacked of social privilege and elitism. Only personal piety, they declared, and fidelity to Qur'anic values (on which they had a distinctive take), entitled a person to exercise any kind of authority in the ideal Muslim community.

Some factions of the Khawarij (for they soon split into many) believed on the basis of their radical egalitarianism that all property should be communally held. One faction, the Sufriyya, were of the opinion that women could assume the caliphate as well. Extant Khariji poetry eloquently records for us the litany of pietistic grudges they held against the Umayyads in this early period.[13]

On account of their militancy and refusal to acknowledge non-Kharijis as Muslims, the number of Khawarij dwindled rapidly through the Umayyad period, becoming inconsequential by the beginning of the 'Abbasid period. The decisive defeat inflicted upon them by 'Ali at Nahrawan had already considerably enfeebled them. Although remaining a persistent nuisance throughout the Umayyad period, they were never serious rivals of the Umayyad rulers. Two major Khariji uprisings, one by the faction known as the Azariqa in Basra and another led by one Shabib ibn Yazid in Kufa, were successfully thwarted by al-Hajjaj, the governor of Basra. The latter-day descendants of the Khawarij, known as the Ibadiya, adopted political quietism and today they live peacefully in parts of North Africa, notably in Tunisia.

At first, 'Abdullah ibn al-Zubayr made common cause with the Khawarij, who were as disgruntled with the Umayyads as he was. But it soon became clear that a wide gulf existed between their programmatic goals and worldviews. Ibn al-Zubayr terminated his alliance with the Kharijiyya and established a viable counter-caliphate in Mecca against the Umayyads in the power vacuum that ensued after the death of Yazid and of Mu'awiya II shortly thereafter. Ibn al-Zubayr won the support of practically all the Muslims, except for those in central and southern Syria. The politics of piety that he engaged in clearly resonated with the overwhelming majority of Muslims, who appear to have identified with the Medinan "old-guard," mainstream values that he represented. Ibn al-Zubayr's rebellion led to the second *fitna* or civil war to engulf the Muslim polity.

The Umayyad succession crisis was resolved when Marwan ibn al-Hakam, an uncle, finally acceded to the throne after the battle of Marj Rahit in 684. This battle fought between the Qays (northern) and Kalb (southern) tribes effectively ended the Sufyanid line of caliphs and inaugurated the Marwanid one. Both Marwan (known as Marwan I) and his son 'Abd al-Malik moved swiftly against Ibn al-Zubayr and his supporters. The attack led by 'Abd al-Malik's formidable governor, al-Hajjaj, in 692 against

Mecca, during which the Ka'ba caught fire, led to Ibn al-Zubayr's death at the age of seventy and the dismantling of his ill-fated counter-caliphate. The second *fitna* was over.

The very popular Zubayrid revolt and the two earlier 'Alid uprisings led by al-Husayn and Mukhtar appear to have convinced the Umayyads that they too, at least publicly, had to assert their Islamic credentials in order to establish their political legitimacy and hold onto their power. This realization very likely prompted 'Abd al-Malik to undertake the building of the Dome of the Rock in Jerusalem, completed in 692, on the site where the Prophet, according to tradition, commenced his ascension to the heavens.[14] Another example of overtly religious activity is afforded by 'Abd al-Malik's loyal governor, al-Hajjaj, who is credited in some of the sources with adding diacritics to the unpointed Qur'anic text so as to standardize its reading. Al-Hajjaj is also said to have undone the changes made to the structure of the Ka'ba by Ibn al-Zubayr and restored it to its former appearance. It is possible to read this latter action as claiming both physical and symbolic ownership of Islam's most sacred, central site and thus asserting undisputed legitimacy on both religious and political grounds.

In the aftermath of the second civil war, 'Abd al-Malik, with the help of his governor al-Hajjaj, instituted a highly centralized government which asserted more direct control over the people. Several important administrative developments occurred in this period. The language of the chancellery (*diwan*) was officially changed from Greek into Arabic, an extensive postal system (*al-barid*) was established (which came in useful for keeping an eye on various subjects, especially in far-flung areas, as well), and new coinage with Islamic religious formulae replacing the Byzantine and Sassanian coins was struck. Some of these measures clearly served the purpose of bolstering the now consciously cultivated Arabo-Islamic identity of the Marwanid dynasty.

The people's aspirations for a recognizably pious and thus legitimate ruler, as may be ascertained from the popularity of 'Abdullah ibn al-Zubayr's counter-caliphate, were amply met in the person of 'Umar ibn 'Abd al-'Aziz, a cousin of 'Abd al-Malik, who ruled for a mere three years (717–20) before being killed. Short though his tenure as caliph may have been, 'Umar the second, as he is often referred to, made a deep impression on the minds and loyalties of his subjects and of those who came after his generation. On account of his personal piety, adherence to Islamic principles of egalitarianism, and holding himself accountable to the people, 'Umar the second is fre-quently described in the sources as the fifth Rashidun caliph. Since we will soon focus on him as one of the most memorable Successors, we will now move ahead with our brief recounting of the rest of Umayyad history and the rise of the 'Abbasids.

THE THIRD CIVIL WAR

There were six more Umayyad caliphs after 'Umar ibn 'Abd al-'Aziz: Yazid II (ruled 720–24); Hisham(724–43); Walid II (743–44); Yazid III (744); Ibrahim(744); and Marwan II (744–50). The remaining thirty years of the Umayyad dynasty were marked by continuing political and social turmoil, with disaffected groups like the Shi'a and the Khawarij occasionally instigating rebellions against the government. After having won considerable redress for their grievances and recognition of specifically their fiscal rights during the brief interregnum of 'Umar II's rule, the non-Arab *mawali* went back to being a disgruntled group after his death. The Umayyads largely ignored the discontent of this group at their peril and took very few measures to alleviate their concerns. The resulting escalating hostility of the *mawali* would play a major role in fomenting the 'Abbasid revolution and its success.

The third *fitna* or civil war is described in the sources as lasting between 744–47; that is, between the time of Walid II's accession to power after the death of Hisham and the assumption of the caliphate by Marwan II. Walid II was appointed by his father, Yazid II, to be Hisham's successor. When Hisham died, Walid II did in fact become caliph, but the situation became complicated by the fact that Hisham during his tenure had wished to appoint one of his sons as his successor. Walid II moved swiftly and resolutely to crush those who had opposed his succession, executing some in the process and imprisoning his cousin, Sulayman ibn Hashim. Walid II also named his two minor sons as his successors, further incurring the wrath of some powerful Umayyads who harbored different succession plans.

A son of al-Walid I, who became Yazid III, emerged as Walid II's rival to the caliphate. In the spring of 744, Yazid and his supporters seized Damascus while the caliph was sojourning elsewhere. Yazid had the support of a "south-ern" coalition composed largely of Kalbi and Yemeni tribesmen, joined by some "northerners" from the Qaysi and Mudari tribes. Walid II fled to his fortified residence near Palmyra but was hunted down by Yazid's forces and killed.

Yazid III's reign is remarkable for its appeal to piety and its claim to adhere to what was now recognized as the hallmarks of legitimate government. The new caliph declared that he was justified in opposing Walid II because the latter would not respond to his appeals for consultation or *shura* to resolve the succession crisis. The sources report that Yazid III gave an inaugural speech, which seems reminiscent to a degree of the address given by the first Rashidun caliph Abu Bakr. In this speech, Yazid III stressed his accountability to the people and vowed to avoid the various abuses of power attributed to his predecessors. He assured his audience that he would step down if he failed to fulfil these promises and accept whomever they chose in his stead as their leader in such circumstances.[15]

The full implications of this speech and thus of Yazid III's religio-political orientation has not been fully appreciated or given its due in our sources. His speech clearly implies that the early Islamic ideals of a righteous, legitimate government were not effaced during Umayyad dynastic rule but rather appears to have gained strength in defiance of Umayyad practices. Yazid III's acknowledgment of the salience of the principle of *shura*, the assertion of his accountability to his subjects, and his attempts to treat the *mawali* and the Arabs on an equal basis in matters of taxation and disbursement of stipends further represented his bid to win the kind of acclaim that Umar II had won on account of his adherence to similar principles. Yazid III in fact is said to have expressed fulsome admiration for Umar II. He was very likely genuinely sincere in the public expression of these sentiments and objectives. But he may have further simultaneously realized that, pragmatically speaking, courting public sentiment in this manner and placating the pietistic groups constituted the best way to ensure the continuity of his political power.[16]

In Yazid III's speech, we discern the influence of a contemporary theological faction known as the Qadariyya or the Ghaylaniyya. It has been noted by historians that there was a close connection between this group and the caliph. The name Ghaylaniyya derives from one Ghaylan al-Dimashqi[17] who had served in some administrative capacity under 'Umar II. They are also termed the Qadariyya, a precursor of the later Mu'tazila, because they spurned the idea of divine predestination (*qadar*) and believed in human free will. It has been convincingly suggested that the free will vs. predestination debate at this time was politically motivated, since proponents of free will were more likely to be inclined to oppose governments perceived as unrighteous and thus illegitimate, such as the Umayyads, whereas those in favor of predestination would lean toward political quietism and acceptance of the status quo. Certain conflicting reports regarding the prominent Successor al-Hasan al-Basri suggest that there is some validity to this assumption, as will be explored below.[18] The Ghaylaniyya also supported the equality of *mawali* and Arab Muslims and believed in the limited powers of the caliphate, neither of which was an overwhelmingly popular notion with the majority of the Umayyad rulers. The espousal of free will and egalitarianism thus cast the Qadariyya/Ghaylaniyya in an oppositional role to most of the Umayyads. Ghaylan himself fell out with the caliph Hisham who had the former executed for his subversive views.

These new policies could barely be implemented because Yazid III died suddenly toward the end of 744 after having ruled for only six months. His death plunged the empire into near total chaos. Yazid III had appointed his brother Ibrahim as his successor but Marwan ibn Muhammad, grandson of Marwan ibn al-Hakam, the fourth caliph, emerged as the strongest candidate to assume power. After successfully defeating the various forces assembled in opposition to him, notably those of Sulayman ibn Hisham, a son of the tenth caliph, Marwan ibn Muhammad entered Damascus in 744, somewhat dramatically on an ass, and declared himself to be the new *Amir al-Mu'minin*. Ibrahim, the former heir-apparent, fled to Palmyra in Syria together with Sulayman and his largely *mawali* army.

One of Marwan's first actions as caliph was to move the seat of his dynasty to Harran in Mesopotamia. This seems to have been prompted by a need to be closer to the Qaysi ("northern") troops loyal to him on the Mesopotamian frontier, since most of the troops in central and southern Syria were Kalbi ("southern") and thus hostile to him. Marwan also reversed the pro-Qadari and pro-*mawali* policies of Yazid III. Such reactionary measures drove a further wedge between him and the non-Arab Muslims.

THE 'ABBASID REVOLUTION

Marwan II's major troubles were, however, only just beginning. Distracted by ongoing opposition to him from various quarters in Syria and Iraq, he seemed not to have fully gauged the extent and significance of the rebellion now brewing in Khurasan in Iran and its environs that would bring his dynasty to an end. The forces and ideological trends that ultimately brought the 'Abbasids to power are complex and the narration of all the details known to us (some of them imperfectly) would prove too lengthy for our purposes. We will, therefore, confine ourselves to a brief description of the most central personalities and events that led to the 'Abbasid revolution culminating in the demise of the Umayyad dynasty.

The 'Abbasid revolution was essentially engineered by a group known as the Hashimiyya, whom we had occasion to meet before in connection with Mukhtar's revolt starting in 685. The Hashimiyya drew their strength from both the Arab and non-Arab Muslim population of Khurasan. In many ways, the situation was somewhat unique here in terms of the interaction of these two groups. The Arabs since the earliest period of their settlement in the last quarter of the seventh century had become quite assimilated with the local Iranian population since no garrison town had been established, as in Kufa and Basra, to sequester the Arab army from the local people. At this point in history, most of the Arab settlers were well assimilated into Persian society. Many of them spoke Persian, had married Persian women, and observed local Persian customs and holidays, like the Persian New Year. Conversion among the Iranian population had also proceeded at a much higher rate in Khurasan than in western Iran, for example. Thus the *mawali* and Arab Muslims had somewhat uniquely forged strong social alliances and consequently assembled a powerful political coalition as well against the Umayyads.[19]

The slogan of the anti-Umayyad movement was *al-rida min al Muhammad*, roughly "[for the sake of] an acceptable member of the house of Muhammad," indicating a fusion of 'Alid legitimist demands with the revolutionary socio-political platform of the 'Abbasids. The 'Abbasid movement gained momentum in Khurasan under a shadowy and charismatic leader named Abu Muslim, who was appointed a personal representative of the Hashimi-'Abbasid Imam at that time, Ibrahim ibn Muhammad, a descendant of al-'Abbas, the Prophet's uncle. The assumed name of this key personality as occurs in the sources – in full, Abu Muslim 'Abd al-Rahman ibn Muslim al-Khurasani – stresses mainly his Muslim ascription and his Khurasani background. There is deliberately no indication in this name of his tribal affiliation or whether he was an Arab or a *mawla*, a harbinger of the more egalitarian socio-political order promised by the 'Abbasid revolution for all Muslims regardless of their tribal or ethnic background.

In 747, Abu Muslim and his cohorts unfurled the black banners of the 'Abbasid movement in Merv and were joined by about 7,000 men in slightly over a month. Nasr ibn Sayyar, the aging governor of Khurasan, and his army proved to be no match for Abu Muslim and his Yemeni coalition forces. The former fled to Nishapur in 748 in order to regroup and launch a new attack against Abu Muslim and his followers. In the meantime, Abu Muslim entered Merv and took control of the situation. He dispatched the Khurasani army which in less than two years defeated three Marwanid armies assembled against him, including that of Nasr ibn Sayyar, and triumphantly entered Kufa in 750. Shortly thereafter, Nasr ibn Sayyar fled to Hamadan where he died.[20]

In the same year, the revolutionary army met the Marwanid forces in the battle of the Zab and the latter were utterly routed. Marwan II fled first to Syria and Palestine. Failing to gather any support there, he fled to Egypt where he was apprehended seven months after the battle of the Zab and put to death. The Umayyad dynasty was forever ended in the East. However, 'Abd al-Rahman (ruled 756–88), a grandson of Hisham ibn 'Abd al-Malik, the tenth Umayyad caliph, escaped from the 'Abbasids and fled to Cordoba, Spain. There, in 756, he established the Western branch of the Umayyad dynasty which lasted until 1031.

Soon after the victory of the revolutionaries, visible cracks began to appear in the 'Alid–'Abbasid alliance around the question of who should be recognized as the new Imam or *Amir al-Mu'minin*. Once his role in the Hashimi-'Abbasid movement had been discovered, the Imam of the Hashimiyya, Ibrahim ibn Muhammad had been imprisoned and then killed in Harran in 749. The Khurasani army upon its arrival in Kufa was welcomed by Abu Muslim's mentor, Abu Salama, who now assumed the title of *Wazir Al Muhammad* ("assistant of the family of Muhammad"). The rest of the 'Abbasids soon flocked to Kufa but Abu Salama treated them with less than complete enthusiasm, even though Abu 'l-'Abbas 'Abd Allah ibn Muham-mad, the brother and heir-apparent of Ibrahim, the murdered Imam, was among them. Abu Salama's relationship with both the 'Alids and the 'Abbasids was bedeviled by the question of the imamate. He is said to have subsequently offered the imamate to prominent members of the Prophet's family in the Hijaz, among them, Ja'far al-Sadiq, 'Abd Allah ibn al-Hasan, and 'Umar ibn 'Ali ibn al-Hasan, all of whom refused.

Finally, the Khurasanians, impatient with the indecision which had lasted for more than two months, forced upon Abu Salama their choice of Abu 'l-'Abbas as the caliph (*khalifa*), the official title conferred upon the first 'Abbasid ruler. Abu Salama agreed and was allowed to continue as the *wazir* under the terms of the agreement with the Khurasanis but was soon executed in 750 when he grew uneasy with this arrangement.

Abu 'l-'Abbas, who ruled for almost five years (749–54), acquired the epithet *al-Saffah*, "the Shedder of Blood" on account of the fact that he had every living member of the Umayyad dynasty who could be found put to death. He was succeeded by his older brother, Abu Ja'far 'Abd Allah ibn Muhammad, known as al-Mansur. Under the first Abbasid caliph, the Khurasanians had retained control of the military, thus severely curtailing the administrative powers of the Amir al-Mu'minin. Upon his accession, al-Mansur wrested military control away from the Khurasanians in a bid to aggrandize the powers invested in his office. He also executed Abu Muslim, the former loyal lieutenant of the 'Abbasid revolution, a move which signaled a decisive rupture with the 'Alids and their religious-legitimist aspirations. Shi'i unhappiness with this state of affairs is manifested in a number of their revolts during al-Mansur's reign. The 'Abbasids had clearly struck out on their own and the Shi'a would be left to pursue their own course and quest for political legitimacy.

PROMINENT SUCCESSORS

The capsule of events recorded above may convey the impression that the Umayyad period was only marked by political dissension, sectarian strife, and military campaigns against internal and external foes. This is hardly the whole picture. The Umayyad era was also marked by significant ideational and intellectual trends that would bear important fruit during the subsequent 'Abbasid period. The foundations of jurisprudence, systematic theology, and mysticism were laid in this period. At the same time sectarian tendencies posed a challenge to the unity of the polity. We will briefly delineate these major trends by focusing on five distinctive personalities from the generation of the Successors whose legacies have molded the Islamic tradition in distinctive ways and whose lives in sharper focus illuminate a crucial chapter in the intellectual and political history of Islamic civilization.

'Umar ibn 'Abd al-'Aziz (d. 720): the pious ruler and renewer of the faith

'Umar ibn 'Abd al-'Aziz ('Umar II) was the fifth Umayyad caliph who ruled from 717 to 720. He was born circa 682, in Medina according to some reports, while others claim that he was born in Egypt. His father was 'Abd al-'Aziz, the governor of Egypt and the younger brother of caliph 'Abd al-Malik. 'Umar had an even more illustrious ancestor in his great grandfather, the second Rightly-Guided Caliph 'Umar ibn al-Khattab, also referred to as 'Umar I. Unlike previous Umayyad rulers, 'Umar II, as the cousin of the caliph before him, did not succeed his immediate predecessor but was appointed to his caliphal office.[21]

'Umar II grew up in Medina. When his father 'Abd al-'Aziz died, he was brought to Damascus by his uncle 'Abd al-Malik and married off to his daughter Fatima. When 'Abd al-Malik died shortly thereafter, 'Umar II was appointed governor of Medina by his cousin Walid I who had assumed the caliphate. In contradistinction to general Umayyad practice, 'Umar II administered the province with the help of a consultative council. The sources praise his governorship in Medina as being marked by fairness and justice toward the people, so much so that hardly any grievances were filed against his administration in Damascus. Medina in fact proved to be a refuge for people escaping from Iraq, now under the harsh rule of the Umayyad governor, al-Hajjaj ibn Yusuf. Displeased with 'Umar's popularity with the Iraqis, al-Hajjaj prevailed upon Walid to dismiss 'Umar from his post, much to the chagrin of the people of Medina.

After his dismissal, 'Umar continued to live in Medina during the rest of Walid's reign and, after the latter's death, under the reign of Walid's brother, Sulayman. Sulayman was 'Umar's cousin and admired the latter for his statesmanship and noble personal qualities. When it was time for Sulayman to designate his successor, he chose 'Umar above his own brothers and son. After an unsuccessful attempt to change Sulayman's mind, 'Umar reluctantly agreed to assume the caliphate. 'Umar II would rule for barely three years but within this short time span, he carved out a unique niche for himself in Islamic history. His fabled piety, self-effacing humility, and simplicity of lifestyle endeared him to the common people and revived in them the memory of the era of the Rightly-Guided Caliphs. Like the Rashidun caliphs, he is said to have made over his salary to the public treasury. He wore ordinary, even patched garments, and refused to take up residence in the caliphal palace, allowing instead his predecessor's family to continue to live there.[22]

His administrative and fiscal policies reversed to a large extent the self-aggrandizing policies of his Umayyad predecessors. 'Umar emphasized his accountability to the people and encouraged them to replace him with some-one of their liking if he should fail to live up to their expectations. On the rare occasion that he accepted gifts, he is said to have made them over to the pub-lic treasury and redistributed among the people estates confiscated earlier by various Umayyad authorities. He initiated the practice of reciting at the end of the Friday sermon the following Qur'anic verse: "Indeed God prescribes justice, the doing of good, and the giving of alms to relatives" (Qur'an 16:90). He showed particular interest in collecting *hadith* at this early date and is said to have commissioned some scholars to "look for what there is of the *hadith* of the Apostle and of his Sunna."[23]

Unlike most of his predecessors, 'Umar II was not preoccupied with con-quest and territorial expansion. He lifted the siege on Constantinople and with-drew his forces from the Byzantine frontier. He did, however, successfully repel an attack by the Turks in Azerbaijan and quelled a number of Khariji uprisings. In a bid to promote religious harmony between the Sunnis and the Shi'a, he stopped the disagreeable Umayyad practice of cursing 'Ali from the pulpits. He continued and expanded the state welfare programs already in place under his predecessors for the poor and the needy. He is said to have shown a particular solicitude for "the protected people" (*ahl al-dhimma*), that is, the non-Muslims under Muslim rule, and taxed them lightly. Thus, in Egypt, he apparently ordered his governor there to charge each Coptic Christian who owned taxable property only twenty dinars in com-parison with the forty dinars levied on the Muslim property owner.[24] Like 'Umar I, 'Umar II is portrayed in later sources as having been on occasion harsh toward non-Muslims. Many of these reports must similarly be taken with a grain of salt, which reflect rather the spirit of a later, more sectarian period.[25]

Needless to say, much as the people loved him, many among his powerful fellow Umayyad royals were alarmed by 'Umar's self-effacing personality and his popularity. As some of the sources inform us, a disaffected person from among the Umayyads bribed a servant to poison 'Umar's food. 'Umar succumbed to the poison but, while he lay dying, he learned of the details of the conspiracy and is said to have forgiven his murderer. He died in Aleppo in 720 and was succeeded by his cousin Yazid II.

'Umar II after death more than made up for the brevity of his reign on earth. His compassion and love for his people, which was amply recipro-cated, guaranteed that he would remain indelibly enshrined in people's memories. There was no higher accolade for a Muslim ruler than to be called one of the Rightly-Guided leaders, and this title was duly bestowed on him by posterity. 'Umar II became for all purposes the fifth Rashidun caliph, the seal of righteous rulers, and, inaugurating a new tradition, the renewer of the faith (*mujaddid*) at the beginning of the second century of Islam after years of decay and moral turpitude under the worldly, corrupt Umayyads. That God would not abandon Muhammad's salvific community to relentless moral degeneration became pious belief. Rather, He would send every hundred years a reviver of the faith who would cleanse the Muslim community of inevitable accretions and dangerous innovations, restoring the pristine faith and the true practices of the community. Henceforth, the centennial renewer would become part and parcel of the Islamic tradition, infusing the community with optimism and imparting to believers a certitude in God's solicitude for their welfare. This development, perhaps more than anything else, defines Umar II's enduring moral legacy.

Al-Hasan al-Basri: conscientious critic and early mystic

His full name occurs in the sources as Abu Sa'id ibn Abi 'l-Hasan Yasar al-Basri, who lived between 642–728. His father, a Persian by the name of Peroz, was imprisoned in Iraq during the period of conquest and brought to Medina by Zayd ibn Thabit, the Prophet's secretary, and there set free. Al-Hasan was born in Medina during the reign of 'Umar ibn al-Khattab after his father married a woman by the name of Khayra, who was a freedwoman of Umm Salama, one of the Prophet's wives. Al-Hasan grew up in Wadi al-Qurra, and later moved to Basra.

One of the best known Successors, al-Hasan al-Basri achieved renown as a preacher in Basra during the Umayyad period. Some of his eloquent sermons and hortatory speeches have been recorded by belle-lettrists, such as al-Jahiz, on account of their moving literary quality. He is portrayed in the sources as having displayed great moral courage in criticizing the Umayyad rulers and their excesses. He enraged al-Hajjaj, the tyrannical governor of Basra, when he criticized the latter for having founded the town of Wasit in 705. As a con-sequence he had to go into hiding until the governor's death in 714.[26]

In contrast to such verbal challenges to tyranny, al-Hasan al-Basri is also depicted in the sources as having advocated political quietism and non-militancy in confronting the injustice of certain Umayyad rulers. A particularly revealing anecdote is recorded by Ibn Sa'd in his entry on al-Hasan al-Basri. According to this anecdote, a group of Muslims once came to al-Hasan al-Basri seeking approval from him to start an armed rebellion against al-Hajjaj. They asked al-Hasan's opinion regarding "fighting against this tyrant who has shed blood, usurped wealth unlawfully, abandoned prayer, and so forth." Al-Hasan replied that in his opinion they should not take up arms against al-Hajaj. "If this is a punishment from God," he counseled, "then you will not be able to remove it with your swords. If this is a trial from God, then be patient until God's judgment arrives, for He is the best of all judges." But this group of people disregarded al-Hasan's advice and rose up in revolt against al-Hajjaj who put them to death. Al-Hasan remarked afterwards that if people would endure patiently the trials visited upon them by unjust rulers, then God would soon provide a way out for them. But regretfully, "they always rush towards their swords, so they are left with their swords. By God! Not even for a single day did they bring about any good."[27]

What is noteworthy about this anecdote is that its implications are at odds with other accounts which impute adherence to the doctrine of free will to al-Hasan. As we have had occasion to remark above regarding the Ghaylaniyya or the Qadariyya, the concept of human free will militated against political quietism, since free will allowed for human agency in changing socio-political circumstances. Wed to the Islamic principle of enjoining what is right and forbidding what is wrong (cf. Qur'an 3:104, 3:110), a Qadari (pro-free will) point of view might even be understood to mandate active opposition to injustice and tyranny by various means. There is a fair body of evidence which establishes al-Hasan's Qadari or free will credentials. He is said to have maintained that humans were fully responsible for their actions and that the sinner alone was to blame for his or her wrongful deeds. This led him to propound the doctrine that the individual who committed a major sin was a hypocrite (*munafiq*). We have also already indicated above his propensity to publicly criticize Umayyad rulers, like al-Hajjaj, who had promulgated unpopular policies, all of which attest to a measure of overt political resistance on his part. It is possible to reconcile these apparently contrarian positions by suggesting that al-Hasan, in keeping with a Qadari orientation, endorsed active resistance to political tyranny which stopped short of militancy.

It must also be borne in mind, however, that a highly popular, exception-ally pious, morally upright, and prominent figure from the second genera-tion of Muslims, such as al-Hasan al-Basri, is likely to be claimed by many groups as their progenitor or forerunner. And indeed, al-Hasan has been claimed by diverse groups from the later period, such as the Mu'tazila, the Sufis, and the Sunnis in general, who each saw their fully developed doctrinal positions prefigured in his thought and practices.[28]

Al-Hasan al-Basri takes his place among prominent *mawali* exegetes of the Qur'an in this early period, such as Sa'd ibn Jubayr, Mujahid ibn Jabr, Tawus ibn Kaysan, Wahb ibn Munabbih (d. ca. 732), and Wasil ibn 'Ata' (d. 749). However, among *hadith* scholars al-Hasan's reputation suffers. He is regarded as a careless transmitter of prophetic reports without due regard for their reliability and was even accused of fabricating reports. It is more prob-able that certain groups of people with specific motivations circulated spuri-ous reports in a later period which were then attributed to al-Hasan so as to gain in authoritativeness.

Al-Hasan is best remembered for his robust piety, his scholarship and preaching, and trenchant criticism of the worldly Umayyads. His simple, abstemious lifestyle was upheld as worthy of emulation by later Sufis. So beloved was he that when he breathed his last in Basra on October 10, 728, people from all walks of life are said to have thronged to his funeral abandon-ing the mosques and their usual haunts, an event described as unprecedented by the biographer Ibn Khallikan (d. 1282).[29]

THE CONSOLIDATION OF SHI'I THOUGHT

The Battle of Karbala' in 680 represents one of those turning points which reshapes history for all time. After their humiliating defeat and decimation at the hands of Yazid's army, the early 'Alids at this juncture were willy-nilly cast into a pietistic, oppositional role vis-à-vis the despised Umayyad gov-ernment, although their opposition henceforth would primarily take a quie-tist turn. This was particularly true of early Shi'ism's distinguished scholars and thinkers who, disheartened by the general socio-political circumstances, turned inwards toward a life of the mind and of the spirt, escaping from the corruption of political affairs.

Arguably the most illustrious Shiʻi name from this early period was that of Jaʻfar al-Sadiq, revered by both the Shiʻa and the Sunnis for his extensive learning and personal piety. His life and contributions are discussed further below.

Jaʻfar al-Sadiq (d. 765): righteous scholar and jurisprudent

Abu ʻAbd Allah Jafar ibn Muhammad, known as al-Sadiq ("the truthful") became the sixth Shiʻi Imam after the death of his father, Muhammad al-Baqir (d. ca. 735). He was born in Medina in 702, a direct descendant of the Prophet Muhammad on his father's side through Fatima and ʻAli. His mother, Umm Farwa, was a great grand-daughter of the first Rightly-Guided caliph, Abu Bakr. He was roughly thirty-seven years old when his father, the fifth Imam, died.[30]

Jaʻfar al-Sadiq studied with his father and grandfather, the fourth Imam, Zainul ʻAbidin ʻAli ibn al-Husayn. He became one of the most prominent authorities of his time on the Qurʼan, *sunna*, and the law. His legal rulings form the basis of the Jaʻfari school of jurisprudence, sometimes counted as a fifth *madhhab* (school of law) along with the four Sunni schools of jurisprudence. Two of the Sunni eponyms of these schools, Abu Hanifa and Malik ibn Anas, studied with him. Among his other well-known students were Wasil ibn ʻAtaʼ, who is credited with having started the Muʻtazili school of thought and Jabir ibn Hayyan, the alchemist known as Geber in Europe. Jaʻfar's scholarly reach, therefore, was quite extensive and testifies to the widespread respect he commanded among all stripes of people, regardless of their sectarian sympathies. Sunni scholars in general had a high opinion of Jaʻfar as a *hadith* transmitter; al-Shafiʻi, for example, regarded him as a highly reliable authority in *hadith* (*thiqa*).[31] In this period, Sunnis and Shiʻa often frequented each other's learning circles, a tendency that became more pronounced in later times.[32]

Jaʻfar's tenure as Imam was punctuated by some of the most tempestuous events to engulf the Muslim world. These events included the revolt of Zayd ibn ʻAli in 740, the ʻAbbasid uprising against the Umayyads starting in 747, and the ʻAlid rebel Muhammad al-Nafs al-Zakiyya's campaign against the ʻAbbasids in 762. Like his father and grandfather before him, Jaʻfar refused to become involved in these insurgencies, maintaining a traditional quietist stance. He was reportedly offered the caliphate by Abu Salama, the leader of the ʻAbbasid revolt, which he turned down.

In later fully developed Imami Shi'i doctrine and historiography, Ja'far al-Sadiq is presented as the undisputed Imam of his time. But it is not clear from earlier sources whether Ja'far claimed to be the rightful Imam publicly or if this was widely acknowledged even among his supporters. His contribution to the evolving Shi'i doctrine of his day appears to have been substantial. Ja'far is believed to have expanded upon three important doctrinal principles that his father, al-Baqir,[33] is said to have already adumbrated: (1) the principle of *nass*, which states that the legitimate Imam must be explicitly designated by his predecessor; (2) the principle of *'ilm*, according to which the rightful Imam is endowed with comprehensive, including supernatural, knowledge; and (3) the principle of *taqiyya* ("precautionary dissimulation") which allowed the Shi'a to dissemble on matters of faith in dangerous circumstances. Ja'far is said to have further expounded on the principle of *walaya* – "loyalty to the Prophet's family" – now being foregrounded in Shi'i thought. According to a report recorded by the well-known seventeenth century traditionist Muhammad Baqir al-Majlisi (d. 1699), Ja'far said,

> The first questions that will be asked of the believer when he stands before the Almighty will be concerning the obligatory prayers, the obligatory alms, the obligatory fasts, the obligatory pilgrimage, and about the *walaya* due to the Prophet's family. If he acknowledges the *walaya* due to us and dies upon that belief, then his prayers, his fasting, his alms, and his pilgrimage will be accepted from him. If he does not acknowledge the *walaya* due to us before God the Almighty, then the Almighty will not accept any of his works.[34]

The notion of loyalty or allegiance to the Prophet's family – that is, to Fatima, 'Ali, their two sons, al-Hasan and al-Husayn, and subsequently, to the rightful Imams among their progeny – would continue to grow in importance so that it would become the soteriological cornerstone of fully articulated Shi'i doctrine by the ninth century. This remains an important doctrinal difference between the Sunnis and Shi'a. Although Sunnis too profess great reverence for the family of the Prophet, they attach no salvational significance to it.

In spite of Ja'far's refusal to become involved in sectarian politics, he was kept under surveillance by the new 'Abbasid rulers and was imprisoned a few times. After their fallout with the 'Alids, the 'Abbasids were fearful of Ja'far's popularity, his scholarly renown, and acclaimed descent from the

Prophet, all very attractive traits in a potential rival claimant to power. Ja'far breathed his last on December 4, 765, at about sixty-three years of age. His partisans staunchly maintain that he was poisoned. He is buried in the famous Baqi' cemetery in Medina where many members of the Prophet's family lie buried.

His death was followed by a severe dispute regarding his successor, which divided the Shi'i community further. Those who came to be known as the Isma'ilis or the Seveners supported the designation of Ja'far's eldest son, Isma'il, as the next Imam. Isma'il, however, had predeceased Ja'far. Consequently, the Seveners recognized Isma'il's eldest son as the next legitimate Imam. Those who would go on to form the *Imami/Ithna 'Ashari* (Twelver) faction recognized a younger son of Ja'far, Musa ibn Kazim, as their Imam after Isma'il's and Ja'far's deaths. The division between the Seveners and the Twelvers has persisted to this day.

THE RISE OF LAW AND JURISPRUDENCE AMONG THE EARLY SUNNIS

After the death of the Prophet, the Qur'an and the *sunna* were the commonly accepted sources (*usul*) of law for the early legal specialists, to which additional sources of consensus (*ijma'*) and analogical reasoning (*qiyas*) would be added later in the eighth century. In a well-preserved letter composed by the second caliph 'Umar ibn al-Khattab and sent to Abu Musa al-Ash'ari, his governor in Basra, three of the four jurisprudential principles – Qur'an, *sunna*, and *qiyas* – are already mentioned in it, according to which the jurist may exercise his personal opinion (*ra'y*). In the period we are currently discussing (the first three quarters of the eighth century), the situation was in considerable flux. The early jurists continued to resort to personal opinion, sometimes under the rubric of juristic preference (*istihsan*), and appealed to the *sunna* of the Companions as a normative source for legal formulations, in addition to the *sunna* of the Prophet. Furthermore, customary law ('*urf*, '*ada*) also won limited recognition in judicial decision-making, although not officially recognized as a legal source.[35]

From the first two generations of Muslims, we have references to the so-called "seven lawyers (*fuqaha'*, sing. *faqih*) of Medina" – Abu Bakr ibn 'Abd al-Rahman (d. 712), 'Ubayd Allah ibn 'Abd Allah ibn 'Utba (d. 716), 'Urwa ibn al-Zubayr (d. 712), Qasim ibn Muhammad (d. ca.728), Sa'id ibn al-Musayyib (d. 712), Sulayman ibn Yasar (d. ca. 728), and Kharija ibn Zayd ibn Thabit (d. 717). Their interpretations of the Qur'an and the *sunna* were regarded as authoritative. Their activities point to the existence of a respectable body of opinion on juridical matters already at this very early date in the latter part of the first century of Islam. Their renown was such that judges are said to have refused to render their verdict until they had consulted with the "seven lawyers."[36] Very little of their work, however, has survived. In Kufa, we have the names of Ibrahim al-Nakha'i (d. between 713–15) and Hammad ibn Abi Sulayman (d. 738), two of the most prominent Successors who engaged in judicial activity. But none of their legal writings has reached us either. The *Majmu' al-fiqh* ("The Compendium of Jurisprudence") of Zayd ibn 'Ali (d. 740), eponym of the Zaydi Shi'a, is the oldest legal manuscript to have survived, albeit in a later, highly redacted form which clearly shows the influence of Hanafi thought. Chronologically, the next major jurist of the eighth century is the celebrated Abu Hanifa, followed by Malik ibn Anas, both of whom we dwell upon next.

Abu Hanifa (d. 767): exemplary interpreter of the law

Abu Hanifa al-Nu'man ibn Thabit ibn Zuta, theologian and jurist, is the eponymous founder of the Hanafiyya, one of the four recognized Sunni legal schools (*madhahib*) today. He was born in Kufa circa 699 and died in 767 in Baghdad at the age of 70. During the reign of 'Ali, the fourth Rashidun caliph, his grandfather Zuta was brought over as a slave from Kabul (other places of origin also mentioned) to Kufa, where he settled after being set free. Abu Hanifa's father Thabit is said to have met 'Ali ibn Abi Talib, who invoked blessings upon him and his offspring.[37]

Abu Hanifa's education began quite early in Kufa. He first memorized the Qur'an and studied *qira'a* (Qur'an recitation) with the famous Qur'an reader 'Asim ibn Bahdala, whose recitation remains one of the most followed today. Abu Hanifa also acquired scholarly training in the religious law and *hadith*, studying with prominent scholars such as Hammad ibn Abi Sulayman (d. 738), the leading jurist in Kufa, and 'Ata' ibn Abi Rabah (d. ca. 744) in Mecca. Abu Hanifa is said to have taken part in debates with members of various theological factions, such as the Jahmiyya, Qadariyya, and the Mu'tazila, in Kufa and Basra, the two leading intellectual centers of the period.

After Hammad ibn Abi Sulayman died, Abu Hanifa gained fame as the foremost scholar of religious law in Kufa but never served as *qadi* ("judge"). He was offered, however, several judgeships by various rulers during the waning days of the Umayyad dynasty. One such ruler who approached him was Yazid ibn 'Amr, the Umayyad governor of Iraq during the reign of the last Umayyad caliph, Marwan ibn al-Hakam (d. 750). When Abu Hanifa turned down his offer, Yazid had him whipped and the former escaped to Mecca where he stayed for five or six years, until the Umayyads were overthrown. Abu Hanifa, like many of the pious notables of his time, kept aloof from the Umayyad rulers who were widely regarded as impious and too worldly. After the 'Abbasids came to power, the caliph al-Mansur often presented Abu Hanifa with gifts hoping to induce him to serve as judge under him, but the latter is said to have always refused them.

In addition to his great scrupulosity (*wara'*) and abstemiousness (*zuhd*), Abu Hanifa is said to have been greatly inclined to charity. His generosity toward the members of his household as well as the poor in general became legendary. He would also meet the financial needs of his poor students. Abu Hanifa's day was typically given over to teaching and prayer. His daily routine began with the morning prayer in a mosque, after which he would answer his students' questions until about noon. After the noon prayer, he would teach again until the night prayer. Then he would return home and, after a short rest, return to the mosque and worship until morning prayer. He is said to have recited prodigious amounts of the Qur'an regularly and, according to some sources, performed the pilgrimage to Mecca fifty-five times.

Abu Hanifa himself did not leave behind substantial works on religious law but his legal thought may be reconstructed from the writings of his students. His best-known students are al-Shaybani (d. 749) and Abu Yusuf (d. 798), who have preserved Abu Hanifa's teachings in their works. From these works it becomes apparent that Abu Hanifa's legal thought was based to a considerable degree on his personal opinions (*ra'y*) and conclusions derived through legal reasoning (*qiyas*). This rationalist orientation remains the Hanafi school's distinctive characteristic. The Mu'tazila, the rationalist theologians of Islam, are even said to have claimed Abu Hanifa as one of their own.

In his theology, Abu Hanifa showed concern for maintaining the unity and harmony of the Muslim community during the divisive period in which he lived, by seeking a middle ground between two extremes. In this propensity Abu Hanifa shows the influence of the Murji'a ("those who defer"), a group which rose in the last third of the Umayyad era, as we mentioned earlier. The Hanafi-Murji'i attitude seminally shaped the political and theological attitudes of the later fully formed *ahl al-sunna*. In Abu Hanifa's letter to the Basran jurisprudent 'Uthman al-Batti, which scholars regard as authentic, the former defends his adherence to Murji'i principles. In the creedal statement attributed to him, known as *Fiqh al-Akbar*, Abu Hanifa articulates ten articles of faith which take issue with the positions of the Khawarij, the Shi'a, the Qadariyya and the Jahmiyya, the latter being two groups which believed in unfettered free will and in that sense were the predecessors of the Mu'tazila. Abu Hanifa probably did not compose this statement himself but the *Fiqh al-Akbar* is deemed to be an accurate summation of his theological views.

Abu Hanifa's detractors in the later period attributed to him certain unpopular beliefs derived not only from the Murji'a but also from the Jahmiyya, so that he is described as having maintained, contrary to his true positions, that the Qur'an was created and that hell was not eternal. Biographical works on *hadith* transmitters (*rijal* works) regularly included Abu Hanifa among the weak transmitters of *hadith*. *Hadith* scholars in general attacked his perceived excessive reliance on personal opinion and legal reasoning. His staunch supporters from among the later Hanafi jurists defended him against these accusations. Thus his student Abu Yusuf stressed that Abu Hanifa was exceptionally learned in *hadith* and the Hanafi jurist Abu Ja'far al-Tahawi (d. 933) wrote a work titled *Manaqib Abi Hanifa* ("The Excellences of Abu Hanifa") which recorded and praised the virtues of his legal school's eponym.

We have conflicting reports about why Abu Hanifa was imprisoned in late life. Some reports say it was on account of his having refused to serve as a judge under the 'Abbasid caliph al-Mansur, while others suggest that it was his rather open criticism of al-Mansur during an 'Alid revolt, which led to his imprisonment. According to some accounts, he eventually died in prison in 767.

Abu Hanifa is counted among the most illustrious of the Successors. Some of the sources relate that he met several Companions of the Prophet, including Anas ibn Malik and 'Abd Allah ibn Abi Awfa in Kufa, Abu 'l-Tufayl Amir ibn Wathila in Mecca, and Sahl ibn Sa'd al-Sa'idi in Medina. This close connection with the Companions conferred on Abu Hanifa and his scholarly activities great merit. The honorific usually applied to him is *al-Imam al-A'zam* ("the Greatest Leader"), from which the neighborhood around his mausoleum in Baghdad derives the name al-A'zamiyya. Under the Saljuq sultan Malikshah in the eleventh century, one of his viziers had an elaborate dome built over his grave. His mausoleum was restored several times under the Ottomans, who officially adopted the Hanafi legal school. This act consequently led to the displacement of the other legal schools from most parts of the Islamic world.

Today the Hanafi school remains the most prevalent in Islamic societies. Abu Hanifa's thought has particularly influenced the Sunni Maturidi school of thought, which initially spread in the Eastern realms of the Islamic world, particularly in Samarqand and Transoxania.[38] The Maturidis derive their name from Abu Mansur al-Maturidi al-Samarqandi (d. 944) and came to constitute one of the two principal "orthodox" schools of theology in Sunni Islam, the other being the Ash'aris, named after the former Mu'tazili theologian al-Ash'ari (d. 935). Unlike the Ash'aris, the Maturidis continued to emphasize the rationalist basis of Hanafi thought. They maintained that reason, independent of revelation, could arrive at religious truths and that there was no basic incompatibility between the two. In contrast, the Ash'ari school gave primacy to revelation over reason and asserted that "good" and "bad," for example, can be known only through revelation. Maturidi thought, however, has considerably colored the later Ash'ari school of thought and mitigated to a great extent the latter's tendency toward fideism. The influence of Maturidi rationalism is evident in the writings of the nineteenth-century reformer Muhammad 'Abduh (d. 1905), to whom we will be referring in a later chapter.[39] In Tunisia, the Hanafi school enjoys equal status with the Maliki, while in Egypt, traditionally dominated by the Malikis, the Hanafi school is now the recognized school of law. It remains predominant in Central Asia, South Asia, Turkey, and the Levant.

Malik ibn Anas (d. 795): fount of learning

Malik b. Anas is one of the most highly respected and earliest scholars of *fiqh*, the eponym of the Maliki *madhhab* in Sunni Islam. Known as "the Shaykh of Islam," "Proof of the Community," and "Imam of the Abode of Migration," he was born in Medina in 714. His family was originally from Yemen, but either his great-grandfather, Abu 'Amir, or grandfather, Malik ibn Abi 'Amir, moved with his family to Medina. Abu 'Amir may have been a Companion and transmitted *hadith*s from 'Uthman, the third caliph. His son, Malik ibn Abi 'Amir, that is, Malik ibn Anas' grandfather, was one of the better known Successors who transmitted *hadith*s from prominent Companions such as 'Umar, and 'Uthman, the two caliphs. He is also said to have been among those who copied out the Qur'an during the time of 'Uthman and was one of the four individuals who made arrangements for the slain caliph's funeral.

Living in Medina gave our Malik access to some of the best known scholars of the period. Among his best known teachers were 'Abd Allah ibn Yazid ibn Hurmuz, a younger Successor who was regarded as one of the most learned people in Medina at his time. Another influential teacher was the older Successor, Nafi', the *mawla* (freedman) of the Companion 'Abd Allah ibn 'Umar, the son of 'Umar I. Malik had much faith in the reliability of the *hadith*s transmitted by Nafi' and the chain of transmission (*isnad*) "Malik – Nafi' – Ibn 'Umar" was considered by later scholars of *hadith*, including al-Bukhari, as a "golden chain," on account of its excellence.[40] As mentioned earlier, Malik studied for a while with the Shi'i scholar Ja'far al-Sadiq as well.[41] Malik excelled in the Qur'anic and *hadith* sciences, with a particular interest in law.

Malik, like many other scholars, avoided fraternizing with the rulers of his day and was outspoken in his political views. He made public pronouncements against pledging allegiance to the 'Abbasid caliph al-Mansur, and was consequently flogged for his "obstreperousness." Al-Mansur later apologized to Malik, and offered him financial inducements to leave Medina and take up residence in Baghdad, but Malik refused to do so. Later, Harun al-Rashid requested that Malik visit him while the former was performing the pilgrimage. Typically, Malik refused, and instead invited the caliph to attend his classes. This anecdote conveys to us the distance scrupulous scholars are said to have maintained between their reified world of learning and the worldly lures of the caliphal court.

Malik is best remembered for his work entitled *al-Muwatta'*, "The Smoothed Path," which was both a work of law and a collection of *hadith*. If we except the legal work of Zayd ibn 'Ali, *al-Muwatta'* is the oldest extant manual of law which has survived in the standard and complete editions by Yahya ibn Yahya al-Masmudi (d. 848) and Muhammad al-Shaybani (d. 904).[42] Al-Shafi'i (whom we will be discussing in the next chapter) studied *al-Muwatta'* with Malik, for which work the former professed the greatest admiration. The *Muwatta'* contains 898 reports attributed to the

Companions and about 822 *hadiths* from the Prophet, which were deemed authentic by virtue of the fact that these *hadiths* reflected the actual practice (*'amal*) of the Medinese. The *Muwatta'* reflects the point of view of the Medinan scholars that the true *Sunna* of the Prophet was attested by their own continuous practice which

> became the final arbiter in determining the content of the Prophet's Sunna. The literary narrative of *hadith* acquired validity only to the extent that it was supported by this local usage. In other words, *hadith* lacking foundations in practice was rejected, while established, past practice (*sunna madiya, al-amr al-mujtama' 'alayhi 'indana*, etc.) constituted an authority-statement fit to serve as the basis of legal construction even if not backed by *hadith*.[43]

Thus it was the actual consensual practice of the Medinan scholars assumed to be historically continuous with the Prophet's which conferred legitimacy on a certain act or legal precept. This position did not discount *hadith* narratives as such but made them secondary to "their own living experience of the law" which accorded with the prophetic past.[44] When a Medinan practice and a *hadith* were at odds, preference was given to the former. This preference for Medinan *'amal* or practice is what distinguishes the Maliki legal school from all other legal schools. In a letter that Malik wrote to a fellow Medinan jurist, Layth ibn Sa'd, Malik counsels the latter not to give legal opinions which contradicted the practice of Medina because of its authoritative nature, closely associated as it was with the practice of the Prophet. Malik counseled,

> All people are subordinate to the people of Medina. To it the emigration was made and in it the Qur'an was revealed, the lawful made lawful and the forbidden made forbidden. The Messenger of God, may God bless him and grant him peace, was living among them and they were present during the very act of revelation. He would tell them to do things and they would obey him, and he would institute *sunnas* for them and they would follow him, until God took him to Himself and chose for him what is in His presence, may God bless him and grant him peace.[45]

In this letter, Malik categorically lays down the superiority of the legal decisions based on Medinan practice over those of the other schools, because of the reservoir of first-hand knowledge of the prophetic *sunna* to which only the Medinans had access and to which the learned people of other cities could not lay claim.

As we shall soon see in the next chapter, al-Shafi'i would reverse Malik's order of preference and make the texts of recorded *hadiths* the final arbiter of the authenticity and legitimacy of prophetic practice. When neither practice nor *hadith* could be adduced as evidence, Malik resorted to personal discretionary opinion (*ra'y*), for which, like Abu Hanifa, he was subjected to criticism by his anti-*ra'y* opponents.

After *al-Muwatta'*, the most important early Maliki legal treatise is the *Mudawwana* ("The Recorded [Document]") by 'Abd al-Salam ibn Sa'id al-Tanukhi, known as Sahnun (d. 845), in which Malik is referred to as one of the foremost authors of legal doctrines and opinions. The Maliki legal school was predominant until recently in the Maghrib (Tunisia, Algeria, Morocco, and Muslim Spain in the pre-modern period) and in Muslim societies in the rest of Africa.

Malik breathed his last in Medina in 795 when he was about eighty-five years old. He was buried, like Ja'far al-Sadiq, in the Baqi' cemetery across from the Prophet's mosque. The governor of Medina at the time, 'Abd Allah ibn Zaynab, led the funeral prayer.

After Malik we are in the period of "the Successors to the Successors," a critical time in the life of the polity when much of the intellectual, political, and social struggles of this period began to bear fruit. In civilizational terms the best was yet to be, the description of which will occupy us for the next few chapters.

The Successors to the Successors I: Administration, Leadership, and *Jihad*

Islam as a faith, intellectual tradition, and world civilization started coming into its own in this period (ca. 796–855). The third generation of Muslims, called the "Successors to the Successors" (*atba' al-tabi'in*) inherited a changed world after the 'Abbasid revolution, and in general, a more optimistic one for most.[1] Important ideological, administrative, cultural, political, and socio-economic developments and changes were ushered in after the overthrow of the Umayyads in 750.

THE FOUNDING OF BAGHDAD

Our historical narrative in the previous chapter had ended with the accession to power by the third 'Abbasid caliph, al-Mansur, in 754. The city of Baghdad, also referred to in the literature as *Madinat al-salam* ("the City of Peace"), was founded under him in 762. A year later, the caliph and his entourage moved from his temporary base in Kufa to his new capital Baghdad, which in a matter of years would rise to unrivaled splendor in western Asia and be second only to Constantinople in size. Al-Mansur also built for himself what is usually called "the Round City" in western Baghdad, also known as *Madinat al-Mansur* ("the City of Mansur"). In the center of the "Round City" stood al-Mansur's famed great palace called "the Golden Gate" or sometimes

referred to as "the Palace of the Green Dome." It contained a large congregational mosque, called the "Mosque of Mansur," which for the next five centuries was used for Friday prayers. The considerable sums spent in building
these new cities and their palatial residences for the royal family convey to us
the enormous wealth pouring into the imperial coffers from the various
conquests at this time and from revenues generated by taxes and trade.[2]

STATECRAFT, ADMINISTRATION, AND LEADERSHIP: ACQUIRING
A PERSIAN FLAVOR

In comparison with the Umayyad period, one of the most important transformations which occurred in the 'Abbasid period was in the conceptualization of membership in the umma or the supra-national Islamic community.
There was a marked, dramatic improvement in the status of non-Arab
Muslims (mawali) vis-à-vis Arab Muslims, bringing them much closer to the
egalitarianism promised to all believers in the Qur'an, the realization of
which principle the mawali had long agitated for under the previous administration. The tribal-ethnic sense of superiority displayed by the Umayyads
toward their non-Arab "client" subjects was remarkably lacking in the early
'Abbasid period. This helped dissipate to a considerable extent the dis-
gruntlement of the mawali evident under Umayyad rule, consequently
making of them eager participants in the new social order.

The group that benefitted the most from this sea change were the Persians, a significant number of whom assumed important official positions in
various 'Abbasid administrations and who wielded significant political as
well as cultural influence. The Persian family of viziers (wazir, a "minister" in
the political sense), called the Barmakids, assumed key administrative roles
under the early 'Abbasid caliphs until ousted from this position by Harun al-
Rashid in 803. The influential class of scribes and secretaries (kuttab, sing.
katib) under the 'Abbasids was composed of a majority of Persians who were
Muslims and Islamicized, yet who retained to a considerable extent a strong
sense of their ethno-national identity.[3] A prominent example of such a scribe
who started his career under the Umayyads and continued for a few years
under the 'Abbasids is Ibn al-Muqaffa' (d. 756). He was not only a gifted
administrator but a skilled translator and prose writer as well, contributing
to the rise of a new, lucid prose style particularly suitable for official

correspondence and chancery communications. Ibn al-Muqaffa' is best remembered for his translation of a Middle Persian literary work of animal fables (originally written in Sanskrit) into Arabic titled *Kalila wa Dimna* ("Kalila and Dimna," the name of the two fox-protagonists). This work became a literary masterpiece in Arabic on account of its engaging and wise tales and was a popular "mirror of princes" work meant to instruct young princes and other notables in the skills of statecraft and leadership.

Under this skilled and educated administrative elite, the vast 'Abbasid imperial bureaucracy became highly organized and professionalized. By the mid-ninth century, the administrative machinery was composed of several separate departments, each called a *diwan*, which employed thousands of personnel. Among the departments was the treasury, an intelligence bureau, and a special court of appeal under the caliph's jurisdiction, known as *mazalim*.

The army too underwent a number of transformations, becoming more tightly-knit in the process and better-trained as full-time professional soldiers. The army was dominated in this period by the *abna' al-dawla* ("the Sons of the Revolution"), who were Khurasanians (from Persia), some of whom were Arab in origin. Under the caliph al-Mu'tasim (ruled 833–42), segments of the army now began to consist of Turkish mercenaries, some of whom were slaves (*mamluks*) or freed slaves. This growth in the professional army would continue for a while, enabling certain factions within it to grow strong to the extent that they could occasionally pose a challenge to the caliphs, as first happened under al-Mutawakkil (d. 861), who was deposed and assassinated by some of his military commanders.

A strong military was seen as essential to protecting the world of Islam and securing its borders against external enemies. In deference to this worldview which regarded the non-Islamic world as a chronic threat, a powerful religiously legitimizing concept was harnessed in its service — *jihad*. It is to the discussion of this emotive term that we turn next.

THE CONCEPT OF *JIHAD*: QUR'ANIC ANTECEDENTS AND THE CLASSICAL JURIDICAL DOCTRINE

The classical juridical doctrine of *jihad* as military activity to protect Islamic realms was articulated in the 'Abbasid period. This doctrine was based on exegesis of key Qur'anic verses, *hadith* pertaining to *jihad*, and realpolitik. In our own time, there is much discussion regarding what is Qur'anic – and thus authentically Islamic – about this classical conception of *jihad* and what is extraneous to this Qur'anic substratum. The different legal and ethical artic-ulations of war and peace that have emerged in Islamic thought testify to the different – and conflicting – ways of reading and interpreting the principal Qur'anic verses dealing with this topic. Some of these variant ways of under-standing the sacred text will now be outlined below. A comprehensive understanding of the Qur'anic treatment of the term *jihad* and other related terms is a necessary prelude to a discussion of an evolution in the meanings of this critical term.

The Qur'anic discourse on jihad

The specific Qur'anic terms that are invoked in discussions of warfare in Islam are *jihad*, *qital*, and *harb*. *Jihad* is a much broader term and its basic Qur'anic signification is "struggle," "striving," and "exertion." The lexeme *jihad* is frequently conjoined to the phrase *fi sabil allah* (lit. "in the path of God"). The full locution in Arabic, *al-jihad fi sabil allah*, consequently means "struggling/striving for the sake of God." This translation points to the poly-semy of the term *jihad* and the potentially different meanings that may be ascribed to it in different contexts, since the phrase "in the path of/for the sake of God" allows for human striving to be accomplished in multiple ways. *Qital* is the term which specifically refers to "fighting" or "armed combat" and is a component of *jihad* in specific situations. *Harb* is the Arabic word for war in general. The Qur'an employs this last term four times: once to refer to illegitimate wars fought by those who wish to spread corruption on earth (5:64); twice to refer to the thick of battle between believers and non-believers (8:57, 47:4); and, in one instance, refers to the possibility of war waged by God and His prophet against those who would continue to practice usury (2:279).[4] This term is never conjoined to the phrase "in the path of God" and has no bearing on the concept of *jihad*.

READING THE QUR'AN IN CONTEXT

Many of the Qur'anic strictures pertaining to both non-violent and violent struggle against wrongdoing and to uphold what is good cannot be properly understood without relating them to specific events in the life of the Prophet. A significant number of Qur'anic verses are traditionally understood to have been revealed in connection with certain episodes in Muhammad's life. Knowledge of the "occasions of revelation" (*asbab al-nuzul*), as obtained from the biography of the Prophet, *hadith*, and exegetical literature, is indispensable for contextualizing key verses that may at first sight appear to be at odds with one another.[5] A specific chronology of events thus needs to be mapped out so that the progression in the Qur'anic ethics of warfare may be understood against its historical backdrop, to which we proceed next

The Meccan period

According to our sources, from the onset of the revelations to Muhammad in circa 610 until his migration to Medina from Mecca in 622 during the period known as the Meccan period, the Muslims were not given permission by the Qur'an to physically retaliate against their persecutors, the pagan Meccans. Verses revealed in this period counsel the Muslims rather to steadfastly endure the hostility of the Meccans. While recognizing the right to self-defense for those who are wronged, the Qur'an maintains in this early period that to bear patiently the wrong-doing of others and to forgive those who cause them harm is the superior course of action in resisting evil. Three significant verses (42:40–43) reveal this highly significant, non-militant dimension of struggling against wrong (and, therefore, of *jihad*) in this early phase of Muhammad's prophetic career:

> The requital of evil is an evil similar to it: hence, whoever pardons and makes peace, his reward rests with God – for indeed, He does not love evil-doers.
>
> Yet surely, as for those who defend themselves after having been wronged – no blame whatever attaches to them: blame attaches but to those who oppress people and behave outrageously on earth, offending against all right; for them is grievous suffering in store!
>
> But if one is patient in adversity and forgives, this is indeed the best resolution of affairs.

In Qur'anic discourse, patience (*sabr*) is thus a component and a manifestation of the *jihad* of the righteous; quietist and activist resistance to wrong-doing are equally valorized. For example, one Qur'anic verse (16:110) states, "As for those who after persecution fled their homes and strove actively (*jahadu*) and were patient (*sabaru*) to the last, your Lord will be forgiving and merciful to them on the day when every soul will come pleading for itself." Another (47:31) states, "We shall put you to the test until We know the active strivers (*al-mujahidin*) and the quietly forbearing (*al-sabirin*) among you." Quietist, non-violent struggle is not the same as passivity, however, which when displayed in the face of grave oppression and injustice, is clearly marked as immoral in the Qur'anic view. "Those who are passive" (*al-Qa'idun*) earn divine rebuke in the Qur'an (4:95).

The active inculcation of patience is frequently insisted upon in the Qur'an, for which generous posthumous rewards are promised. For instance, Qur'an 39:10 states, "Those who are patient will be given their reward without measure;" and Qur'an 25:75 states: "They will be awarded the high place [in heaven] for what they bore in patience ... abiding there forever." This high Qur'anic estimation of the moral attribute of patience is reflected in a statement attributed to the Prophet found in the two sound *hadith* compilations of al-Bukhari (d. 870) and Muslim (d. 875), which states that humans have not been given anything better or more abundant than patience.[6]

The verses quoted above underscore the non-violent dimension of *jihad* during the Meccan period which lasted thirteen years compared to the Medinan period of ten years. The Qur'anic verses which were revealed during this period and dictated the conduct of the Prophet and his Companions are thus of extremely important consideration in any discussion on the permissibility of engaging in armed combat within the Islamic context. As these early verses show, the Muslims were allowed to engage in self-defense but without resorting to fighting in the early period. For the most part, this meant resisting the Meccan establishment by first secret and then active, public propagation of the faith, through manumission of slaves who had converted to Islam, and, for some, by emigration to Abyssinia/Ethiopia whose Christian king was sympathetic to the early Muslims, and later to Medina.[7]

Both Muslim and non-Muslim scholars, medieval and modern, however, have tended to downplay the critical Meccan phase in the development of the Qur'anic doctrine of *jihad*. It is, however, practically impossible to contextualize the Qur'anic discourse on the various meanings of *jihad* without taking the Meccan phase into consideration. The introduction of the military aspect of *jihad* in the Medinan period can then be appropriately and better understood as a "last resort" option adopted when attempts at negotiations and peaceful proselytization among the Meccans had failed during the first thirteen years of the propagation of Islam. When we add to the Meccan period the first two years after the *hijra* when fighting had not yet begun, we arrive at a total of roughly fifteen years of non-militancy as compared to eight years in the Medinan period during which fighting took place.

The Medinan period

In 622 CE, which corresponds to the first year of the Islamic calendar, the Prophet received divine permission to migrate to Medina, along with his loyal followers. There he set up the first Muslim polity, combining the functions of prophecy and temporal rule in one office. The Medinan verses, accordingly, now have increasingly more to do with organization of the polity, communitarian issues and ethics, and defense of the Muslims against Meccan hostilities. A specific Qur'anic verse (22:39–40) permitting fighting was revealed in Medina, although its precise date cannot be determined. The verse states:

> Permission [to fight] is given to those against whom war is being wrongfully waged, and indeed, God has the power to help them: those who have been driven from their homes against all right for no other reason than their saying, "Our Provider is God!" For, if God had not enabled people to defend themselves against one another, monasteries, churches, synagogues, and mosques – in all of which God's name is abundantly glorified – would surely have been destroyed.

Another verse states (2:217):

> They ask you concerning fighting in the prohibited months.[8] Answer them: "To fight therein is a serious offence. But to restrain men from following the cause of God, to deny God, to violate the sanctity of the sacred mosque, to expel its people from its environs is in the sight of God a greater wrong than fighting in the forbidden month. [For] discord and strife (*fitna*) are worse than killing."

Until the outbreak of full-fledged war a little later in the same year, the Qur'an, in this and other verses previously cited, refers to the reasons – *jus ad bellum* – that justify recourse to fighting. In verses 42:40–43, where self-defense is allowed but not through violent means, the reasons are the wrongful conduct of the enemy and their oppressive and immoral behavior on earth. In verses 22:39–40 quoted above, a more explicit reason is given: wrongful expulsion of the Muslims from their homes for no other reason than their avowal of belief in one God. Furthermore, the Qur'an asserts, if people are not allowed to defend themselves against aggressive wrong-doers, all the houses of worship – it is worthy of note that Islam is not the only religion indicated here – would be destroyed and thus the word of God extinguished. The verse thus implies that Muslims may resort to defensive combat even on behalf of non-Muslim believers who are the objects of the hostility of non-believers.[9] In the final verse cited (2:217), the Qur'an acknowledges the enormity of fighting during the prohibited months but at the same time asserts the higher moral imperative of maintaining order and challenging wrong-doing. Therefore, when both just cause and righteous intention exist, war in self-defense against an intractable enemy may become obligatory.

> Fighting (al-qital) is prescribed for you, while you dislike it. But it is possible that you dislike a thing which is good for you, and that you love a thing which is bad for you. God knows and you know not. (2:216)

The Qur'an further asserts that it is the duty of Muslims to defend those who are oppressed and who cry out to them for help (4:75), except against a people with whom the Muslims have concluded a treaty (8:72).

With regard to initiation of hostilities and conduct during war (jus in bello), the Qur'an has specific injunctions. Qur'an 2:190 which reads, "Fight in the cause of God those who fight you, but do not commit aggression, for God loves not aggressors," forbids Muslims from initiating hostilities. Recourse to armed combat must be in response to a prior act of aggression by the opposite side.[10] The Qur'an further counsels (5:8), "Let not rancor towards others cause you to incline to wrong and depart from justice. Be just; that is closer to piety." This verse may be understood to complement 2:190 in spirit and intent, warning against excesses that may result from an unprincipled desire to punish and exact revenge.

During the month of Ramadan in the third year of the Islamic calendar (624 CE), full-fledged hostilities broke out between the Muslims and the pagan Meccans in what became known as the Battle of Badr. In this battle, a small army of Muslims decisively routed a much larger and more experienced Meccan army. Two years later, the Battle of Uhud was fought in which the Muslims suffered severe reverses, followed by the Battle of al-Khandaq in 627. Apart from these three major battles, a number of other minor campaigns were fought until the Prophet's death in 632. Some of the most trenchant verses exhorting the Muslims to fight were revealed on the occasions of these military campaigns. One such verse is 9:5, which has been termed the "sword verse" (*ayat al-sayf*). It states:

> And when the sacred months are over, slay the polytheists wherever you find them, and take them captive, and besiege them, and lie in wait for them at every conceivable place.

Another verse (9:29) is often conjoined to the above, which runs:

> Fight against those who – despite having been given revelation before – do not believe in God nor in the Last Day, and do not consider forbidden that which God and His messenger have forbidden, and do not follow the religion of the truth, until they pay the *jizya* with willing hand, having been subdued.

The first of the "sword verses" (9:5), with its internal reference to the polytheists who may be fought after the end of the sacred months, would circumscribe its applicability to only the pagan Arabs of Muhammad's time. This is, in fact, how many pre-modern scholars, such as Mugatil ibn Sulayman[11] and al-Tabari,[12] understood the verse. The second of the "sword verses" (also called the *jizya* verse) is seemingly directed in general at the People of the Book, that is, Jews and Christians. But a careful reading of the verse clearly indicates that it does not intend all the People of the Book but only those from among them who do not, in contravention of their own laws, believe in God and the Last Day and do not forbid wrongdoing. This understanding is borne out by comparing verse 9:29 to verses 3:113–115, for example, which state,

> They are not all the same. Among the People of the Book are a contingent who stand [in prayer] reciting the verses of God at all times of the night while they prostrate.

> These are they who believe in God and the Last Day and enjoin what is right and forbid what is wrong. They hasten to [perform] good deeds and they are among the righteous.

> And whatever they do of good will not be rejected [by God] and God knows best who are the God-fearing.

The Qur'an in another verse (2:193) makes unambiguously clear that should hostile behavior on the part of the foes of Islam cease, then the reason for engaging them in war also lapses. This verse states:

And fight them on until there is no discord (*fitna*) and religion is only for God, but if they cease, let there be no hostility except toward those who practice oppression.

The harshness of the two "sword verses" is thus considerably mitigated and their general applicability significantly restricted by juxtaposing to them conciliatory verses, such as the ones cited above and other such verses. Among other such verses is the one that has been characterized as the "peace verse" (8:61):

> If they incline toward peace, incline you toward it, and trust in God. Indeed, He alone is all-hearing, all-knowing.

And,

> Slay them wherever you catch them, and turn them out from where they have turned you out; for persecution is worse than slaughter ... But if they cease, God is Oft-forgiving, Most Merciful. (2:191–92)

> God does not forbid you from being kind and equitable to those who have neither made war on you on account of your religion nor driven you from your homes. God loves those who are equitable. (60:8)

These verses make fighting against those who oppose the propagation of the message of Islam and consequently resort to persecution of Muslims contingent upon their continuing hostility. Should they desist from such hostile persecution and sue for peace instead, the Muslims are commanded to accede to their request. It should be pointed out that Qu'ran 2:191–2 have been understood by commentators as referring specifically to the events at al-Hudaybiyya. Thus Muqatil ibn Sulayman states explicitly that these verses only concern the "Arab polytheists" (*mushriki 'l-'arab*).[13] Qur'an 60:8 further makes clear that non-Muslims of good-will and peaceableness cannot be the targets of hostility simply on account of their different religious backgrounds.

LATER UNDERSTANDINGS OF *JIHAD*

By the period under discussion here (late second century of the Islamic era/early ninth century of the Common Era), *jihad* as primarily "armed combat" had become the accepted meaning in influential circles, particularly in the administrative and juridical ones. This occurred despite the fact that the term *jihad* in Qur'anic usage is clearly a multivalent word, and as even a cursory reading of some of the related literature reveals, was understood as such by early religious authorities and scholars. Exegetical glosses from the early period on the full Qur'anic phrase *al-jihad fi sabil allah* (translated as "striving" or "struggling in the path of God") explain it as referring to a wide array of activities other than military defense of Islam, such as giving charitable alms, embarking on the pursuit of knowledge, and earning one's livelihood by licit means, among other activities. Parallel extra-Qur'anic literature (primarily exegesis and *hadith*) records various perspectives on martyrdom (*shahada*, a term which does not occur in the Qur'an in this sense) which reflect the multiple meanings of the term *jihad*. An individual who met death while struggling in any licit and noble pursuit during one's mundane existence on earth could be regarded as a "martyr" (*shahid*, pl. *shuhada'*).[14]

NEGOTIATING THE POLYVALENCE OF THE TERM *JIHAD*

The scholarly literature from the first three centuries of Islam reveals that there were competing definitions of how best to strive in the path of God, engendered by the polyvalence of the Qur'anic term *jihad*. Recent rigorous research has established that there was a clear divergence of opinion regarding the nature of *jihad* and its imposition as a religious duty on the believer through the first century of Islam and into the second half of the second century. Meticulous scholarship has established that during the Umayyad period, there were multiple and conflicting perspectives on *jihad* and its purview held by jurists from the Hijaz (from the province of western Arabia that includes Mecca and Medina) and jurists from Syria.[15] Hijazi jurists, like Ibn Jurayj (d. 762), tended to place greater emphasis on religious practices such as prayer and mosque attendance and did not consider *jihad* obligatory for all. Another early jurist Sufyan al-Thawri (d. 778) was of the opinion that *jihad* was primarily defensive, and that only the defensive *jihad* may be considered obligatory on the individual.[16] On the other hand, Syrian jurists like al-Awza'i (d. 773) held the view that even aggressive war may be considered obligatory. No doubt this last group was influenced by the fact that the Syrian Umayyads during his time were engaged in border warfare with the Byzantines and there was a perceived need to justify these hostilities on a theological and legal basis.[17] It would not be an exaggeration to state that expressing support for expansionist military campaigns during the Umayyad period was to proclaim one's support for the existing government and its policies.[18]

By the early 'Abbasid period, roughly mid to late eighth century, the military aspect of *jihad* would receive greater emphasis in many circles. In the opinions of some jurists, this aspect was understood to override the other non-militant spiritual and social significations of this term. *Jihad* from this period on would progressively be conflated with *qital* ("fighting"), collapsing the distinction that the Qur'an maintains between the two. As the jurists and religious scholars in general became consolidated as a scholarly class and accrued to themselves commensurate religious authority by the tenth century, they arrogated to themselves the right to authoritatively define *jihad* and circumscribe the range of activities prescribed by it. With the powerful theory of abrogation (*naskh*) at their disposal, some of the jurists effectively rendered null and void the positive injunctions contained in the Qur'anic verses which explicitly permitted the conclusion of truces with foes and counseled peaceful co-existence with particularly the "People of the Book." One of the most important verses declared by a number (by no means all) of these scholars to have been abrogated or superseded is Qur'an 2:256, which forbids compulsion in religion, by verses which give the command to fight.[19]

This, however, does not mean that these scholars henceforth regarded coercion of non-believers to embrace Islam as valid.[20] But since Qur'an 2:256 had been adduced as a proof-text by those who inveighed against the concept of an offensive *jihad* – for that might lead the way to coercive conversions – the opposite camp felt impelled to declare the injunction contained in this verse (and other verses which advocated peaceful, non-militant relations with non-Muslims) to be abrogated or at least superseded by other verses, such as the so-called "sword verse"[21] or by Qur'an 9:73.[22] In the opinion of these jurists, such an act of abrogation or supersession would remove scripture-based proscriptions against the waging of offensive battles in order to extend the political realm of Islam. Once conquered, non-Muslims could be given the choice of either embracing Islam or paying the poll-tax. Usually compliance with the second option (in the absence of any desire to convert) meant that the third option created by this camp of jurists for non-Muslims – "to be put to the sword" – who refused to accept Islam was unlikely to be exercised, and the jurists in all probability envisioned that this is how matters would turn out. Thus even these jurists could not have conceived of *jihad* as "holy war," as this term is often carelessly translated, to effect the conversion of non-Muslims. They could in fact be described as doing just the opposite – that is, of politicizing and secularizing *jihad* so that it came to refer to expansionist war which could be launched to further the state's imperial objectives to territorially expand and extend its political reach. The monovalent and belligerent understanding of *jihad* promoted by such scholars within the context of international relations clearly undermined the rich diversity of meanings associated with the term in Qur'anic and early *hadith* discourse.

The jurist al-Shafi'i (d. 820) is said to have been the first to permit *jihad* to be launched against non-Muslims as offensive warfare, although he qualified non-Muslims as referring only to pagan Arabs and not to non-Arab non-Muslims. He further divided the world into *dar al-islam* ("the abode of Islam") and *dar al-harb* ("the abode of war") referring to non-Muslim territories, while recognizing a third possibility *dar al-'ahd* ("the abode of treaty") or *dar al-sulh* ("the abode of reconciliation"), referring to non-Muslim states that may enter into a peace treaty with the Islamic state by rendering an annual tribute.[23] In the absence of actual hostilities, the Shafi'i school of thought posited an existing state of "cold war" between the abodes of Islam and of war, which required constant vigilance against the latter.[24] Political theorists after al-Shafi'i would enshrine this concept in their writings by averring that one of the duties of the caliph was to launch *jihad* at least once a year, although others were of the opinion that this duty could be fulfilled by simply being in an adequate state of military preparedness to forestall enemy attacks.[25]

Al-Shafi'i's perspective on *jihad* was, in many ways, a marked departure from earlier juristic thinking and reflects a certain hardening of attitudes toward non-Islamic states by his time (late eighth and early ninth century). This is quite evident when his views are compared with those of jurists from the earlier Hanafi school of law. Early Hanafi jurists, for example, did not subscribe to a third abode of treaty, as conceptualized by al-Shafi'i, but were of the opinion that the inhabitants of a territory which had concluded a truce with the Muslims and paid tribute to the latter became part of the abode of Islam and entitled to the protection of the Islamic government.[26] The Hanafis also adhered to the position that non-believers could be fought only if they resorted to armed conflict, and not simply on account of their different belief system.[27] This would become a principle of contention between early Shafi'i and Hanafi jurists.

It is worth emphasizing that the concepts of *dar al-islam* and *dar al-harb* have no basis in the Qur'an nor in the *sunna*. The invention of these terms and the resulting aggrandizement of the military aspect of *jihad* were based rather on ad hoc juristic interpretations of particularly verses 9:5 and 9:29, largely in deference to realpolitik in the 'Abbasid period. The 'Abbasid state, in control of a vast and diverse political realm, had to develop a sophisticated law of nations, termed in Arabic *al-siyar* (lit. "motions," "travels"). From the vantage point of realpolitik, *jihad* could be understood as defensive or offensive fighting whose primary purpose was to allay the security concerns of the state. Thus as we saw during the Umayyad period (661–750), the constant border skirmishes with the hostile Byzantines predisposed Syrian jurists in particular to endorse the concept of an offensive *jihad* (in opposition to Medinan and Meccan jurists living far away from the metropole) as an effective military strategy against a perceived intractable enemy.

The politicization and secularization of *jihad* is further indicated by the titles of works on the law of nations during the early 'Abbasid period, such as *Kitab al-jihad wa 'l-siyar*, signaling the yoking of a religious concept (*jihad*) to the exigencies of imperial foreign policy (*siyar*), while acknowledging the historically separate bailiwicks of each.[28] It should not come as a surprise to us that on account of the sensibilities of the day, politically expedient considerations had to be couched in religious rhetoric and morally legitimized (a proclivity that is not exactly unknown to us today). It is necessary for us to interrogate the ostensible religious purposes advanced for aggressive military activity and the rhetoric of religio-political triumphalism engaged in by certain Muslim jurists and scholars of this period. Such a line of inquiry would be revealing of more mundane and politically expedient motivations for expanding the semantic and legal purview of *jihad* to include expansionist war fought for political and/or patriotic ends, clothed in religious garb, at particular times in history. Suspicion of such worldly motives is already apparent in reports contained in early *hadith* works such as the *Musannaf* of 'Abd al-Razzaq (d. 827). One such report specifically expresses anxieties about joining the military campaigns of those "who fight seeking [the gains of] the world."[29]

Lacking a scriptural basis, the legal division of the world into bipolar spheres is not doctrinally binding in any way. And, in fact, by the sixth century of Islam/twelfth century of the Common Era, these terms had fallen into desuetude since they no longer accurately described contemporary historical and political realities. Accordingly, juristic thinking in this period, in accommodation of these changed realities, came to consider *jihad* as a caliphal duty that was basically in abeyance, but which could be revived in times of crisis. The famous philosopher Ibn Khaldun (d. 1406) would characterize this change in the juristic conception of *jihad* as reflective of a "change in the character of the nation from the warlike to the civilized stage."[30]

It is worthy of note that in the process of politicizing *jihad*, the daring abrogation of the critical Qur'anic verse 2:256 (which forbids compulsion in religion) advocated by some scholars was by no means accepted by all. Two celebrated Qur'an commentators from a later period, Muhammad ibn Jarir al-Tabari (d. 923)[31] and Ibn Kathir (d. 1373)[32] resolutely maintained that this verse had not been abrogated and its injunction remained valid for all time. It is significant that al-Tabari's well-known juridical work *Ikhtilaf al-fuqaha'* ("the Differences of the Jurists") does not list Qur'an 9:5 as an abrogating verse;[33] and neither does the late work on the Qur'anic sciences by al-Suyuti (d. 1505).[34] It is therefore obvious that as late as the fifteenth century there was by no means a scholarly consensus on the status of Qur'an 2:256 and that the most influential commentators of the pre-modern period continued to maintain the normative applicability of this verse.

MANY PATHS TO MARTYRDOM

As previously mentioned, the Qur'an does not have a single word for "martyr" or "martyrdom," two concepts that are intrinsically linked to the development of the concept of *jihad* primarily as armed combat against the enemies of Islam. One of the Qur'anic verses (3:169; cf. 47:4, 2:154) that has been construed to refer to the special status of the military martyr runs thus, "Do not think that those who were slain in the path of God are dead. They are alive and well provided for by their Lord." Early exegetical and *hadith* works, however, make clear that the phrase "slain in the path of God," was not understood to be restricted to those fallen in battle, but could be glossed in several ways, as discussed below.

The common Arabic word now for martyr is *shahīd*. In the Qur'an, this word is only used, interchangeably with *shāhid*, to refer to "a legal" or "eye-witness."[35] Only in later extra-Qur'anic tradition does this word acquire the meaning of "one who bears witness for the faith," particularly by laying down his life. Extraneous, particularly Christian, influence may be suspected here.[36] Muslim encounters with Levantine Christians in the late seventh century very likely contributed to this development. There is evidence for the probable influence of the cognate Syriac word for martyr-witness *sahēd* on the Arabic *shahīd* and the latter's subsequent acquisition of the secondary and derivative meaning of "martyr."[37] The fact that we encounter the term *shahid* in the sense of martyr-witness only in the *hadith* literature already implies the later development of this strand of meaning.

The original broad purview of *shahid* finds reflection in early *hadith* works. Thus the *Musannaf* of ʿAbd al-Razzaq (d. 827), which was compiled earlier than al-Bukhari's authoritative collection of *hadith*, contains a number of Companion reports (that is, reports which go back to a Companion of the Prophet only rather than directly back to Muhammad) which relate competing definitions of *shahid*. A few examples will suffice. One report attributed to the Companion Abu Hurayra states that the *shahid* is one who, were he to die in his bed, would enter heaven.[38] The explanatory note that follows states that it refers to someone who dies in his bed and is without sin (*la dhanb lahu*). Another report is related by Masruq ibn al-Ajdaʾ who states, "There are four types of *shahada* or martyrdom for Muslims: the plague, parturition or delivery of a child, drowning, and a stomach ailment."[39] Significantly, there is no mention of martyrdom being earned on account of dying on the battlefield in this early report. An expanded version of this report, however, originating with Abu Hurayra, quotes the Prophet as adding to this list of those who achieve martyrdom, "one who is killed in the way of God (*man qutila fi sabil allah*)."[40] It is this expanded version containing the full, five definitions of a *shahid* that is recorded later in the authoritative *hadith* work of al-Bukhari.[41]

The early eighth-century *hadith* compilation titled *al-Muwatta'* of the Medinan legal scholar we encountered earlier, Malik ibn Anas (d. 795) states: "The martyrs are seven, apart from death in God's path. He who dies as a victim of an epidemic is a martyr; he who dies from drowning is a martyr; he who dies from pleurisy is a martyr; he who dies from diarrhea is a martyr; he who dies by [being burned in] fire is a martyr; he who dies by being struck by a dilapidated wall falling is a martyr; and the woman who dies in childbed is a martyr."[42] This report and the one cited above assigns martyrdom to the believer who suffers a painful death from a variety of debilitating illnesses, or a difficult labor for women in particular, or being victim to an unfortunate accident such as being crushed to death by a falling wall, in addition to falling on the battlefield.

The multiple, non-combative significations of the phrase *fi sabil Allah* ("in the way of God"), particularly in the early period, is further clear from a noteworthy *hadith* recorded in 'Abd al-Razzaq's *Musannaf*. According to this report, a number of the Companions were sitting with the Prophet when a man from the tribe of Quraysh, apparently a pagan and of muscular build, came into view. Some of those gathered exclaimed, "How strong this man looks! If only he would exert his strength in the way of God!" The Prophet asked, "Do you think only someone who is killed [sc. in battle] is engaged in the way of God?" He continued, "Whoever goes out in the world seeking licit work to support his family is on the path of God; whoever goes out in the world seeking licit work to support himself is on the path of God. Whoever goes out seeking worldly increase has embarked, however, on the way of the devil."[43]

Jihad as spiritual struggle against one's carnal self is reflected in another prophetic statement found in the relatively early *hadith* works of Ahmad ibn Hanbal (d. 855) and al-Tirmidhi (d. 892), which states, "One who strives against his own self is a *mujahid*, that is, carries out *jihad*."[44] A *hadith* recorded by Muslim similarly emphasizes the internal, spiritual aspect of striving for God; it affirms, "Whoever strives (*jahada*) with his heart is a believer."[45] Another report praises the commission of charitable deeds as a commendable act of *jihad*, as recorded by three of the most authoritative Sunni *hadith* compilers, al-Bukhari, Muslim, and al-Tirmidhi. In this *hadith*, the Prophet declares, "the one who helps widows and the poor are like the fighters in the path of God."[46] The range of meanings indicated by these statements is to be expected since the daily struggle of the individual to live his or her life "in the way of God" infuses even the most ordinary activities with moral and spiritual significance and thus meeting with divine approbation. Therefore, one who perished while engaged in such mundane but morally commendable acts could be and was considered a martyr.

Lastly, it should be mentioned that there are *hadith*s found in authoritative ninth-century compilations which counsel against military zeal and the courting of martyrdom. Al-Bukhari records reports in which the Prophet counsels that it is forbidden for an individual (1) to wish for death, and (2) to wish for an encounter with the enemy.[47] Saving one's life and the lives of others is a high ethical priority in the Qur'an (5:32), even to the extent that the Qur'an expressly permits the believer to abjure his or her faith publicly under duress, as long as one's heart remains firm in belief (16:106). The willful seeking of martyrdom is forbidden in Islam's normative texts and is regarded as a form of suicide or self-destruction, categorically proscribed in the Qur'an (2:195, 4:29) and in *hadith*.[48]

In this early period, as we see, *jihad* had still not been almost completely collapsed with *qital* (fighting), as we find in later legal works, and martyrdom had both non-combative and combative inflections. Early *hadith* and exegetical works preserve a much broader spectrum of meanings for these two terms and thus remain indispensable sources for our understanding of the historical development and transformation of these terms.

CHANGES IN CONCEPTIONS OF LEADERSHIP

There were dramatic changes in the concept and nature of leadership occurring in this period as well. The concept of the caliph ruling practically infallibly and invincibly with some measure of divine protection is exogenous to Islam. Recent, careful scholarship has shown that such notions seeped into the Islamic milieu through infiltration of ancient Persian and Greek ideas of divine or sacred kingship.[49] Our discussion so far reveals that the early egalitarian Islamic community largely recognized differences among the faithful on the basis of personal piety and moral excellence alone, tending to devalue kinship and social status in conscious contradistinction to the pre-Islamic period.[50] Such a moral attitude found broad reflection in the socio-political organization of the early polity as well. Leadership positions mostly (although not always) tended to devolve upon those who had already distinguished themselves for their exceptional piety and meritorious service to the Islamic community. A case in point was Salman al-Farisi, a non-Arab convert to Islam without a distinctive lineage, appointed to the governorship of Persia by 'Umar, the second caliph. In the Sunni conception of the caliphate, the caliph, *primus inter pares*, was, certainly in theory, liable to be deposed for wrong-doing and could be chided (and sometimes was) for straying from good governing practices or for failing to confer with those he governed.

The first caliph Abu Bakr's inaugural address, recorded in many sources, remains a model of humility and accountability to the people. To reprise a significant point he makes in this key address, he is quoted as counselling the people gathered before him, "You must be Godfearing, for piety is the most intelligent practice and immorality is the most foolish. Indeed I am a follower, not an innovator; if I perform well, then help me, and if I should deviate, correct me."[51]

The conception of legitimate leadership adumbrated in this key address is referenced by the Qur'anic view that the most morally excellent were the most qualified for political stewardship on earth, as we have discussed earlier. Abu Bakr accordingly argues his case before the public, establishing his credentials for the office, and asserts his accountability before those he will govern. Conspicuously lacking in this speech and in the accounts that follow of Abu Bakr's investiture is any notion that unreflective obedience would consequently be due to him from the populace.

This early emphasis on personal piety as the primary criterion for assessing an individual's moral and social standing never fully eradicated the pre-Islamic (*Jahili*) valorization of noble descent and tribal affiliation. This valorization remained in uneasy tension with Islam's radical egalitarianism for most of the formative period. With ideas of political absolutism and hierarchical social customs of particularly Persian provenance gaining ascendancy under the 'Abbasids from the eighth century onwards, Jahili notions of showing deference to the high-born and the politically prominent began to make a diffident comeback as well. 'Abbasid adoption of titles, such as "God's deputy on earth" and "God's shadow on earth" are all reflective of this transformative trend. The title *Khalifat Allah* ("God's deputy on earth") had already been adopted by the Umayyads in a self-aggrandizing vein but they still maintained a certain Arab approachability vis-à-vis their subjects. The 'Abbasid caliphs, however, progressively grew inaccessible to their public and adopted in large measure the trappings and pageantry of the Persian imperial court. The pious would be aghast at such developments; we have their dissenting voices recorded in primarily the ethical and mystical literature of the period deploring these changed circumstances.[52] Over time, political theorists would lend an Islamic patina to such autocratic notions, allowing for a comfortable accommodation with political reality. This tendency becomes strongly apparent when one compares early and late exegeses of the critical Qur'anic verse which counsels believers to "Obey God and the Messenger, and those possessing authority among you" (4:59), as we now proceed to discuss.

With regard to the "people possessed of authority" (*ulu 'l-amr*), early Qur'an commentaries give us a very good idea of how the early Muslims understood this term. One of the earliest works of exegesis we have at our disposal is the one by the late seventh/early eighth-century Qur'an commentator Mujahid ibn Jabr (d. 720), from the generation of the Successors. In his commentary, Mujahid states that this verse was revealed in reference to "those endowed with critical insight into religion and reason" (*uli 'l-fiqh fi 'l-din wa-'l-'aql*). A second variant report relates that the phrase refers to "those possessing critical insight, knowledge, [sound] opinion and virtue."[53] Particularly noteworthy in these glosses is the emphasis on knowledge, independent reasoning, and critical discernment on the part of the *ulu 'l-amr*.

Another early exegete, Muqatil ibn Sulayman al-Balkhi (d. 767), also a Successor, records in his *tafsir* work that the key phrase *ulu 'l-amr* was revealed specifically in reference to the military commander Khalid ibn al-Walid in a particular historical context, and, more broadly, refers to the commanders of military contingents in general.[54] Muqatil refers to an unnamed military campaign during which Khalid ibn al-Walid and 'Ammar ibn Yasir had a disagreement regarding the status of a prisoner of war as the specific context for the revelation of this verse. Muqatil compares Qur'an 4:59 to 24:51, which helps to further clarify the meaning of the former. Qur'an 24:51 states, "For those who obey God and His messenger and fear God and heed Him, they are the ones who are victorious." In comparison with 24:51–52, Muqatil understands obedience in 4:59 to be due only to God and His messenger, with the *ulu 'l-amr* excluded.[55]

The ninth-/tenth-century exegete al-Tabari (d. 923) gives an account of the various meanings attributed to this phrase and gives us a sense of the evolution in its interpretation up to his time. In his commentary on verse 4:59, al-Tabari refers to a number of early authorities who understood the phrase *ulu 'l-amr* as referring in general to "people of knowledge and insightful understanding," with many variant reports being recorded.[56] Other commentators, according to al-Tabari, were inclined to understand this verse as referring to all the Companions of Muhammad (*ashab Muhammad*).[57] Al-Tabari also quotes the Companion Ubayy ibn Ka'b as saying that the verse was a reference to the political rulers (*al-salatin*),[58] an interesting anachronistic usage of this word here since sultans did not rise in the Islamic world until about the tenth century, well after the time of the Companions.[59] He further cites the opinion of several Companions that this verse referred to specific military commanders during the time of the Prophet, such as 'Abd Allah ibn Hudhafa, Khalid ibn al-Walid, and 'Ammar ibn Yasir.[60]

This brief survey of early exegetical works – from the late seventh to the tenth century – clearly establishes that the earliest meanings associated with the word *amr* had no political overtones in the early period.[61] Accordingly, the phrase *ulu 'l-amr* during at least the first two centuries of Islam did not refer to wielders of political authority, as became the common understanding by the fourth century of Islam, but rather broadly to "people of insight and understanding," and/or to specific military commanders during the Prophet's time.

We find the reflection of a similar trend in political treatises. One of the earliest monograph-length political treatises at our disposal is the *Risalat al-'Uthmaniyya* of al-Jahiz (d. 869). This treatise composed in the early ninth century (circa 820) still preserves for us the full gamut of the meanings ascribed to this phrase in the early works of *tafsir* and also provides new insights into the semantic trajectory of this term in this period. In this work al-Jahiz indicates the range of possible interpretations of this verse. Some Qur'an exegetes, he says, have understood the phrase *ulu 'l-amr* to have a restricted application and to apply only to specific agents (*'ummal*) of the Prophet, to his specific delegates or representatives (*wulat*), and/or to specific commanders of his armies, such as Abu Musa al-Ash'ari. Others have understood it to refer to political rulers (*salatin, umara'*). Yet others have interpreted this phrase to refer more broadly to the Companions of the Prophet as a group, and/or to Muslims in general.[62] In the early ninth century, al-Jahiz's important but relatively unknown political treatise still does not show a preference for the meaning of *amr* as "political authority;" rather his work continues to document the broad range of meanings that were ascribed to the word over time. The last exegetical gloss recorded by al-Jahiz would invest the entire Muslim community (or, at the least, its righteous members) with moral and political authority.

The standard and better known political treatises of the later period do, in fact, increasingly begin to restrict the term *ulu 'l-amr* to the political rulers of the various Muslim communities. The Shafi'i jurist al-Mawardi (d. 1058) in his influential political treatise *al-Ahkam al-sultaniyya* ("The Governmental Ordinances") refers to verse 4:59 and explicates it as ordaining virtually unquestioning obedience on the part of Muslims to their appointed leaders (*al-a'imma al-muta'ammarun*).[63] He cites in this case a well-known *hadith* from Abu Hurayra in which the Prophet states: "After me there will be rulers/ governors, the righteous with his righteousness and the corrupt with his corruptness; listen to them and obey them in what is in accordance with the truth. If they should rule wisely or justly then it counts in your and their favor. And if they should act unjustly, then it counts in your favor and against them."[64] It is pertinent to note that this *hadith* counseling political subservience is attributed to Abu Hurayra, whose reputation as a *hadith* transmitter is mixed at best, and which reputation should impel us to regard the reliability of this report (and others like it attributed to him) as less than completely assured.[65] It seems clear that once the word *amr* came to be understood as primarily referring to political authority by sometime in the ninth century, prophetic reports (of varying degrees of reliability) advising against causing social upheaval (*fitna*) by engaging in political rebellion would be associated with Qur'an 4:59 and thus marshaled as religious warrants for promoting political quietism and authoritarianism.

It is fashionable in certain circles these days to promote an essentialist view of Islam as largely inflexible and frozen in its tracks on account of being beholden to an assumed immutable religious law. According to this view, this state of affairs affects not only religious belief and practices within Islam but its political culture as well. Thus the entrenchment of political authoritarianism in the ninth century is ahistorically regarded in these circles as always having existed in the Islamic world and due directly to scriptural injunctions. One of the more prominent proponents of such views is the historian Bernard Lewis. Lewis bases his conclusions on Qur'an 4:59, which he however misreads and mistranslates. Thus he renders the critical phrase *ulu 'l-amr minkum* in Qur'an 4:59 as "those in authority over you" rather than "those in authority among you" (the Arabic preposition *min* means "among" rather than "over"). The latter correct translation suggests a significantly different conception of authority, which is more egalitarian and diffuse in nature than top-down. Lewis compounds his mistake by then proceeding to grandly pronounce on the intrinsically authoritarian nature of the Islamic political tradition, since, he maintains, Qur'an 4:59 teaches that "the primary and essential duty owed by the subjects to the ruler is obedience." Furthermore, he opines, "the duty of obedience … is a religious obligation, defined and promised by Holy Law and grounded in revelation."[66]

Careful, historical surveys based on a close reading of early and later texts help disabuse us of such jejune, essentialist notions and contribute to the realization that Islamic civilization, like any other, is the product of many external variables – social, historical, political, and economic – as it was equally the result of competing ideational and ideological currents, the most important of which understandably was the Islamic one with all its permutations. The rubric *Islamic* blinds us to the many extra- and non-Islamic threads which held together the fabric of Islamic civilization. But, we would argue at the same time, that did and does not make it any less Islamic. In the heyday of its civilization in the pre-modern period, the umbrella term *Islamic* made room for everything and anything that could be accommodated within its capacious world-view and broad conceptualization of moral order. Within its conception of political order, it also progressively made room for various administrative notions out of sheer pragmatism, which sometimes, as we have seen, violated some of its core moral precepts.

It was this capacious world-view that contributed to the rise of a distinctive Islamic humanism, termed *adab*, at the same time that the study of the religious law was intensifying and becoming institutionalized. A good sense of the intellectual history of our period, therefore, challenges the pat bromide that humanistic pursuits must of necessity have been alien to the assumed pre-modern theocentric Islamic consciousness. In the next chapter, we continue our discussion of intellectual history during the lifetime of the third generation of Muslims, a landmark period in the development of the cultural life of the polity.

The Successors to the
Successors II: Humanism,
Law, and Mystical Spirituality

THE RISE OF HUMANISM

The early 'Abbasid period witnessed the flourishing of various disciplines and sciences, chief among them the religious sciences: Qur'anic studies, *hadith*, theology, and law. These sciences were traditionally called "the transmitted sciences" (*al-'ulum al-naqliyya*), to which were added ancillary linguistic and literary sub-disciplines, including grammar, syntax, and poetry. These subjects were initially taught in the larger "teaching" mosques of the period in informal study circles (*halqa*). By our period, a new academic institution, the mosque-hostel complex (*masjid-khan*), was coming into being which provided accommodation for out-of-town students and teachers. By the eleventh century, the institute of higher education, called *madrasa* in Arabic, would develop from this mosque-hostel complex and become widespread in the Islamic world under the patronage of many powerful rulers and wealthy benefactors. It is the *madrasa* that is believed to have influenced the structure and curriculum of the medieval European university starting in the twelfth century.[1]

Persian influence, as we saw, was most strongly felt in the area of statecraft but also progressively highly noticeable in the adoption of certain cultural practices, literary tastes, and culinary arts. A vibrant humanistic, literary tradition emerged in the 'Abbasid period under the rubric of *adab* ("belles-lettres," also "manners"). This humanistic tradition owes its impetus to the translation activities of the eighth and ninth centuries which made the literary heritage of the ancient civilization of Greece, and to a lesser extent of Persia, India, and the ancient Near East, accessible to an Arab audience. In three-quarters of a century after the establishment of Baghdad the Arabic-reading world was in possession of the chief philosophical works of Aristotle, the leading neo-Platonic commentators, and most of the medical writings of Galen, as well as of Persian and Indian scientific works. In several decades Arab Muslim and Christian scholars would assimilate what had taken the Greeks centuries to develop. In absorbing the main features of both Hellenic and Persian cultures Islamic civilization occupied an important place in the medieval cultural unit which linked southern Europe with western Asia. This culture may be regarded as being "fed by a single stream, a stream with sources in ancient Egypt, Babylonia, and Phoenicia, all flowing to Greece and now returning to the East in the form of Hellenism."[2] This stream would later be redirected toward Europe, particularly by Muslims in Spain and Sicily, where it helped create the Renaissance in Europe.

A very significant development in 751 aided in the proliferation and dissemination of knowledge in the Islamic world. In this year, paper-making technology learned from Chinese prisoners of war was introduced, causing all other writing materials to be supplanted by it in the early decades of the 'Abbasid period. The 'Abbasid elite actively promoted the use of paper and different kinds of paper were developed, often named after some of the key translators of this period.[3]

In the rise of wisdom literature and mathematics, India acted as an early source of inspiration. About 771 CE, an Indian traveler introduced into Baghdad a treatise on astronomy which, by order of the caliph al-Mansur, was translated by Muhammad ibn Ibrahim al-Fazari (d. circa 796). Al-Fazari subsequently became the first astronomer in the Islamic world. The stars had of course interested the Arabs since pre-Islamic times, but no scientific study of them had yet been undertaken. Islam added its impetus to the study of astronomy as a means for fixing the direction of prayer (*qibla*) toward the Ka'ba. The famous al-Khwarizmi (d. 850), from whose name "algorithm" is derived, based his widely known astronomical tables (*zij*) on al-Fazari's work. Other astronomical works were translated in this period from Persian into Arabic, especially during the time of Harun al-Rashid by al-Fadl ibn Nawbakhti (d. 815), his chief librarian. The Indian traveler mentioned above had also brought a treatise on mathematics by means of which the numerals that in the West are called Arabic numerals and which the Arabs called Indian numerals entered the Muslim world. In the ninth century, the Indians made another important contribution – the decimal system – to Arab mathematical science.

Other disciplines, such as the physical sciences, medicine, astronomy, and philosophy, proliferated under the 'Abbasids. In 765, the caliph al-Mansur, afflicted with a stomach disease which had baffled his physicians, summoned from Jundishapur (Gondishapur) in Persia a man named Jurjis ibn Bahktishu', the dean of its hospital there. His name Bahktishu' (meaning "Jesus [Yashu'a] has delivered") conveys that he was one of the Nestorian (East Syrian) Christians who predominated in Iraq. Jundishapur was noted for its academy of medicine and philosophy said to have been founded about 555 by the great Persian king Anushirwan. The science of the institution was based on the ancient Greek tradition, but the language of instruction was Aramaic. Jurjis soon won the confidence of the caliph and became the court physician, though he retained his Christian faith. It is reported that when he was invited by the caliph to embrace Islam, he retorted that he preferred the company of his fathers, be they in heaven or in hell.[4] (He seems not to have suffered any ill consequences from this bold and candid remark.) In Baghdad, Ibn Bakhtishu' became the founder of a brilliant dynasty which for six or seven generations, covering a period of two centuries and a half, exercised an almost continuous monopoly over medical practice at the caliph's court. Jurjis's son Bakhtishu' (d. 801) and his grandson Jibril (Gabriel) served as court physicians to Harun al-Rashid.

At the time of the Arab conquest of the Fertile Crescent, the intellectual legacy of Greece was unquestionably the most precious treasure at hand. The various 'Abbasid forays into the land of the Byzantines, or as the Arab chroniclers say, "the land of the Romans," (bilad al-Rum) resulted in the introduction, among other objects of booty, of Greek manuscripts (chiefly from Amorium and Ancyra [Ankara]). Al-Ma'mun is said to have sent emissaries as far as Constantinople, to the Byzantine Emperor Leo the Armenian himself, in search of Greek manuscripts. In response to his request, the Byzantine emperor sent him a number of books, including those of Euclid.[5] Since Arab Muslims were not able to read the Greek originals, they depended on translations made primarily by Nestorian Christians who did know Greek. The Nestorians first translated the Greek works into Syriac and then from Syriac into Arabic.

The peak of Greek influence was reached under al-Ma'mun, an activist caliph who took strong ideological positions on many issues. First and foremost, al-Ma'mun considered himself a rationalist, having adopted the Mu'tazili position that there was no contradiction between the revealed religious law and reason. The Mu'tazila sprang up in the early part of the eighth century and argued that revelation or scriptural truth could and should be affirmed through rational inquiry. They were greatly influenced by classical Greek methods of logical and philosophical argumentation. One source relates that one night Aristotle appeared to al-Ma'mun in a dream and assured him that there was no real difference between reason and the revealed law.[6] This likely apocryphal but significant anecdote is meant to convey the importance of rational inquiry for al-Ma'mun (and, by extension, for the Mu'tazila) and to establish its primacy in the religious realm.[7] Even after the Mu'tazila faded away, their intellectual legacy endured in the dialectical approach to knowledge adopted by most theological factions, signaling the far-reaching epistemic revolution in Islamic thought that they had wrought.

One of the most important achievements under al-Ma'mun's rule was the establishment of the then famous *Bayt al-Hikma* ("the House of Wisdom") in 830. The House of Wisdom was a combination library, academy, and translation bureau. It was probably the most important educational institution to be established since the foundation of the Alexandrian Museum in the first half of the third century BCE. Under al-Ma'mun, it became the center of the translation activity that would last through the early tenth century. As custodians of this repository of ancient wisdom, Arab Muslims and Christians working together preserved, redacted, and intensely cultivated the valuable learning of antiquity. The inclusion of Arab Christians in the intellectual life of this period by their Muslim patrons points to the spirit of ecumenism that pervaded at least the world of learning in this period. A modern scholar has described the Graeco–Arabic translation movement of Baghdad as "a truly epoch-making stage, by any standard, in the course of human history;" "… equal in significance to … that of Pericles' Athens, the Italian Renaissance, or the scientific revolution of the sixteenth and seventeenth centuries, and it deserves to be recognized and embedded in our historical consciousness."[8]

The translation of Greek works into Arabic had already started under the second 'Abbasid caliph al-Mansur. The translator's name most associated with this early period is that of the Syrian Christian Abu Yahya ibn al-Batriq (d. between 796 and 806), who translated for al-Mansur most of the works of Galen and Hippocrates (fl. ca. 436 BCE). He is also said to have translated the *Elements* of Euclid and the *Almagest*, the great astronomical work of Ptolemy. Apparently these early translations were not properly done and had to be revised under Harun al-Rashid and al-Ma'mun. Another early translator was the Syrian Christian Yuhanna ibn Masawayh (d. 857) who is reported to have translated several medical manuscripts for Harun al-Rashid and for his successors.

The *shaykh* or the "chief" of the translators, as the Arabs called him, was Hunayn ibn Ishaq (d. 873), one of the most distinguished scholars of the age.[9] Hunayn was a Nestorian Christian from Iraq who was appointed by al-Ma'mun as the director of the *Bayt al-Hikma*, where he also trained his son and nephew in the art of translation. In many cases, Hunayn would do the initial translation from Greek into Syriac and his colleagues took the second step and translated from Syriac into Arabic. For instance, Aristotle's *Hermeneutica* was first translated from Greek into Syriac by Hunayn; his son, Ishaq, translated the Syriac version into Arabic. The son Ishaq ibn Hunayn became known as the greatest translator of Aristotle's works. Hunayn is reported to have translated *Plato's Republic*, several works of Aristotle, and almost all of Galen's scientific output. Seven books of Galen's anatomy, lost in the original Greek, were fortunately preserved in Arabic. The translators were often handsomely rewarded by the caliphs for their efforts. Hunayn, for example, is said to have received about 500 dinars per month; al-Ma'mun is said to have paid him in gold the weight of the books he translated. Hunayn reached the summit of his glorious career when he was appointed the personal physician of the 'Abbasid caliph al-Mutawakkil (847–861).[10]

Another very important and later group of translators should now be mentioned beside the Nestorians. The leading name in this second group of translators is Thabit ibn Qurra (ca. 836–901), recruited from the Sabians of ancient Harran in Mesopotamia. The Sabians were pagans who were star-worshipers; as a consequence, they had a strong interest in astronomy and mathematics. The Qur'an (2:59) refers to a group of people called the Sabians, who cannot be the same as the Sabians of Harran, since the Qur'an clearly indicates that this group is to be classed with Jews and Christians as monotheists and are thus to be regarded as one of the People of the Book. The 'Abbasids took advantage of this verse, however, and declared the Sabians of

Harran to be the same as the Qur'anic Sabians and granted to them the status of the *ahl al-dhimma*, the protected group of monotheistic faith. This would set an important precedent for the future. Muslims through time would extend this concept to other peoples and religions not mentioned in the Qur'an, and even though not strictly or hardly monotheistic. Thus, in the Indian subcontinent, Muslim rulers extended the protected status to Hindus, and in Persia it was extended to the Zoroastrians, the fire-worshipers of ancient Persia.

Before the age of translation came to an end, practically all the works of Aristotle that had survived to that day had been translated into Arabic. No less than a hundred works of Aristotle, called by the Arabs "the philosopher of the Greeks," had been translated. Some of these works attributed to Aristotle, however, are now known to be forgeries. All this was taking place while Europe was almost totally ignorant of Greek thought and science. One modern historian has remarked that "while al-Rashid and al-Ma'mun were delving into Greek and Persian philosophy, their contemporaries in the West, Charlemagne and his lords, were reportedly dabbling in the art of writing their names."[11]

The philhellenic attitude gained ground among Muslim intellectuals to the point where some of them spoke with disdain of "inferior" peoples who made little or no use of the learning of classical antiquity, such as the Byzantine Christians. Thus, the well-known historian al-Mas'udi (d. 956) had this to say about them:

> The sciences continued to be in great demand and intensely cultivated until the religion of Christianity appeared among the Byzantines; they then effaced the signs of philosophy, eliminated its traces, destroyed its paths, and they changed and corrupted what the ancient Greeks had set forth in clear exposition.[12]

The superiority of Muslims in this case over the Byzantine Christians was constructed on epistemic grounds rather than theological. As Dimitri Gutas has remarked, the conclusion one was expected to draw from al-Mas'udi's statement was that "were Muslims to reject the Greek sciences they would be no better than the Christian Byzantines: the superiority of Islam over Christianity in this context, therefore, is solely based on the Muslim acceptance of the fruits of the translation movement."[13]

The humanistic sciences were spawned by the study of literature (poetry, belles-lettres, prosody) and the linguistic sciences (grammar, syntax, philology). In the field of belles-lettres and the arts, the Persian contribution was the strongest. The earliest literary prose work in Arabic that has come down to us is the previously mentioned *Kalila wa Dimna*, a translation of a wisdom tale from Pahlavi (Middle Persian), which in turn was a translation from the original Sanskrit. The original work was brought to Persia from India, together with the game of chess, during the reign of the Persian King Anushirwan (531–78). What gives the Arabic version special significance is the fact that the Persian version was lost, as was the Sanskrit original. The Arabic version, therefore, became the basis of all existing translations into some forty languages, including several European tongues such as Latin, and then Italian, Greek, Icelandic and several Slavonic languages, as well as Turkish, Hebrew, Ethiopic, and Malay. The book *Kalila and Dimna* was part of the burgeoning mirrors-of-princes literature and intended to instruct princes in the art of administration by means of animal fables. The previously mentioned Ibn al-Muqaffa', the Arabic translator of *Kalila wa Dimna*, a Persian Zoroastrian convert to Islam, was a member of the powerful, highly educated secretarial class which was in large measure responsible for the emergence and development of *adab*.[14]

As Islamic realms expanded and a sophisticated, complex bureaucracy evolved, the epistolary (prose-essay) genre arose which eventually would spawn a rich secular, administrative literature. Many from among the class of royal secretaries and courtiers who were of Persian descent continued to provide adaptations and translations of Indian-Persian wisdom literature for the entertainment and edification of the upper class. Among the translated works were ancient histories and legends, fables and proverbs – almost anything that appealed to the literary sophisticate and social dilettante. Poetry had dipped in popularity in the early Islamic period but began to enjoy a resurgence in the eighth century. Pre-Islamic poetry in fact was minutely studied by Muslim philologists and religious scholars in this period because of the proximity of its language to that of the Qur'an and thus for its beneficial role in elucidating abstruse words or locutions in the sacred text.

The attraction toward "foreign" literary traditions was, unsurprisingly, not to everyone's liking. There is no need to recapitulate here in great detail the *Kulturkampf* that would ensue for at least three centuries (eighth through tenth) pitting Persian ethno-cultural sentiments against similar Arab sensibilities in the movement known as *al-Shu'ubiyya*.[15] Suffice it to say that it resulted in a much more cosmopolitan, one could even say multi-cultural, Islamic civilizational identity, which was not necessarily predicated on a particular (specifically Arab) ethnic or even religious affiliation. Some have described this multi-cultural, multi-ethnic, and multi-religious civilization as Islamicate rather than Islamic, underscoring the fact that Islam as a religion and world-view was but one seminal component of the rich cluster of values, ideas, imaginaries, and perspectives that shaped it.[16] Late eighth- through ninth-century 'Abbasid society was the crucible in which these contested, hybrid identities would coalesce to a considerable extent.

As a consequence of these intellectual and cultural trends, a specifically Islamic humanism or *adab* emerged, which, according to probably the most famous belle-lettrist in Arabic literature, Amr ibn Bahr al-Jahiz (d. 869) whom we encountered before, may be defined as "(1) the total educational system of (2) a cultured Muslim who (3) took the whole world for his object of curiosity and knowledge."[17] *Adab*, according to the first part of this definition, is the equivalent of the Greek notion of *paideia*, which referred to a holistic education that contributes to the moral development of the individual. The latter two components allow us to speak of a multiplicity of humanistic trends (humanisms) in this period of extraordinary intellectual and cultural floruit. These trends may variously be characterized as: (1) Intellectual humanism, practiced mainly by the Mu'tazila predicated on the belief that Islam is a rational religion in full accordance with the laws of logic; (2) Literary humanism, which has been described as the product of an "aristocracy of the mind,"[18] resulting from a formal, broad-based humanistic education with an emphasis on language studies that led to the acquisition of refined cultural and social ideals appropriate to the courtier, statesman, religious dignitary, and diplomat, for example; (3) Religious humanism, which may be characterized as a "serene contentment with the non-transcendental aspects of Islamic life alongside an unreserved acquiescence to all the conditions of the faith, thus integrating a human and satisfying earthly existence with the hope of eternal salvation;" and, finally, at a more embryonic level in this period but more pronounced from the end of the ninth century on, (4) Legalistic humanism, engendered by the fact that the Shari'a, the religious law, being comprehensive in its scope, requires the jurist and other legal practitioners to be concerned with the complexities of human nature at the spiritual and temporal levels, allowing for the emergence of a certain humanistic perception and insight.[19]

The broad conceptualization of *adab* which takes the universe as the focus of its inquiry linked the various academic disciplines together. The *adib* ("litterateur," "well-bred person") was regarded as someone who was well-versed in various branches of knowledge in contrast to the *'alim* who was usually a specialist in a single branch.[20] The thirteenth-century scholar Ibn al-Sid al-Batalyawsi (d. 1127) indicated the function of *adab* as the common thread running through the various fields of study when he remarked: "the lower [or: more obvious] goal of *adab* is to acquire the skills which enable one to compose poetry or prose; the higher goal is the interpretation of the Qur'an and *hadith*, and this is what the theorists of Islamic law have in mind when they engage in the study of *adab*."[21] The study of law thus could not be severed from the overall humanistic perspectives in which it is firmly grounded. There is no stronger rebuttal than this classical view of the broad purview of legal studies to the claim common especially today in certain circles that the religious law (*al-Shari'a*) somehow exists in splendid hermetic isolation from other disciplines, its interpretation uninfluenced by mundane and humanistic concerns. A brief look at the rise of law and jurisprudence through the lives of its most famous early practitioners now follows.

THE FLOURISHING OF LAW AND JURISPRUDENCE

This era, in combination with the immediately preceding one, is the era of some of the greatest jurists of Islam. In the previous chapter, we dealt with the lives of the two earlier eponyms of the final four Sunni schools of law (*madhahib*) – Abu Hanifa (d. 767) and Malik ibn Anas (d. 795). We also looked at the life and teachings of Ja'far al-Sadiq, who spawned the Shi'i Ja'fari legal school of thought. The two remaining eponymous founders of the Sunni law schools are al-Shafi'i and Ibn Hanbal, who will now be the focus of our discussion in this order.

Al-Shafi'i (d. 820), the master architect of jurisprudence

Abu 'Abdullah Muhammed ibn Idris al-Shafi'i al-Qurashi was born in Gaza or Asqalan in Palestine in 767 and died in Cairo in 820. As his *nisba* indicates, he was from the Quraysh tribe of Mecca. Following the death of his father, al-Shafi'i moved to Mecca with his mother at two years of age. He started his education there where he memorized the Qur'an, learned language and poetry, *hadith* and jurisprudence (*fiqh*). Al-Shafi'i is said to have studied traditional Arabic poetry during his residence with the tribe of Hudhayl in Mecca. He also studied the *Muwatta* of Malik at a very early age.[22]

When he was about twenty years old, al-Shafi'i moved to Medina to study law under Malik ibn Anas. When Malik died in 795, he moved to Baghdad to study with prominent legal scholars there, such as the Hanafi jurist Muhammad ibn Hasan al-Shaybani (d. 804). In Baghdad he developed his own legal system, which was transmitted by Ibn Hanbal, al-Zafarani, and Abu Thawr. In the year 814, al-Shafi'i left for Egypt where in response to his changed circumstances he devised a new legal school of thought, transmitted by al-Buwayti, al-Muzani, and al-Bulqini. The Iraqi school came to be known among jurists as "the old" (al-qadim) and the Egyptian school "the new" (al-jadid). This fact is much repeated in modernist literature to point to the essential malleability and rational basis of Islamic jurisprudence and the social and historical contingencies which determine its application.

Al-Shafi'i's undoubted masterpiece is al-Risala fi 'l-usul ("Treatise on Legal Principles"). Although not yet offering a comprehensive legal theory, the Risala adumbrated basic legal principles that came to henceforth characterize Islamic jurisprudence and thus represented a significant paradigm shift in legal thinking up to this point. Among these seminal legal principles were (1) that law had to be derived exclusively from revealed text; (2) that the sunna of the Prophet was a normative, binding source of law; (3) that there is no contradiction between the Qur'an and sunna nor among Qur'anic verses nor among hadiths; (4) that the Qur'an and the sunna are in hermeneutic agreement; (5) a legal ruling derived from unambiguous and extensively transmitted (mutawatir) sources was not subject to questioning while a ruling obtained through ijtihad (reasoning) and qiyas (analogy) could be so subjected; and (6) ijtihad and qiyas, along with the consensus that it can engender, are mandated by scripture. Through his Risala, al-Shafi'i thus achieved an important modus vivendi between unrestricted use of personal opinion (ra'y), a hallmark of the earlier Hanafi school of thought, by requiring that legal reasoning be grounded in actual religious texts, and the excessive traditionalism of early Hanbali and Zahiri thought which restricted the use of qiyas in the absence of clear scriptural injunctions.[23]

Al-Shafi'i, however, was against the methods of juristic preference (istihsan), which he criticized as too subjective and leading to ad hoc manipulation of the law in accordance with one's desires (taladhdhudh). His landmark contribution to the future trajectory of legal thought lies in the fact that he redefined sunna as the sunna of the Prophet only, and rejected the customary practices of the Companions as a source of law, as was common among earlier jurists. He further categorically limited the normative component of *sunna* to the texts of attested *hadith*s only, that is to the recorded textual evidence of the Prophet's statements. In other words, a reported practice of the Prophet had no normative weight if not supported by an actual *hadith*. We may regard this as an anti-*salafi* stance on the part of al-Shafi'i which discounted the *'amal* ("praxis" or "living tradition") of the Companions as a source of law. His stance is also an indication of the progressive transition to a literate, text-based society from primarily an oral one at this juncture in history.

Among his other important works are the *Kitab al-umm* ("the Source-book"), which contains his legal responsa (*fatawa*) given in Egypt while his *Kitab al-hujja* ("Book of [Legal] Evidence") records his responsa made in Baghdad. Later generations of scholars have attributed much influence to his writings during his lifetime and considered him to be the first to formulate the basic principles of jurisprudence (*usul al-fiqh*). Thus Fakhr al-Din al-Razi (d. 1209) was of the opinion that "al-Shafi'i was to *usul al-fiqh* what Aristotle was to logic."[24] The evidence shows, however, that this recognition of the profundity of al-Shafi'i's legal formulations did not happen right away but occurred rather toward the end of the ninth century when a genuine synthesis between rationalism and traditionalism had taken place. In this propitious atmosphere, al-Shafi'i's *Risala* which "represents the first attempt at synthesizing the disciplined exercise of human reasoning and the complete assimilation of revelation as the basis of the law," could be more favorably assessed.[25] The acceptance of this reconciliation between revelation and reason is signaled in the writings of the Shafi'i jurist Ibn Surayj (d. 918), who played a pivotal role in raising the Shafi'i school to prominence in the tenth century.[26]

The Shafi'i school of thought became prominent in Egypt, Greater Syria (Syria, Jordan, Palestine, and Lebanon), Iraq, the Hijaz, Indonesia and South Asia and was the official school under the Ayyubids in Egypt and remained prominent during the subsequent Mamluk period. The Ottoman era starting in 1517 displaced Shafi'ism from most of these areas and replaced it with the Hanafi school of thought.

As mentioned earlier, al-Shafi'i's conceptualization of an essentially polarized world and his views on the nature and role of *jihad* were influential from the ninth century on. Recent attention has focused on his exposition of this topic and subjected to a strong critique, something we will have occasion to refer to in greater detail in the following chapters.

Ahmad Ibn Hanbal (d. 855), stalwart defender of the faith

Abu 'Abdullah Ahmad ibn Muhammad ibn Hanbal al-Shaybani al-Marwazi was born in Baghdad in 780 and died there in 855. As his relational names suggest, he was a member of the Shayban tribe and his family originally came from Merv before moving to Baghdad. His genealogy as recorded in the sources reaches to one of the grandfathers of the Prophet, Nizar. His own grandfather Hanbal ibn Hilal was a governor of Sarakhs during the reign of the Umayyads, who supported the 'Abbasid revolution and then served in the 'Abbasid army. Ahmad ibn Hanbal was initially educated in Baghdad where he memorized the Qur'an and studied Arabic grammar, jurisprudence and *hadith*. He continued his education with eminent teachers such as 'Abd al-Rahman ibn Mahdi, Sufyan ibn 'Uyayna, Yahya ibn Sa'id al-Kattan, and al-Shafi'i. From the last he learned jurisprudence and legal methodology. He is also said to have frequented the study circles of the leading Hanafi scholar of the time, Abu Yusuf (d. 798), under whom he studied *hadith* and jurisprudence. Ibn Hanbal's association with Abu Yusuf has been questioned by some since the latter was one of "the people of discretionary opinion" (*ahl al-ra'y*), whereas Ibn Hanbal would later become known for his opposition to the practice of *ra'y*.[27] Among his most illustrious students were four out of the six compilers of the authoritative Sunni collections of *hadith*: al-Bukhari (d. 870), Muslim (d. 875), al-Tirmidhi (d. 892) and al-Nasa'i (d. 915).[28]

When the 'Abbasid caliph al-Ma'mun (813–33) accepted the Mu'tazili dogma of the createdness of the Qur'an, he pressured Ibn Hanbal to accept it. Ibn Hanbal refused to accept this dogma, which he considered to be contrary to "orthodox" belief. Because of his refusal, he was persecuted and imprisoned. The caliph al-Mu'tasim (833–42) adopted the same position as his predecessor and Ibn Hanbal remained in prison where he is said to have been tortured. His imprisonment continued into the period of al-Wathiq (842–47), who similarly subscribed to this Mu'tazili position. When al-Mutawakkil (r. 847–61) reverted to the doctrine of the uncreated Qur'an, Ibn Hanbal was able to resume his teaching activity.[29]

For Ibn Hanbal, the attributes and names of God are eternal. Considering the issue of human action, he adopted a middle approach between the doctrine of the Mu'tazila and the Jabriyya, that is, between those who advocated complete free will and predestination respectively. Ibn Hanbal regarded the

Qur'an as the eternal speech of God and uncreated. For him faith is manifested in inward acceptance by heart, outward expression, and action. Although the sinner is liable to punishment, he or she remains a believer in spite of the commission of grave sins. Faith can increase with good action and decrease with bad actions. His theological views were developed and defended by scholars of the following generations, such as Abu Sa'id al-Darimi, Ibn Abi Ya'la, Ibn Taymiyya, and Ibn Qayyim al-Jawziyya.

A number of works have been attributed to Ibn Hanbal. Among them only the *Musnad*, which is a collection of around 30,000 *hadiths*, was definitely his composition. As the title suggests, the *hadiths* are listed according to the names of the transmitters rather than the subject matter. Other works were collected and written by his son 'Abd Allah ibn Ahmad ibn Hanbal and by his other students upon his death. These included the *Kitab al-sunna* ("Book of Prophetic Practice"), *Kitab al-'ilal wa ma'rifat al-rijal* ("Book of Deficiencies and Knowledge of Narrators), and *al-Radd 'ala 'l-jahmiyya wa al-zanadiqa* ("The Refutation of the Jahmiyya and the Heretics"). Ibn Hanbal assigned *hadith* a key role in Islamic law and theology. His legal methodology emphasized the centrality of the Qur'an, *hadith*, and sayings of the Companions as sources for legal rulings.

Ibn Hanbal was regarded primarily as a scholar of *hadith* rather than a jurist by later scholars, such as al-Tabari and the Maliki jurist Qadi 'Iyad (d. 1149). But other scholars like al-Nasa'i (d. 914) regarded Ibn Hanbal as someone who combined knowledge of *hadith* with jurisprudence.[30] Several works dealing with specific topics in jurisprudence are attributed to him, such as *Ahkam al-nisa'* ("Legal Rulings Pertaining to Women") and *Kitab al-salah* ("Book of Prayer"). More than 130 of his disciples have also transmitted his juridical views, collected together as *Masa'il al-imam ahmad* ("The Juridical Questions of the Imam Ahmad").

In roughly the tenth century, the Hanbali school became established in Syria and later spread to Egypt but did not gain much of a following in other parts of the Islamic world as did the other legal schools. Hanbalism's general conservatism and discouragement of independent reasoning have contributed to its limited appeal. The Hanbali school is now genealogically connected with Wahhabism, the religio-political ideology associated with Muhammad ibn 'Abd al-Wahhab (d. 1791), the activist reformer of the eighteenth century whose activities are integrally connected with the rise and development of Saudi Arabia. To this day, the Hanbali school remains the official school of Saudi Arabia and Qatar. The puritanical strain and intolerant zeal for the moral reformation of society conceived along very narrow lines that have been attributed to Wahhabi thought, however, cannot be fairly ascribed to Ibn Hanbal and his early students. These trends owe their genesis rather to the vicissitudes of history and political circumstances starting in the eighteenth century, whose full treatment is beyond the temporal purview of this book.[31]

THE RISE OF *TASAWWUF* (SUFISM)

Sufism is the Anglicized name given to Islamic mysticism, called *tasawwuf* in Arabic. The Arabic word is based on *suf* meaning "undyed wool" in Arabic, because these mystics were apparently accustomed to wearing rough woollen clothes. We could regard the woollen garment of the Sufi as an emblem of pious protest against the luxury and opulence of the upper classes in the 'Abbasid period and of their attempt to ward off the moral deterioration of their times. Sufis are often described in Western literature as "ascetics," which can be misleading since asceticism is linked to monks and monasticism in the Christian context. Monasticism based on renunciation of the world is prohibited in Islam; communal life and convivial fellowship are integral to a Muslim's place in the world. Sufis thus do not withdraw completely from the world. They may retreat from it for short periods of time but they almost always re-emerge to engage it in the expectation of transforming it as one's heart has been transformed through inner reflection and purification. Indeed, Sufis themselves sometimes prefer to explain the etymology of *tasawwuf* as linked to the root *s-f-y* meaning to "purify," first themselves and then others. Their activist mission often compels them in the direction of public preaching and sermonizing. Their experience of God is for them something to be shared with the rest of their community, even though they realize that not everyone can follow them along the Sufi path. The early folk preachers and the pietists who are often designated in the literature as "storytellers" (*qussas*), "sermonizers" (*wu "az*), and abstemious individuals in general (*nussak* or *zuhhad*), were the mystically inclined who in a later period would be called Sufis, as Sufism began to be institutionalized in the tenth century.[32]

One may fruitfully compare certain aspects of the mood of the Sufi movement with the Romantic mood of early nineteenth-century Europe. Sufism, like Romanticism, represented a revolt against the formalism and intellectual dogmatism that seemed to them to dominate the lives of their co-religionists. Ritualism and reason were no longer adequate as expressions of the totality of religious experience. Most Sufis would claim that they have transcended intellectual knowledge itself (*'ilm*) and to have attained a very special type of knowledge called by them *ma'rifa*, or *'irfan*, referring to gnostic or experiential knowledge. The locus of this special immediate and experiential knowledge is the heart which "is the synonym of the intellect."[33]

In our early period, before the mid-ninth century, Sufism was still in an embryonic, amorphous form. In the following century, the Sufi brotherhoods (*tariqa*) began to be formed and conventicles or lodges (*zawiya*) for these brotherhoods started to emerge. In our period, the term *tasawwuf* itself had not been coined but the phenomenon to which it refers – an intense cultivation of one's inner, spiritual life and God-centeredness – certainly existed. As the eleventh-century mystic al-Hujwiri (d. 1071) remarked, "In the time of the Companions of the Prophet and their immediate successors, this name did not exist, but its reality was in everyone. Now the name exists without the reality."[34] Al-Hujwiri's remark is meant to underscore the natural inclination of the virtuous *salaf* of the first two generations to *tasawwuf*, which he implies was more genuine and sincere than those who practiced it in his generation in a more formal and apparently superficial manner. Ibn Khaldun was also of the opinion that the first three generations of Muslims automatically and naturally practiced *tasawwuf*, which, since it was so widespread, did not require a special designation. But "when worldliness spread and men tended to become more and more bound up with the ties of this life, those who dedicated themselves to the worship of God were distinguished from the rest by the title of Sufis."[35]

On account of his deep piety and attachment to God, avoidance of a self-indulgent life, and suspicion of worldly privilege and authority, the Successor al-Hasan al-Basri, whom we referred to earlier, is counted among the early Sufis, although his conventional biographies do not refer to him as such – that would have been an obvious anachronism. Pious men and women of this period who are counted among the early Sufis include, besides al-Hasan, Bayazid al-Bistami (d. 874), Dhu Nun al-Misri (d. 856), and the celebrated Rabi'a al-'Adawiya (d. 801; see further below). Bayazid al-Bistami's single-minded devotion to God and awe of Him became legendary. He is said to have complained that he made no spiritual progress while praying and fasting constantly nor by associating with the pious nor by standing with the warriors in the path of God. Then one night al-Bistami had a dream in which he asked of God, "How does one find the way to You?" And He replied, "Leave your self and come to me." Al-Bistami commented afterwards, "I then shed my self as a snake sheds its skin."[36]

Despite the antinomian tone to this anecdote, al-Bistami is on record as having called for strict adherence to the obligatory religious duties and counseled the avoidance of innovation. He is, however, credited with having promulgated the concept of *fana'*, self-annihilation in contemplation of the Divine Being, a standard teaching of many Sufi orders which is often denounced by the more conventional as dangerous "monism" (*wahdat al-wujud*).

Rabi'a al-'Adawiyya (d. 801): mediating piety and gender

Al-Hasan al-Basri's close friend and even mentor at times, as many of the sources report, was the legendary Rabi'a al-'Adawiya (despite the discrepancy in time span). Rabi'a's life in particular illumines for us issues of piety and gender in the late eighth century.

The famous twelfth-century mystic Farid al-Din al-'Attar (d. 1220) memorably remarked,

> The true explanation of this fact [that women count for as much as men among the saints] is that wherever these people, the Sufis, are, they have no separate existence in the Unity of God. In the Unity, what remains of the existence of "I" or "thou?" So how can "man" or "woman" continue to be?[37]

"Saints" above is the English rendition of the Arabic term *awliya'* (sing. *wali*), which literally means "friends" or "intimates" of, by implication, God. The concept and place of "sainthood" in Islamic culture is markedly different from that in Catholic or Orthodox Christianity, primarily because such a notion grew up outside mainstream Islam, is not recognized doctrinally, and is often assumed to be dangerously veering towards (if not actually being) heretical innovation (*bid'a*). As a part of popular or folk Islam, the *awliya'*, however, have played and continued to play a rich role in the lives of ordinary people, serving as mediators between their humdrum, banal existence and the spiritual world full of transcendent possibilities. In this sense, the *awliya'* share a parallel function with the Christian saints but the analogy breaks down when pressed beyond this point. We would be guilty of a disservice in communicating the flavor of the roles of the *awliya'* in various Islamic societies if we conflated them with Christian saints. Thus we prefer to refer to them either by their Arabic referents or the more general term "mystics" so as not to elide the full spectrum of meanings nestled in these terms (for example, the counter-cultural and anti-establishment connotations inherent in the original term *awliya'* not necessarily conveyed by "saints").

To return to our celebrated subject, Rabi'a of Basra was a freedwoman from the tribe of Qays ibn 'Adi, on account of which she was called al-'Adawiyya. Born into a modest home in Basra between 713–17, Rabi'a ("fourth") was so called because she had three older sisters. Her life was struck by tragedy at a very young age when she lost both her father and mother. A famine ensued in Basra and she was separated from her sisters. One day she was seized by a strange man and sold into slavery for the paltry sum of six dirhams to a man who worked her very hard. In his hagiography of Rabi'a, Farid al-'Attar records many wondrous deeds and miracles attributed to her. One of them was the cause of her release from slavery. According to al-'Attar, Rabi'a was inclined to fast all day and pray through the night. She was generally not given to complaining, but one night as she prayed, she could not help but remonstrate with her Friend, "O my Lord, you know that my heart's desire is to obey you and that the light of my eye is in the service of your kingdom. I would not refrain for even an hour from serving you, if the matter were up to me, but you have placed another creature over me." It so happened that her owner had awakened that night and had stood watching her as she prayed. When Rabi'a uttered the above words, he is said to have seen a lamp appear suspended in mid-air without chains, illuminating the entire house. This deeply affected her master and the next day he let her go free.[38]

Rabi'a is then said to have wandered off into the desert, seeking solitude and contemplation of the divine, eventually acquiring a cell upon her return from the desert, where she dedicated herself solely to worship of God. An anecdote relates that one day she stuck her head outside her cell and her servant addressed her, encouraging her to "come out and see what the Maker has wrought." Rabi'a instead invited her in to see the Maker, for "the contemplation of the Maker pre-occupies me, so that I do not care to look upon what He has made."[39] She is said to have lived in constant poverty and refused the well-meaning help of her friends, remarking, "God knows that I am ashamed to ask Him for this world, though He rules it, and how shall I take it from one who does not rule it?"[40]

Unlike most mystics in Islam, Rabi'a never married and is said to have refused many offers of marriage in her life. Celibacy has never been an ideal in Islam and is regarded as a form of excessive self-denial in the absence of extenuating circumstances, since one unnecessarily denies oneself the licit pleasures and benefits of conjugal life. Sufi biographies, however, speak admiringly of her rejection of various suitors, including al-Hasan al-Basri, who, as we have mentioned, has been improbably linked to her. Many of her friends and confidants were in fact men like Sufyan al-Thawri, Malik Dinar, and, less credibly, Dhu al-Nun al-Misri (d. 856), and al-Hasan, who seem to have freely visited her and sought her advice on many matters.

Rabi'a's love for her friends was tough and hard-headed; she is said to have sternly lectured some of her friends for their indulgence in worldly pleasures. She also took exception to Sufyan al-Thawri's expertise in *hadith*, considering it to be a distraction from the real pursuit of the love of God.[41] In the context of piety and worship, the camaraderie between Rabi'a and her male colleagues appears not to have raised eyebrows in a society that had by now begun (or would soon begin) to more stringently regulate social mixing between the sexes not closely related to one another.

Rabi'a was almost ninety when she died in 801 and was buried in Basra. All her life she had been in preparation for her final meeting with the Beloved. Her shroud is said to have been always placed before her in her customary place of worship. According to 'Attar, she gave posthumous testimony to two visitors to her grave that she had in fact "attained that which I saw."[42]

Some later non-Sufi biographers had ambivalent views of Rabi'a and her contribution to scholarship. Thus, al-Dhahabi (d. 1348) praises her abstemiousness and God-fearing character (*al-zahida al-khashi'a*) but did not put much stock in reports attributed to her.[43] Earlier non-Sufi authors, like al-Jahiz who was a younger near-contemporary of Rabi'a, were more favorably disposed toward her.[44] Sufi biographers, however, hold her in practically universal high esteem and extol her single-minded devotion to God and uncompromising stoicism. They also often grant her a much higher spiritual status than her distinguished male contemporaries or near-contemporaries, such as al-Hasan al-Basri and Sufyan al-Thawri. Such glowingly favorable assessments of distinguished women by male authors occur in the relatively early accounts of the female Companions of the Prophet but grow progressively rare in later works, particularly in reference to non-Companion women. Through her exceptional piety and learning, Rabi'a transgressed the usual boundaries erected for women, demonstrating through her life (even when viewed under the layers of legendary accretions) that a general veneration for piety and learning, regardless of whom they may be lodged in, remained a predictable constant of societies influenced by the Islamic *Weltanschauung*. Even later in the Mamluk period, a woman scholar could rise above the many restrictions placed in general on the members of her sex and win a considerable amount of recognition from her learned male peers and even be granted a measure of religious leadership (*riyasa*) on account of her exceptional learning and achievements.[45]

We have now come to the end of our broad survey of the first three generations of Muslims, the *salaf* revered by posterity and invoked by it to maintain, however tenuously, a continuous link with the "authentic" Islamic past. Some want to merely "recreate" a reasonable enough facsimile of it (the hows and wherefores of such a project are not fully explained), while others wish to retrieve the spirit and world-view which animated it and to mold them to the exigencies of today. How this process of retrieval should proceed is being debated urgently and sometimes heatedly in the contemporary period. As in the eighth and ninth centuries, Muslims once again are faced with a rapidly changing, almost unrecognizable world for which their existing religious and intellectual traditions cannot always provide pat answers. Is it back to the drawing-board for them on a number of critical issues? Will their twenty-first century sensibilities and fragmented, even besieged, cultures prove as resilient and creative as those of the first three centuries of Islam, and perhaps go beyond? In the next two chapters, we hope to explore these highly charged questions and their implications for Muslims in this century.

Constructing the Pious Forbears I: Historical Memory and the Present

THE ISLAMIST CONSTRUCTION

We have had occasion to mention earlier that the first three generations of Muslims, the focus of our study, are called in full al-Salaf al-Salih ("the Pious Forbears"). Muhammad 'Abduh (d. 1905), the great reformist rector of al-Azhar University, was of the opinion that the *umma*, the Muslim community in his time, ought to be like the early community of the elders, that is the *salaf*.[1] His student and loyal colleague Rashid Rida maintained that a genuine revival of Islam would occur through following the Qur'an, the true *Sunna*, and the guidance of the Pious Forbears.[2] 'Abduh's and Rida's statements nicely encapsulate for us the general Muslim idealization of the Pious Forbears and their status as the moral exemplars par excellence for subsequent generations of believers.

We referred earlier to the well-known *hadith* in which the Prophet Muhammad affirms that the first three generations of Muslims are the best; those who follow them (*al-khalaf*) are not expected to be of the same moral caliber. The *concept* of the "Pious Forbears" very likely originates in this report but the *hadith* itself does not use the actual Arabic term al-salaf al-salih. What may be the earliest usage of this compound term, although not in these precise words, occurs in a *hadith* recorded in the *Musnad* of Ahmad ibn Hanbal (d. 855). According to this *hadith*, when his wife Zaynab died, the

Prophet said at her funeral, "Cling [addressing the deceased Zaynab] to 'Uthman ibn Maz'un, our virtuous and pious predecessor (*salafina al-salih al-khayr*)."[3] 'Uthman ibn Maz'un was known for his ascetic piety and monotheistic inclinations even before Islam. He won distinction in Islam for his early conversion, emigration to Abyssinia, and abstemious habits. So inclined was he to praying and fasting that Muhammad had to counsel him to be more moderate in such practices. "Indeed," said the Prophet, "your eyes have their rights over you, and your body has its rights, and your family has its rights. So pray, and sleep, and fast, and break fast."[4] Generous prophetic praise for the predeceased 'Uthman, as encoded in the words *al-salih* and *al-khayr* occurring in the report cited above, testify to his Islamic precedence and moral excellence and harbingers the application of these terms to the Companions in general.

An early work from the late ninth century on jurists, composed by Muhammad ibn Khalaf Waki' (d. 918), refers to the Prophet's Companions as "just leaders," indicating that it was the justice of the *salaf* which commanded respect from posterity and invited mimesis.[5] The late ninth-century Qur'an commentary of al-Tabari (d. 923) does not yet mention the full term *al-salaf al-salih* but provides a strong indication of the idea in progress. In his prefatory remarks to his commentary, al-Tabari refers to "the forbears (*al-salaf*) from among the Companions and the paragons and of those who followed (*al-khalaf*) from among the Successors and the scholars of the community."[6] Here, from the vantage point of al-Tabari, the term *salaf* refers to the first generation of Muslims only. But the Successors who immediately followed them (*al-khalaf*) are also already early Muslims of great standing.

The oldest reference to the *salaf* as paradigmatic role models appears to be a statement ascribed to Abu Hanifa (d. 767) recorded by the fifteenth-century polymath Jalal al-Din al-Suyuti (d. 1505) in one of his works. According to this statement, Abu Hanifa counsels, "Follow the traditions and the way of the *salaf* and be on your guard against new-fangled matters (*bid'a*) for all of that constitutes a departure from the norm."[7] Here we have the express purpose in following the *salaf* clearly articulated – to guard against undesirable innovation and preserve the integrity of the custom of the Prophet and his closest associates. If this ascription is genuine, it is very likely the earliest formulation of the *salafi* doctrine.

By the late pre-modern period, the term and concept of *al-salaf al-salih* in reference to the Companions in particular and the relational term *salafi*, signifying one who followed them, began to occur frequently in Islamic discourses of piety. The early thirteenth-century scholar 'Izz al-Din Ibn al-Athir (d. 1234) remarked that the term *salafi* was derived from *salaf* and signified adherence to their doctrine.[8] In the early fourteenth century, the Hanbali theologian Ibn Taymiyya (d. 1328) would assert that "the Companions and the Successors were better than us."[9] This continuing reverence for the earliest Muslims and their unique role in imparting valuable information to succeeding generations of Muslims about their beloved Prophet led to the amassing of information concerning their activities, personal conduct, and other biographical details by the historians and biographers from a fairly early period. The Companions were reasonably assumed to have emulated the Prophet to the greatest extent in their daily lives. As we mentioned earlier, scholarly evidence establishes that *sunna* for the earliest Muslims was a broad concept that included not only the normative practices and sayings of Muhammad but also those of his closest Companions. Interpretations of scripture, analysis of *hadith*, and the recounting of certain events reliably attributed to the Companions readily invited belief. Divergences in behavior from the reported lifestyles of the *salaf* and acting in contradiction to their transmitted counsel gave the scrupulous Muslim pause.

In the modern period, the term *al-salaf al-salih*, or in short, *salaf*, has become highly evocative of authenticity and legitimacy. Ascription of certain principles and practices to the *salaf* attests to their early provenance and justifies their implementation in the Muslim polity. As indicated in Abu Hanifa's statement above, departure from the practice of *salaf* exposes one to dangerous innovation and, therefore, to error. The adjectival form *salafi* has come to connote varying degrees and forms of attachment to the Pious Forbears. Those who claim such attachment to them and declare themselves to be their followers in some manner and form are collectively called *Salafiyya*, or in its Anglicized form, *Salafis*.

This is a term which by no means implies adherence to a predictable, consistent set of beliefs. As used specifically in the nineteenth and twentieth centuries, it refers to a wide gamut of views that developed in this period. It further reflects an ongoing process of connecting and disconnecting with the past in various projects of renewal (*tajdid*) and reform (*islah*) through this period. Jamal al-Din al-Afghani (d. 1897), a charismatic reformer of self-proclaimed Afghani background (but very likely originally from Iran) and Muhammad 'Abduh, mentioned above, were the most prominent of the early reformist Salafis of the nineteenth century.[10] For them adherence to the example of the Pious Forbears meant the stripping of dubious accretions from the later Islamic tradition and the recovery of what was believed to be the historically authentic beliefs and practices of the *salaf*. Only such beliefs and practices adapted to present circumstances could point the way forward like a beacon, maintained 'Abduh.[11] This early modern *salafi* project of retrieval and recovery was intended to revive the spirit of the times of the Pious Forbears, characterized, as they saw it, by egalitarianism, justice, tolerance, and mercy.[12]

A significant part of the methodology of the early reformist Salafis involved the critical scrutiny of non-Qur'anic material – *hadith*, biography, and exegeses – to determine the probative and historical value of the reports contained therein. Muhammad 'Abduh, for example, rejected the genre of the *isra'iliyyat* (stories of biblical provenance with no basis in the Qur'an which had entered the exegetical literature in particular) and the *fitan* traditions (apocalyptic reports), even when they occurred in reliable *hadith* collections.[13] Rejection of what was spurious and dubious, the early reformist Salafis hoped, would allow the figures of the Pious Forbears and their lives to emerge clearly from the shadows of history and allow Muslims to regenerate themselves by adopting, adapting, and implementing the true values and ideals they represented.

Contraposed to the reformists are the integrist or conservative, and especially now, reactionary Salafis who share the reverence of the reformists for the Pious Forbears and who also believe that the revival of the Muslim community hinges on the faithful emulation of the *salaf* and their practices. However, they eschew the kind of textual and historical criticism advocated by the reformists, and adhere to a rather uncritical acceptance of certain biographical details of the Prophet's life and of his Companions as transmitted by premodern scholars, and tend to follow a literal understanding of specific legal precepts. The Wahhabis of Saudi Arabia, followers of Muhammad ibn 'Abd al-Wahhab (d. 1791), are a prominent example of this latter type. Their trenchant conservatism and puritanical zeal have nearly completely rendered *Salafi* a term of opprobrium in our contemporary period.[14]

Beyond certain core beliefs and precepts, many Muslims throughout time have negotiated and contested almost every issue related to their spiritual, material, and cognitive well-being, a process which has led to dynamic processes of engagement with and interrogation of their contemporary situations, as well as of their past. On the other hand, resistance to such enterprises on the part of others has led to stultifying stalemates in turns. The Pious Forbears configured and reconfigured, have remained germane to intense theological, legal, and political discussions since the early pre-modern period. The relevance of the lives and examples of the Pious Forbears as both historical and "iconic" figures in these processes of negotiation and engagement continues unabated for contemporary Muslims. It is to this discussion we turn next.

IMPLICATIONS AND RELEVANCE OF STUDYING THE LIVES OF THE FIRST MUSLIMS TODAY

There are competing discourses on Islam today. Strands of these discourses are often at loggerheads with one another and struggle to gain center stage. The present rancorous debate on what constitutes "authentic" Islam and who may be considered qualified to speak on behalf of Muslims sometimes takes place in a historical vacuum. A historical, diachronic survey such as ours, even if only of the first three generations, demonstrates that it is clearly untenable to speak of Islam as a reified, monolithic tradition through the generations, severed somehow from Muslim men and women who interpreted and engaged creatively with their scripture, the prophetic tradition, and their ancillary sciences in diverse historical and socio-political circumstances. It is also a mistake to assume that everything Muslims did and said was based on religious imperatives and, therefore, defining of the Islamic tradition. Like any other group of people, Muslims sometimes responded and reacted to the exigencies of their particular situation on the basis of scriptural and *hadith* warrants, considerations of rational and social utility, and pure self-interest. Some of these historically specific and culturally bound responses cannot be considered binding beyond their original limited purview, nor were they meant to be.

This chapter will focus on how the concept of *al-salaf al-salih* is invoked by hard-line (Sunni) Islamists today and by their opposite camp, the reformist or modernist Muslims.[15] It will juxtapose their competing views on a number of critical issues in order to bring into sharp relief their asymmetry. The degree to which their views coincide with or diverge from what the available historical accounts relate to us concerning these issues will be discussed in chapter 11. Our focus on these two polar camps is not intended to elide the existing broad spectrum of views and positions regarding the Pious Forbears. Rather, this focus serves to highlight the most dominant and contentious views regarding the Pious Forbears prevalent today. It further indicates their wider ramifications for the formulation of responses by Muslims of different orientations to modernity and its inherent complexities.

For our purpose, the term "Islamist" refers to activist individuals and groups in various contemporary Islamic societies whose primary wish is to govern and be governed politically only by Islamic principles, understood by them to be immutably enshrined in the *shari'a* or the religious law. "Islamism" refers to a highly politicized version of Islam whose genesis occurred in the early twentieth century largely as a reaction to the abolition of the caliphate by republican Turks in 1924 and to the debilitating effects of Western colonialism in the Islamic world. In 1928, Hasan al-Banna in Egypt established the Muslim Brotherhood (*Ikhwan al-Muslimin*) as a countervailing response to both British colonial rule and secular nationalist politics which unchecked, it was feared, would undermine the traditional Islamic character of Egyptian society.[16] In the Indian sub-continent, Abul A'la Mawdudi (see further below) established the Jamaat-i Islami ("the Islamic Society") party in 1941 to effectively articulate and galvanize a new Muslim political consciousness in reaction to British occupation and Hindu nationalism. Mawdudi emigrated to newly created Pakistan in 1947 and continued to agitate for the establishment of an Islamic state there.[17] To compensate for the loss of the caliphate and what clearly appeared as the political emasculation of Muslims worldwide by hostile Christian Europeans at this time, assertion of a distinctive Islamic political identity and an assumed divinely mandated political agenda that supposedly would command the loyalty of Muslims worldwide was called for, from the perspective of certain Muslim political activists.[18]

Among such activist individuals and groups, we are using the term "Islamist" to refer to particularly hard-line Islamists (also occasionally referred to as "radical" or "militant" Islamists), who have been considerably influenced by the thought of Mawdudi and his prominent disciple, the Egyptian activist Sayyid Qutb. Their attitude toward modernity and its epistemic foundations can fairly be described as "rejectionist," although even the most reactionary Islamists are usually not averse to using technology and other modern appurtenances for advancing their cause.[19] Some have argued that

Islamists of various shades are not rejecting modernity so much as constructing alternative versions of it.[20] Not all radical Islamists are influenced by Qutb's thought; in fact, there are some who specifically reject it.[21] There are also "moderate" Islamists (as they are usually termed), who, while also committed to a highly politicized form of Islam, often subscribe to democratic norms and embrace certain intellectual aspects of modernity. Moderate Islamists are generally not included in our use of the term "Islamist" in this discussion, unless specifically stated to the contrary.

"Modernist" and "reformist" Muslims, in our usage, refer to observant Muslims who, starting roughly in the eighteenth century, began to emphasize the inherent adaptability of Islamic principles and thought to modernity, partially in response to the beginning of the European colonial onslaught. For the most part, we will be using these terms interchangeably. In particularly post-colonial contexts today, modernists argue that certain freshly interpreted Islamic principles can reveal their congruence with modern liberal principles of democratic government, civil society, gender equality, etc., without necessarily being identical to their formulations in the Western context. Like the Islamists, they too would like to usher in social change but their means of effecting change are essentially hermeneutic and educational. Accordingly, they stress the rereading of religious texts, primarily the Qur'an and *hadith*, as a legitimate exercise in *ijtihad* (independent reasoning) to arrive at interpretations appropriate to their historical circumstances without jettisoning the classical heritage and to foster a sense of a continuous critical and dynamic process of engagement with this heritage through education.[22]

Despite their respect for tradition in general, modernists tend to be critical of traditionalists who are perceived as unthinkingly following precedent and stymying the efforts of Muslims to adapt to the modern world. One prominent modernist of the nineteenth century, Sayyid Ahmad Khan, expressed this disdain for traditionalism when he stated that he wished to "clean the black stains of these errors [of traditionalism] from the luminous face of Islam."[23] "Modernists" and "reformists" are also called "liberals" and "moderates" by some.

"Traditionalists," probably the great majority of Muslims who adhere to traditional Islam in their religious observances and sensibilities, figure only marginally in our subsequent discussion since they are usually not active participants in current impassioned debates about engaging modernity. The definitions and nomenclature given here do not, of course, capture all varieties of intellectual and ideological orientations among today's roughly 1.3 billion Muslims, but they allow us to proceed with a functional and adequate framework within which to describe and analyze the most prominent features of the two competing trends of modernism and hard-line Islamism. Length constraints do not allow us to provide a detailed social history of the development of these trends; additional bibliography suggested in the endnotes will direct the reader to appropriate supplementary information.

In this chapter, we will begin with a number of the most prominent issues in which the *salaf al-salih* are implicated in hard-line Islamist discourses, followed in the next chapter by a discussion of the role the Pious Forbears play in reformist and modernist thought.

THE *SALAF AL-SALIH* IN THE ISLAMIST IMAGINATION

A number of persistent assumptions have grown up around particular precedents said to have been set by the *salaf al-salih* that permeate the discourse of most hard-line Islamists today. These precedents are presented in their discourse as paradigmatic and normative for succeeding generations of Muslims. Among them, four topics are the most ubiquitous in Islamist discourses. They are: (1) establishment of the so-called "Islamic State;" (2) the assumed immutable nature of the *shari'a*; (3) the status and role of women; and (4) the nature of *jihad*. These topics create the parameters for the righteous, God-ordained society (and, ultimately, the world) that they have in mind. The kind of proof-texts and arguments they deploy to support their ideological platform are briefly sketched below. The historicity of these claims will be assessed further in chapter 11.

Establishment of the "Islamic State"

A highly politicized version of Islam is the cornerstone of most, if not all, Islamist discourses. According to this version, a full-blown concept of what most Islamists call the "Islamic State" and "Islamic Government" is articulated by the religious law. Such a state, they affirm, has existed since the time of the Prophet and was replicated by particularly Abu Bakr and 'Umar, the first two

Rightly Guided Caliphs. The primary characteristic of the "Islamic State," according to this school of thought, is "divine sovereignty" or "divine governance," termed in Arabic *al-hakimiyya* by the Islamist thinker Abu 'l-A'la Mawdudi (d. 1979). In his writings on political Islam, Mawdudi has maintained in regard to the "Islamic state" (*al-Dawla al-Islamiyya*) that "the basic conception underlying all its outward manifestations is the idea of divine sovereignty." In this Islamic State, its ideal leaders and servants "will all work with a sense of individual and collective responsibility to God [alone], not to the electorate, neither to the king nor the dictator."[24]

These ideas greatly influenced his ideological disciple, the Egyptian activist Sayyid Qutb (d. 1966), who made *al-hakimiyya* the linchpin of his Islamist agenda. In his strident political manifesto *Ma'alim fi 'l-Tariq* ("Signposts on the Path"), Qutb invokes the latter part of Qur'an 4:59 which states, "If you should differ in regard to anything, then refer it to God and the Messenger"[25] and understands it to thereby place an absolute limitation on the authority of human beings. It moreover establishes, according to Qutb, that no one may arbitrarily promulgate a piece of legislation without acknowledging "the supreme sovereignty" (*al-hakimiyya al-'ulya*) of God. This entails recognition that the only source of political authority (*al-sulutat*) is "God, the Almighty, not the people, not the [political] party, not any individual."[26] The verse also makes clear, Qutb asserts, that no human being can claim to speak or to have spoken in the name of God except the Prophet; thus there is no resemblance here to European notions of theocracy or of divine kingship.[27]

While modernist Muslim scholars and activists have argued vigorously in favor of a basic ideational compatibility between the concept of *shura* and Western-style democracy (see next chapter), many Islamists of particularly the Mawdudian/Qutbian school of thought tend to see fundamental differences between the two. They argue that since a democratic government derives its authority from the will of the people and laws enacted by humans, it is immediately at odds with an "Islamic Government" which is understood to derive its authority from God and His revealed laws. Thus Mawdudi states, "Wherever this system [sc. democracy] exists, we do not consider Islam to exist, and wherever Islam exists, there is no room for this system."[28] Members of the Islamic polity are required to obey their ruler as long as he follows Qur'anic and sunnaic regulations, in accordance with Mawdudi's understanding of Qur'an 4:59. He adds that such a ruler in turn derives his legitimacy from the consent and freedom of the Muslims.[29]

Although this last statement sounds quite democratic on the surface, it should be remembered that Mawdudi (and Qutb) had very specific and exclusivist notions of exactly who qualifies as a ["true"] Muslim.[30] Mawdudi in fact subscribed to what he described as "theo-democracy" or a "democratic caliphate." In this conceptualization, the ideal Islamic state is headed by virtuous rulers who govern its contented obedient citizenry consensually and perfectly in accordance with the assumed transparent political mandate provided by the Qur'an and the *sunna*.[31] Needless to say, the transparency of such a scriptural political mandate is only evident to "true" Muslims like Mawdudi and his cohorts and only they are able to implement it.

The immutable shari'a and its political reach

Hard-line Islamists adhere to the notion of a practically immutable religious law, the *shari'a*, regarding whose scope and interpretation all right-thinking Muslims are in perfect accord. The two principal sources of the *shari'a*, the Qur'an and the *sunna*, are held by many of them to admit of a single and uniform, often literal, interpretation, authoritatively established by the Prophet and upheld by his Companions, and thus valid for all times and places. While there still may be room for interpretation in limited cases, reasoned interpretive activity (*ijtihad*) is the province of only a few, preferably of those who subscribe to their particularist views and share their ideological orientation. Hard-line Islamists reject the possibility of multiple, equally valid interpretations of the religious law as expressed in the four Sunni schools of jurisprudence since, in their view, proper interpretation of the law by those who are qualified to do so will yield a single, uniform understanding of it.[32]

Nowhere is the hard-line Islamist perception of the *shari'a* more manifest as absolute and unchanging than in their construction of religious and political authority. In their political discourse (and in that of other groups), the Qur'anic verse (4:59), mentioned above, which states in its first part, "O those who believe, obey God and the Messenger and those in possession of authority (*uli 'l-amr*) among you," is frequently invoked. Sayyid Qutb's incomplete exegesis of 4:59 in his *Ma'alim* referred to above must be supplemented by his commentary in his exegetical work *Fi Zilal al-Qur'an* ("In the Shade of the Qur'an") for us to determine whom he intends by the *ulu 'l-amr* and what role they play in his political schema. These two works taken together tell us that Qutb, like Mawdudi before him, envisaged the *ulu 'l-amr* as those who acknowledged the sovereignty of God in the Muslim polity, and as a consequence, were the best qualified to implement the divine laws conveyed to humankind by the Prophet Muhammad and elaborated upon comprehensively in his *sunna*, as became codified in the *hadith* literature. Unlike classical Islamic jurisprudence which added analogical reasoning and consensus of the community as supplemental sources of jurisprudence in the absence of explicit texts, hard-line Islamists usually recognize no other authoritative sources besides the Qur'an and *sunna* for legislative activity. For them the *shari'a*, simply put, is a legal code which "enacted as it is by God, is unchangeable."[33]

This view allows hard-line Islamists to insist, for example, on the literal application of the *hudud* penalties as spelled out in classical Islamic jurisprudence for major infractions and crimes, such as theft and adultery, in their Islamic State. No leniency is to be permitted in such matters. The immediate implementation of *hudud* laws is of burning importance for them, since that is for them in many ways the most visible manifestation of an Islamic/Islamist identity. In their apotheosis and reification of the religious law, there is no room for accommodation of customary and cultural practices (*'urf*) nor for multiple readings of scripture and ancillary texts. Nor is there room for the historical contextualization of legal rulings as they developed over time nor for the invocation of public commonweal (*maslaha*) as grounds for legal ratiocination, as actually occurred in the praxis of Muslim communities throughout time.[34] The slogan "Islam is the solution" is meant to convey to the world that Islam, as a reified corpus of religious and political commandments, has left nothing unaddressed. Not surprisingly then, Qutb, and those following him, refer to Islam as a "system" rather than as a faith.[35] The *ulu 'l-amr*,[36] among whom Qutb undoubtedly places himself and his cohorts, and who, therefore, constitute the vanguard (*tali'a*) of the "Islamic Revolution" in the making have all the pre-packaged answers yielded by this "system" in the service of the Islamic utopia they ultimately hope to establish.[37]

The status and role of women

The first generation of Muslim women, like their male contemporaries, enjoy the hallowed position of *al-salaf al-salih*. With very few exceptions, the names of second and third generations of women are usually not included among the Pious Forbears. Female Companions of the Prophet from among his family members – wives, relatives, and non-relatives – enjoy a very high status, however, among the first generation of Muslims on account of their precedence in accepting Islam and in the commission of other meritorious activities, their close proximity to Muhammad, and celebrated loyalty to him. Both Muslim men and women, but particularly the latter, are expected to model their behavior on that of their pious female forbears. Social legislation and cultural mores pertaining to women are frequently legitimized and upheld on the basis of the conduct of women Companions.

Among most Islamists, there is a limited range of views on proper female decorum and women's roles, especially in the contemporary public sphere. Like the traditionalists, they too emphasize women's roles as wives and mothers and wish to limit their access to the public sphere, unless absolutely economically necessary or due to certain emergency situations.[38] The story of Adam and Eve as recounted not in the Qur'an but in *hadith* and refracted through the prism of late pre-modern *tafsirs* and modern Islamist commentaries is marshaled to provide a divine undergirding for women's domestic roles. Thus, the popular Egyptian preacher Muhammad Mutawalli al-Sha'rawi draws upon the *hadith* which states that woman was created from Adam's rib. Since the rib is crooked, he says, this endows the woman with an essential "crookedness." But it is this very crookedness, according to Mutawalli, which empowers women to achieve their highest potential as care-givers to their families, particularly children, since such a role requires not rationality but compassion and empathy.[39]

The "Islamic State" is responsible for enforcing what is now known as personal or family law, which regulates the domestic sphere.[40] In the traditionalist and Islamist understanding, Islamic personal or family law prohibits "the unrestricted intermingling of the sexes," mandates veiling for women, recognizes men's guardianship of women, establishes clear laws of divorce and separation, permits "conditional polygamy" and clearly defines the rights and duties of husband, wife, and children.[41] One scholar who finds favor with these groups of people on the subject of feminine propriety is the twelfth-century Hanbali theologian Ibn al-Jawzi (d. 1201). He composed a well-known manual entitled *Ahkam al-nisa'* ("Statutes pertaining to Women"), which counsel women on proper decorum and conduct. Two chapters in particular in this work refer to the desirability of women cloistering themselves in their homes. Chapter 26 is entitled "Cautioning Women from Going Outside the Home," and chapter 27 is "Mention of the Merit of

[Staying] Home for Women."[42] Ibn al-Jawzi prefaces chapter 26 by counseling women to avoid going out as much as possible. If a woman should be obliged to go out, he says, she should do so after obtaining her husband's permission and be attired in shabby, unattractive clothes. She should try to wend her way through empty areas, avoiding busy thoroughfares and marketplaces. She should be careful not to have her voice heard in public and if she should walk in the streets, she should stick to the sides and not walk in the middle of them.[43]

In chapter 27, Ibn al-Jawzi records a report from the Companion 'Abd Allah Ibn Mas'ud who is quoted as remarking that when a woman emerges from her home, and her family members ask her, "Where are you headed?" and she replies, "I am going out to visit the sick," or "to pay my respect to a deceased person's family," then she is accompanied by the devil. Ibn Mas'ud is further quoted as saying that she rather finds favor in the sight of God by staying within the confines of her home and worshiping the Almighty.[44] Another late pre-modern Hanbali theologian Ibn Qayyim al-Jawziyya (d. 1350), popular among Islamists, drives home the point that such attitudes had become firmly entrenched in the Mamluk period, at least among certain theologians. He records (one assumes approvingly) in a manual attributed to him containing information about women that a certain Bedouin man described the ideal woman as being, among other things, "self-effacing" and inclined "to stick to her home ..."[45]

What about the women *salaf* themselves? Can they be invoked to support late medieval construals of "proper" Muslim women who are demure, retiring, and, above all, who prefer seclusion in their homes to activity in the public sphere in the manner described above by Ibn al-Jawzi? From our early selective discussion of women *salaf*, we are readily inclined to think that a number of the women Companions would be particularly "problematic," insofar as they fail to conform to this image. 'A'isha, the Prophet's young widow, who led a political insurrection against the fourth Rightly-Guided Caliph and boldly challenged certain male Companions like Abu Hurayra when they disseminated what she knew to be spurious *hadith*s, would have special difficulty fitting in within the above mold. Not surprisingly, as we previously noted, 'A'isha's image in particular is often "sanitized" in the later literature through the portrayal of an older and wiser version of herself, stricken with remorse over her impetuous, ultimately unfeminine and, therefore, morally unsanctioned actions in the public political sphere.[46]

What about other "difficult" women Companions like Umm 'Umara and Umm Waraqa, who were also unusually active in the public sphere and assumed roles with the full assent of the Prophet that would be considered controversial by the Mamluk period? Since details of the lives of the women *salaf* have been and are still centrally constitutive of traditionalist and Islamist views of the "proper" roles of women in Islamic societies, we will spend a bit of time below comparing the biographical treatment of these two well-known women Companions, Umm 'Umara and Umm Waraqa, by Ibn Sa'd in the ninth century and the prominent fifteenth-century Mamluk historian and scholar Ibn Hajar al-'Asqalani (d. 1449). This will allow us to trace the attitudinal changes concerning public roles of women over time.

Umm 'Umara: the valiant warrior

The accounts of Umm 'Umara's life and their manipulation by various scholars have important ideological ramifications for today. This becomes readily apparent when we compare the differences in details between Ibn Sa'd's and Ibn Hajar's biographical entries on her. These details have a very important bearing on particularly the issue of women's participation in the battlefields of early Islam, a very public and traditional masculine domain. As mentioned earlier (in chapter 5), Umm 'Umara's real name was Nusayba bint Ka'b and she was celebrated for her bravery and martial prowess. She was present at the battles of Uhud, Khaybar, Hunayn, and al-Yamama (633–34) and was present at the signing of the Treaty of al-Hudaybiyya. As a combatant at Uhud, she is said to have sustained twelve wounds to her body, inflicted either by a spear or a sword, while defending the Prophet. Praising her valor, Muhammad said her position on the battlefield on that day was unsurpassed by anyone else.

In comparing the entries on her by Ibn Sa'd and Ibn Hajar in turn, one finds different emphases on different events. In his relatively lengthy entry on her (three and a half pages in a modern printed edition), Ibn Sa'd relates four variant accounts of her valiant defense of the Prophet during Uhud that emanate from different sources.[47] Ibn Hajar's entry on Umm 'Umara is only about a quarter as long in print as Ibn Sa'd's entry, containing only a single account of her brave exploits on the battlefield. The fulsome praise that Umm 'Umara earned from the Prophet on account of her bravery as reported by Ibn Sa'd is not repeated by Ibn Hajar.[48]

To explain Umm 'Umara's diminished stature in Ibn Hajar's recounting of her life, we need to introduce two other women Companions – Umm

Kabsha and Umm Sinan – to ferret out our fourteenth-century biographer's implicit agenda. In the case of Umm Kabsha, Ibn Hajar relates that she asked for the Prophet's permission to accompany a certain army with no reference made to a specific foray. The Prophet responds categorically by simply saying, "No." At this point Umm Kabsha pleads with him and explicitly states that she does not want to fight but only to tend to the wounded and provide water. In Ibn Sa'd's account of this event, she is not quoted as saying that she would not fight. The Prophet then replies, "I would have given you permission were it not for the fact that it would become an established precedent (sunna), and thus it would be said that such and such a female had gone out [sc. to battle]. So remain behind."[49]

Ibn Hajar then points out that the content of this single report is at odds with another report which mentions that our third woman Companion, Umm Sinan al-Aslami, had been granted permission by the Prophet to go to the battlefield. The only way to reconcile these two reports with their contradictory implications is to maintain, according to Ibn Hajar, that the report concerning Umm Kabsha abrogates the report concerning Umm Sinan. The reason Ibn Hajar gives for this is that the Umm Kabsha report is the later one and refers to an incident that occurred after the conquest of Mecca in 630. Since the Umm Sinan report has Khaybar as the backdrop and another report refers to the battle of Uhud, both of which were earlier, the later report, according to Ibn Hajar, must be considered to have superseded the earlier two.[50]

How Ibn Hajar comes to know the historical context of the Umm Kabsha report is not explained. Ibn Sa'd, as I mentioned before, does not indicate a precise chronology for this report. Choosing the period after the conquest of Mecca as the historical locus for this report makes possible the implication that women's participation in battles before the fall of Mecca was unobjectionable because everyone had to rally to the cause under the dire circumstances in which the small community of Muslims found itself at that time. After the fall of Mecca, such participation could be dispensed with as Islam became the predominant religion in the Arabian peninsula and then a world civilization. By picking the post-conquest period to locate the Umm Kabsha report, Ibn Hajar seems to wish to underscore that specific historical exigencies in the early period which had made women's participation in certain battles necessary, had now lapsed, making such participation not only no longer necessary but objectionable.

The fact that Umm Kabsha is cited in Ibn Hajar's version as specifically disavowing armed combat and only desiring to aid the wounded and the thirsty is also very significant. Ibn Hajar leaves no doubt in the reader's mind that it was not potentially a combatant's role that was being denied to Umm Kabsha, but rather her physical presence itself on the battlefield, for even the most humanitarian of purposes. It is interesting to note that Ibn Sa'd in his biographical work describes Umm Kabsha simply as "a woman from [the tribe of] Quda'a," who had requested the Prophet's permission to take part in an unnamed battle. The permission was denied and Ibn Sa'd leaves it at that.[51] Ibn Hajar, however, makes of this event a *cause célèbre*.

With regard to the status of the Umm Kabsha report as an abrogating one, Ibn Hajar does not bring up, or perhaps conveniently does not remember, the case of Umm 'Umara, who is said to have lost a hand while fighting at al-Yamama, a battle that was fought after the fall of Mecca between 633–34. Both Ibn Sa'd and Ibn Hajar mention this historical detail about Umm 'Umara in their entries. One would be justified in remonstrating thus: surely the conduct of a well-known female Companion who had fought in a clearly identified battle after the fall of Mecca should have more of a bearing on Ibn Hajar's discussion of this sensitive issue than the case of Umm Kabsha, especially since the historical details of the latter are obscure at best. The Umm Kabsha episode, therefore, cannot provide a firm basis from which to derive categorical conclusions about the chronology involved, and this would also affect its status as an abrogating report. Ibn Hajar, however, appears to have clearly made up his mind regarding the latter-day propriety of feminine presence on the battlefield, and by extension, in the public sphere in general, and, therefore, produces only the Umm Kabsha episode as a proof-text in defense of this position.

Umm Waraqa bint Abd Allah ibn al-Harith

According to Ibn Sa'd, Umm Waraqa on accepting Islam personally gave her allegiance to Muhammad, and related *hadiths* from him. She is said to have memorized the Qur'an and the Prophet asked her to lead her household in prayer.[52] She also hired a (male) caller to prayer. The Prophet would visit her frequently and conferred on her the epithet "the Martyred Woman" (*al-shahida*). At the time of Badr, Umm Waraqa entreated Muhammad to let her accompany him to the battlefield and tend to the wounded so that "perhaps God may grant me martyrdom." The Prophet assured her that God would grant her martyrdom. Umm Waraqa, Ibn Sa'd further records, continued to lead the members of her household in prayer until two servants, a male and a female, who were under her charge, murdered her during 'Umar's caliphate, for which they were later put to death. 'Umar is said to have remarked that due to her violent and unjust death, she had in fact achieved martrydom.

Turning to Ibn Hajar's account of Umm Waraqa's life, we are struck by the fact that he does not mention that she had led "the people of her household" (ahl dariha; which, since we are not told the contrary, must have consisted of male and female members) in prayer at the express request of the Prophet. He records, however, that she had asked the Prophet's permission to hire a male caller to prayer. Further doctoring on his part of the older version as contained in Ibn Sa'd's work becomes evident when he launches into an explanation of the sobriquet "the Martyred Woman" conferred on her by the Prophet. Ibn Hajar foregrounds the account according to which she asked Muhammad's permission to take part in the battle of Badr as a nurse. In his rendition of this event, the Prophet explicitly forbids her, using Qur'anic diction, "Remain (qurri)[53] in your house; for indeed God will grant you martyrdom [in another way]." In case the import of this directive is lost on the reader, Ibn Hajar supplies a variant account (not occurring in Ibn Sa'd's entry) in which the Prophet is quoted as counseling her even more bluntly, "Sit in your home, for indeed God will grant you martyrdom in your house"[54] (emphasis added). The tragic denouement to Umm Waraqa's life then teleologically falls into place: a woman can achieve the status of a martyr by remaining (and only by remaining) within her home and carrying on her usual domestic activities, like the supervision of her servants.[55]

It is worth bearing in mind that Ibn Sa'd does not record the Prophet's injunction to "remain in your house," in response to Umm Waraqa's entreaty. The only prophetic response he records is Muhammad's assurance to her that she would indeed achieve martyrdom. Ibn Sa'd's version does not rule out the possibility that Umm Waraqa did accompany the Prophet to the battlefield. Muhammad's prescient statement simply presages her tragic end but does not express disapproval of her potential presence at Badr. Given that we are now able to detect a certain editorial tendency on Ibn Hajar's part, it is not surprising that Umm Waraqa's function as the prayer leader of her household, mentioned by Ibn Sa'd, goes unreported by him as well.

The devil, as they, is in the details. It is these relatively minor deviations in detail that are highly revealing of how societal conceptions of women's agency and proper conduct in the public realm came to be progressively defined and restricted in the late pre-modern Muslim world. Most jurists and theologians by then had decided that leadership of prayer of mixed congregations was not an appropriate role for women and that virtuous women best exercised their virtue within the confines of their home. These views, like others, came to be retrojected onto the lives of the earliest Muslim women. Such views from the later period provide valuable ammunition for contemporary hard-line Islamists who wish to curtail women's legal and societal rights on the claim that such views accurately reflect the gender norms of the earliest period.

The nature of jihad

The extremist Islamist view of the world holds that Islam represents a drastic rupture with everything that went before, effaces the validity of prior religious traditions, and mandates its political hegemony over all. Hard-line Islamists signal this kind of "historical" view by their contemptuous use of the term *al-Jahiliyya* which signifies everything that antedated Islam and is not Islamic, as they define it, and therefore morally worthless in their evaluation.[56] What reeks of *al-Jahiliyya* and is assumed to be an obstacle to the spread of Islam must be ruthlessly stamped out. The vehicle for doing this is the "Islamic State" and the means for achieving this goal is *jihad*. Since, according to many Islamists, "Islam is a revolutionary ideology and programme which seeks to alter the social order of the whole world and rebuild it in conformity with its own tenets and ideals," *jihad* then "refers to that revolutionary struggle and utmost exertion which the Islamic Party brings into play to achieve this objective."[57]

Jihad in this sense is arguably the most controversial issue that dominates activist Islamist rhetoric. Of course not all Islamists (or modern Salafis in general) are militants who advocate the use of violence for political gain. Those who are militants, however, tend to understand *jihad* as the waging of unrelenting military activity against non-Muslims deemed hostile to Islam and against those perceived as "lapsed" Muslims until they are politically vanquished.[58] The "true" Muslims, that is themselves, who die waging militant activity against their adversaries are martyrs, who are promised bounteous rewards in the hereafter. Once again, these militant Islamists attempt to justify their positions and rhetoric by asserting that they reflect first-/seventh-century views regarding *jihad* and martyrdom. They refer in particular to the so-called sword verses (9:5 and 9:29) in the Qur'an without any contextualization as scriptural warrants for their militant position. They have developed a cult of martyrdom in justification of which they appeal to the *hadith* genre known as the "excellences of *jihad*" (*fada'il al-jihad*), which tends to contain unreliable and spurious reports in fulsome praise of military activity and the abundant posthumous rewards promised for such activity.[59]

The militant Islamists' novel conception of *jihad* as armed combat directed against other Muslims is predicated on their doctrine of *takfir*:[60] the declaration of Muslims, whom they regard as lukewarm or lapsed, to be unbelievers. A particularly unsavory militant tract titled "The Lapsed Duty" (*al-Farida al-gha'iba*), was penned by an Egyptian extremist 'Abd al-Salam Faraj, who is said to have inspired the assassins of former Egyptian president Anwar al-Sadat. His screed excoriates various Muslim rulers for having "apostatized" from Islam, on which account they must be fought against.

The binary vision of the world articulated by jurists of the ninth century which divided it into the "abode of Islam" and "abode of war" finds considerable resonance among radical Islamists. Despite the fact that these divisions are not to be found either in the Qur'an or the *sunna* (a fact that may not be known to many among them), they tend to promote these categories and the world-view behind them as normatively mandated. They thus appeal to the legal opinions of the ninth-century jurist al-Shafi'i (d. 820) who fully articulated this dichotomous conception of the world, which, however, he had qualified by the addition of a third domain, the abode of treaty or reconciliation (*dar al-'ahd*).[61]

By the twelfth century, this notion of a bifurcated world had become quite passé as it no longer matched the political realities of the time. However, militant Islamists have resurrected the ninth-century concepts of opposed dual spheres or abodes in the contemporary period, preferring to ignore the period before the late eighth century (from the time of the early *salaf*) when these notions had not existed, as well as ignoring the later period when these concepts fell into desuetude. They also prefer the understanding of *jihad* as exclusively "armed combat," a meaning that had gained ascendancy from roughly the ninth century on, once again bypassing the earlier period when this was a much more diverse and polyvalent term, reflecting its

Qur'anic provenance.[62] They also skip over the later period when its spiritual significations became considerably heightened, especially in Sufi circles. Radical Islamists in fact are dismissive of *hadith*s which speak more highly of spiritual and non-combative *jihad* than the combative one, such as the famous one which divides *jihad* into the greater and lesser one.[63] (They further tend to denigrate Sufism in general which is too other-worldly and self-abnegating for them.)[64] The military *jihad* may bring these Islamists untold pleasures in the next world if they should expire in its midst, but the kingdom of this world is their most coveted and preferred prize. The term *jihad* for them primarily serves to yoke the religious to their self-serving political ambitions.

Constructing the Pious
Forbears II: Historical Memory
and the Present

THE SIGNIFICANCE OF THE *SALAF AL-SALIH* FOR THE MODERNISTS

Many modernists and reformists also appropriate to a considerable degree the Pious Forbears as paradigmatic figures for their enterprise of reform and revival of the tradition from within. The historicity and thus authenticity of certain precepts and practices are established by linking them to precedents set by the Pious Forbears, more commonly from the first generation of Muslims than the succeeding two. Modernists tend to be further interested in ferreting out the rationale behind the reported deeds and statements of the Pious Forbears. To this end, they focus as well on historical accounts and biographical literature (*sira*) to contextualize the reported speech and practices of the *salaf* and resurrect the spirit of their times. Compared with the traditionalist *Salafiyya*, their approach toward the Pious Forbears thus tends to be more critical and investigative, seeking to retrieve their more historically credible personas from beneath the layers of legendary detritus. Theirs is often a hard-nosed project of excavation and recovery.

We now proceed to delineate in brief typical modernist positions on the four issues discussed in relation to the hard-line Islamists.

Establishment of the "Islamic State"

Modernists and reformists do not necessarily have a consistent position on this issue. Some modernists may advocate the establishment of a state that would be recognizably Islamic, primarily by upholding the Shari'a, which however, unlike the Islamists, is understood by them to be adaptable to and accommodating of modern life and its complexities. Unlike in the case of the traditionalist Salafiyya and hard-line Islamists, the revival of the caliphate as an institution is not necessarily an integral part of the modernist project, although the revival of the ethical and political principles and the general élan associated with the Rashidun caliphate usually is. Furthermore, unlike the hard-line Islamists, the modernists do not believe that there is a pre-conceived blueprint specifying the structural format of an "Islamic State" as such. Modernists tend to regard any state which guarantees certain basic individual and communal rights and liberties as being in accordance with broad Islamic moral parameters and thus meeting the Islamic litmus test. The actual mode of governance may be decided upon by consultation with knowledgeable people, the consent of the public, and the prevailing historical circumstances, since they believe that there are no specific religious directives concerning this matter.[1]

With regard to legitimate government, modernists tend to insist on three cardinal tenets that are defining of consultative and accountable government, an ideal pursued by the *salaf*, and actually implemented by the Rightly-Guided Caliphs, as they maintain. These three tenets are: (a) *shura* ("consultation") and accountability; (b) *bay'a* ("allegiance," "ratification"); and (c) *ijma'* ("consensus"); these are now discussed further.[2]

(a) *Shura* is a Qur'anic concept and thus sanctified by revelation and rooted in prophetic practice. There are two Qur'anic verses advocating consultation which are frequently quoted in this context. The first (3:158–59) states, "So pass over [their faults], and ask for [God's] forgiveness and consult them in matters; then, when you have made a decision, put your trust in God." The second verse (42:38) runs, "[The believers are] those who answer the call of their Lord and perform prayer, and who conduct their affairs by mutual consultation, and who spend of what We have bestowed upon them."

Consultation on various matters has been considered obligatory by most scholars while others have tended to regard it as a highly recommended practice. The predominant sentiment in the sources – theological, juridical, ethical, and administrative — is that *shura* as mutual consultation in various spheres is the preferred and desirable method of resolving matters. Numerous instances of Muhammad's consultative activities are documented in these literatures. Such attestations from the time of the Prophet have created, in fact, a powerful normative precedent for succeeding generations of the faithful.

Modernists derive more examples from the Rashidun period in order to further buttress their argument that consultation is a mandated practice in all matters, and particularly in the political realm. They point to Abu Bakr's inaugural speech which emphasized governance based on consultation with both the Meccan and Medinan Muslims and his accountability to them, inviting the people to correct him if he should fall short in any way. 'Umar's setting up of the six-man electoral council (*shura*) to deliberate upon the choice of his successor is a powerful arrow in the quiver of the modernists. This *shura* is sometimes understood by them to be the precursor of the modern parliament or legislative assembly, setting a normative example for the translation of broad guidelines of proper governance into administrative reality. Modernists point to these historical instances to make their case that a representative and accountable government that upholds justice and equitable treatment for all its citizens is the only kind permissible within Islam, regardless of what its actual structure and mode may be.[3] Modernists tend to be strong proponents of democracy today, whether in its procedural, constitutional, or liberal forms, since in their perception democratic processes today best satisfy Islamic standards of popular enfranchisement and accountability established in the earliest period.[4]

(b) *Bay'a* ("allegiance," "contract") is established through prophetic practice and the custom of the Rightly-Guided Caliphs. It is well-known that newly converted Muslims, male and female, personally came to the Prophet and gave him their allegiance, which signaled their inclusion in the Islamic community. In the post-prophetic period, this remained a standard practice which served to recognize the importance of the people's explicit or tacit consent to being governed by specific individuals. Thus, Abu Bakr's election could only be ratified by the *bay'a* given by the people present during the Saqifa episode, as were the subsequent choices of the remaining Rashidun caliphs. The practice continued, at least nominally, even when dynastic rule became the norm.

Many modernists tend to interpret the early *bay'a* as the equivalent of the modern ballot whereby an individual is allowed to register his or her opinion regarding the eligibility of specific political candidates.[5] They argue that since the rationale behind the *bay'a* in the Rashidun period was the soliciting of individual opinion in the election of the leader, such a rationale can best be realized in the contemporary period through the modern voting system. It is interesting that the modern Arabic word for voting – *taswit* – reflects this evolution. The verb behind this noun is *sawwata*, which means to raise one's voice or speak up. The voter (*musawwit*) is, therefore, literally one who speaks up and makes his or her opinion heard, as during the noisy debates during the Saqifa episode, a right which is now considered to be enshrined in the modern concept of political enfranchisement.

(c) *Ijma'* ("consensus") is, ideally speaking, the logical denouement of the consultative process and collective decision-making. In addition to *shura* and *bay'a*, modernists underscore the concept of *ijma'* to point to what they perceive as the inherently democratic impulse within Islam. *Ijma'* is not a Qur'anic term but its normativeness is established through the practice of the *salaf*. Modernists thus refer to the process of caliphal selection from the Rashidun period which depended on popular ratification to establish its legitimacy. The manner of election of the caliphs, they affirm, points to the importance of building a broad base of consensus to legitimize key political decisions in particular.[6] Consensus, as we saw, would become one of the sources of jurisprudence, along with the Qur'an, *sunna*, and analogy (*qiyas*), as articulated by al-Shafi'i (d. 820). Consensus, in theory of the people[7] but in reality of the scholars who claimed to represent the people,[8] would over time also come to be regarded as reflective of the divine will; for, surely, as was the pious view, the majority of righteous Muslims through study of their sources, consultation among themselves, and deliberative reflection would decide on the right course of action that would meet with divine approbation.[9]

Modernists and reformists expand the classical purview of the term *ijma'* to include the political sphere in addition to its traditional legal one. Thus the eighteenth-century Indian Muslim scholar Shah Wali Allah al-Dihlawi (d. 1762) regarded *ijma'* as the logical end product of the political process of consultation (*shura*) which involved the caliph and the learned people of the Muslim community.[10]

With regard to the political concept of "divine sovereignty," modernists point to many of the defining characteristics of the early political culture of Islam to counter the Qutbian Islamist understanding of this concept as a divine mandate for a complete way of life with a set of prescribed answers for nearly every imaginable situation, a scenario that leaves little room for human input and interpretation. While acknowledging God's sovereignty over all creation, modernists do not view this as impeding in any way human freedom in determining their course of action in particularly the political sphere under the guidance of broad moral imperatives.[11] The well-known modernist scholar of Islamic thought, Fazlur Rahman, stressed that the Qur'anic concept of God's sovereignty has nothing to do with political or legal sovereignty but rather means that "God has bestowed a certain constitution both to this universe and to man ..."[12]

The Qur'anic designation of human beings as "God's vicegerent" (khalifa) on earth is emphasized by modernists as investing humans with the right and authority to assume custodianship of earth. The example of the Rightly-Guided Caliphs, the modernists assert, clearly establishes that such custodianship was understood in the early period to be predicated on human agency and deliberative reasoning while safeguarding the moral objectives and the spirit of the religious law. 'Umar's bold innovations, for example, in instituting the state register of pensions (diwan), abrogating temporary marriage, establishing the Islamic (hijri) calendar, and modifying inheritance laws are lauded by posterity as reasoned measures whose adoption was prompted by both moral and practical considerations.

Modernists also question hard-line Islamist readings of divinely formulated government into scripture. With regard to the critical Qur'anic phrase ulu 'l-amr that has figured prominently in discussions of religious and political authority, the late nineteenth-/early twentieth-century reformist intellectual Rashid Rida (d. 1935), close friend and disciple of Muhammad 'Abduh, glossed the phrase as referring to "the people who loosen and bind" (ahl al-hall wa-'l-'aqd) among Muslims. They include the political rulers, judges, the religious scholars (al-'ulama'), the leaders of the army, and the rest of the rulers and leaders "whom people resort to in their need and for their general welfare."[13] Rida warns, however, that Qur'an 4:59 does not call for absolute obedience to the ulu 'l-amr but only to God and His Messenger, the reason being that the verse continues with "And if you should differ with regard to a thing, then refer it to God and His Messenger." If the *ulu 'l-amr* rule according to the precepts of God and the *sunna*, Rida contin-ues, then one may obey them. If they do not and in fact resort to tyranny and oppression (*zulm*), then obedience is no longer an obligatory duty but is in fact forbidden.[14]

He continues by saying that the *ulu 'l-amr*, sc. "the people who loosen and bind" (*ahl al-hall wa-'l-'aqd*) include all those in whom the Muslim commu-nity has faith. As such, they would include the scholars, the leaders of the army, and the leaders of various sectors of society who promote the general interests (*al-masalih al-'amma*) of the people. Among these sectors are trade, industry, and agriculture. Therefore, labor union leaders, political party leaders, members of the editorial boards of respectable newspapers and their chief editors are all included in the category of the people "who loosen and bind." Rida asserts that obedience to them constitutes obedience to the *ulu 'l-amr*.[15] Unlike hard-line Islamists, Rida does not see authoritarianism being mandated by an exclusively political reading of Qur'an 4:59. Rather, he understands the verse as referring to different kinds of authority – moral, intellectual, administrative, financial as well as political – dispersed among different groups of people who, with the consensus of the majority, wield collective, benevolent influence for the welfare of the community. On that account they are owed voluntary obedience by the people, which is liable to be withdrawn if the *ulu 'l-amr* fail to live up to their obligations. This kind of non-authoritarian reading of key Qur'anic verses directly challenges the radical Islamist hermeneutic enterprise which is conducive to political absolutism.

The immutable shari'a and its political reach

Unlike radical Islamists, modernists tend to emphasize the application of the intent and overall objectives (*maqasid*) of the religious law more than its lit-eral injunctions, especially when the literal understanding of a specific dic-tum in a particular circumstance would result in unusual hardship and/or violation of an inviolable broader moral imperative. Thus, many of them argue, since the *shari'a* must uphold certain ethical values such as justice and mercy at all times, specific legal injunctions may never violate these fundamental requisites in any given historical and social circumstance.[16] Those injunctions that appear to do so need to be re-examined and reinter-preted.[17] They also place more emphasis on the discernment of the ratio legis (underlying cause; *'illa*) of specific legal precepts than on their literal, textual meaning.[18]

Modernists further believe that since the *shari'a* is essentially flexible and invariably just, it has enough checks and balances built into it to prevent miscarriage of justice. Punitive sanctions that appear on the surface to be harsh are usually difficult to implement since the conditions for proving the commission of the crime for which these sanctions exist are practically impossible to fulfill. The most notable example of this is adultery which can only be punished (by flogging according to the Qur'an; by stoning according to *hadith* alone) if four individuals are eye-witnesses to the actual act of sexual penetration, a condition still virtually impossible to meet, even in our voyeuristic age. Modernists thus hold that such punishments are essentially deterrent in nature and have been carried out infrequently in Muslim societies throughout history.[19] In a rather original manner, Muhammad Shahrour, a Syrian engineer turned exegete, author of the controversial *al-Kitab wa-'l-Qur'an*, has suggested that the *hudud* laws as outlined in classical jurisprudence represent the maximum penalty that cannot be surpassed by the jurists but lesser punishments may be decreed at their discretion. This line of reasoning allows him to conclude that the law as interpreted in the pre-modern period should not be understood nor applied in a literal manner in modern societies.[20]

Modernists argue against the assumed all-pervasive, reified nature of the *shari'a* as maintained by the Islamists and against the notion that the *shari'a* comes with ready-made answers to every imaginable circumstance. They tend to affirm that the reach of the religious law extends to many aspects of human existence while not directly addressing others. Outside worship (*'ibadat*) the *shari'a* offers broad guidelines rather than detailed precepts for proper conduct in various spheres of social and other forms of interaction (*mu'amalat*).[21] The religious law certainly does not, and cannot, have a specific injunction in advance for every possible human situation or contingency. The Qur'an, the principle source of the religious law, "is not a lawbook but is primarily a moral code from which a legal system may be derived."[22] This derived legal system is the result of human reasoning and effort which allows specific legal precepts to be extrapolated from the Qur'anic moral code, as well as from the *sunna*.

The science or the study of law (that is, jurisprudence) which leads to the derivation of legal rulings is called *fiqh* in Arabic. In its basic semantic signification, *fiqh* broadly refers to human understanding and rational discernment. Wael Hallaq has perceptively characterized what we tradition-ally call Islamic law as "jurists' law."[23] Islamists and modernists are essentially in agreement that the *shari'a* must always be respected but they tend to talk past one another when the former mistake *fiqh* for *Shari'a* and/or use the terms interchangeably. Jurisprudence (*fiqh*) is a human intellectual activity and, therefore, fallible and changeable. Specific legal interpretations result-ing from the deliberations of jurists were crafted in response to specific his-torical and social contingencies. Changed circumstances, the modernists insist, necessitate changed interpretations in conformity with the objectives (*maqasid*) of the law. Modernists see a fatal epistemological problem arising from the conflation of jurisprudence with the religious law itself, that is, of *fiqh* with *shari'a* by hard-line Islamists (and often by traditionalists as well).

Thus in opposition to the more fervent Islamists, modernists typically emphasize the malleability of the *shari'a* which allows the faithful to relate to it in creative interpretive ways in different circumstances. The broad parameters of the religious law, they maintain, leave ample room for negotiation and accommodation of its fundamental moral objectives as well as for considera-tions of the common good (*maslaha*) through recourse to independent reason-ing (*ijtihad*). Like *maqasid* ("objectives"), *maslaha* is another key term associated with modernist discourses on the relevance of the *shari'a* in the contemporary period that harks back to the Shafi'i jurist and theologian Abu Hamid Muham-mad al-Ghazali's (d. 1111) exposition of this legal principle.[24] This principle would be further elaborated upon by Abu Ishaq al-Shatibi (d. 1388), whose rational juristic thought has enjoyed a revival among modernists.[25]

These principles are believed by many modernists to be already reflected in certain juridical and administrative decisions made by the earliest Mus-lims, although not necessarily articulated as such in the existing sources. Conforming to the broader objectives of the law in order to promote the common good allowed the *salaf* to effectively legislate innovatively in rapidly changing circumstances as the Islamic realms expanded and became trans-formed over time. Thus 'Umar's abolition of temporary marriage resonated with the first Muslims as being a necessary clampdown on what could other-wise easily pass for legal prostitution. He also determined a fixed penalty for the consumption of alcohol through analogical reasoning although the Qur'an specifies none. However, as we mentioned before (chapter 3), his attempts to impose a ceiling on the value of the bride-gift (*mahr*) were effectively nullified by an older woman's protestations that he was overstepping his authority. This anecdote serves as a proof-text for those who would maintain that the legal decisions of the *salaf* were accepted by their contemporaries when they were perceived as hermeneutically in line with the overall purpose of the *shari'a* and resisted when they were not. This kind of consensual interpretive negotiation over legal rulings in the early period that emerges from a number of sources particularly heartens the modernists in their bid to revive this early *salafi* spirit of engaging the religious law in a creative and democratic fashion.[26] Furthermore, the anecdote has been highlighted by some modernists as pointing to the equal right of women to take part in public debates with men – and in a mosque no less.[27]

Within the hierarchical ordering of the sources of law, modernists and reformists emphasize the supremacy of the Qur'an over the *sunna*, sometimes even the former's sole supremacy vis-à-vis the latter. Thus Rashid Rida maintained that the Qur'an is the main source (*asl*) of religion and that rules derived from the *sunna*, if not directly bearing on religious matters, need not be followed. Such non-religious sunnaic rulings, which have to do with civil, political and military matters, are the result of the Prophet's fallible personal *ijtihad* and are consequently non-binding on the believer. He cites in this context Qur'an 5:101 which states, "O those who believe! Do not ask questions about things which, if made known to you, would cause you harm." Rida comments that this verse implies that the Qur'an deliberately did not address many things, since detailed rulings about a large number of matters would prove cumbersome for humans. Religion should lead to ease and well-being of the people, as indicated in Qur'an 87:8, which says, "We will make it easy for you [to follow] the Easy [Path]." According to Rida, premodern jurists often flouted this basic legal objective (*maqsad*) – to ensure ease in the practice of religion – by devising difficult and arduous applications of the law in matters where, Qur'anically speaking, it had no jurisdiction.[28] This modernist proclivity for privileging the Qur'an considerably above the *sunna* or *hadith* is already apparent in al-Shatibi's legal thought in the fourteenth century, which in turn sought to revive what was believed to be the authentic practices of the *salaf*.[29]

The status and role of women

As previously mentioned, the position (and attire) of women is often the litmus test of religious authenticity in charged Islamist discourses regarding "proper" Islamic societies. The legitimacy of women's presence and activity in the public sphere is a bone of contention between most Islamists (along with the traditionalists who almost always see eye to eye with them on this particular topic) and the modernists. Many Islamist activists may and do recruit (invariably veiled) female cadres of volunteers who take part in political demonstrations and in other highly visible public activities. Nevertheless, these activities are cast as being called forth by exceptional and urgent circumstances (sort of along the lines of Ibn Hajar's argument in his biographical work concerning the women Companions). In the absence of such circumstances, women should ideally adhere to traditional roles in the home and family, regardless of the level of their education. The necessary regeneration of society will follow when the sexes assume their divinely mandated different yet complementary societal roles.

Modernists take exception to this line of reasoning which they say is unsupported by scripture and the historical praxis of the early Muslim community. From their liberal, woman-friendly vantage point, they view scripture and ancillary texts as capable of supporting all or most reasonable and morally defensible notions and activities. From such a liberal perspective they derive a scriptural rationale for creating legislation that would guarantee non-discriminatory social and political rights for women.[30] Thus polygamy which was permissible in societies at a time when women were exclusively reliant on men for financial support should certainly not be encouraged, in their opinion, in the modern period and curtailed since it has outlived its usefulness. Even in the pre-modern period, many modernists argue, the Qur'an only grudgingly tolerated at best the institution of polygamy, temporarily countenancing it, like slavery, since the socio-economic conditions which facilitated these two institutions then could not be reformed overnight. The primary Qur'anic proof-text (4:129) marshaled by them in defense of this understanding states, "You are never able to deal fairly among women, even if it is your ardent desire." Since male human nature is categorically declared in this verse as incapable of being totally fair in polygamous relationships, and since the legitimacy of a polygamous union rests on the completely fair and equal treatment of up to four wives by the husband, then the Qur'an in essence inveighs against polygamy and promotes monogamy as the mandated practice, according to the modernists.[31]

Because of their interest in the historic contextualization of religious texts and of the secondary interpretive literature, modernists avidly try to weed out culturally conditioned understanding of such texts from what they regard as more reliable interpretations warranted by the texts themselves and changed historical circumstances. Modernist scholars like and study history; it is their best ally against ahistorical obscurantism. Thus Fazlur Rahman states that "preference for history over *hadith* proper reverses the bias of the traditionists, who held technical *hadith* superior to historical reports."[32] History provides them with evidence of actual implementation of a precept and better illustrates the spirit of a certain principle. Over and above *hadith* as recorded text, modernists sometimes place more of an emphasis on the actual practices ("living *sunna*" or "tradition") of the Prophet and that of his Companions as described in biographical and historical sources. As we saw earlier, the jurist Malik b. Anas had emphasized this living tradition (*'amal*) as more authentically reproducing the prophetic past and preferred the practices of the Medinan scholars over the actual text of a *hadith* if the two were at odds. Other early sources suggest that the term *sunna* in the earliest period did not only refer to specific precedents set by Muhammad in his speech and conduct, but alluded as well to general principles of justice and righteous behavior as exemplified by the Prophet.[33] To make their case, many modernists appeal to these earlier more elastic and capacious understandings of *sunna* before al-Shafi'i's "reduction" of the concept in the late second century of Islam to mean precedents set by the Prophet only, as evident in recorded statements attributed to him.

As one might imagine, this relative devaluation of textual *hadith* at times makes for radically different approaches to the Islamic tradition, especially on questions of *hudud* punishments involving the death penalty, attitudes toward religious minorities, and women's roles, which have been primarily determined on the basis of *hadith*. On this last issue of women's roles, traditionalist and Islamist resistance to women's greater participation in the public sphere is often regarded by modernists as a vestige of cultural conditioning and not attributable to any specific Islamic, particularly Qur'anic, injunction. This is dramatically evident when modernists turn to the Qur'anic accounts of the creation of Adam and his wife in order to challenge patriarchal notions of familial division of labor. They point out that the Qur'an either exclusively blames Adam or Adam and his wife together for the "Fall" but does not single out the woman for blame. Most pre-modern exegetes, however, drew upon the biblical version of the Creation story and the Fall in order to exonerate Adam of any wrong-doing and place the blame squarely on Eve (named Hawwa' in the exegetical literature). The notion that woman was made from Adam's rib – along with its exegetical implications – is discounted by modernists since it has no Qur'anic pedigree but shows the influence of the biblical creation story.[34] Thus the contemporary feminist Amina Wadud states, "In maintaining the dual form [in referring to both Adam and his wife], the Qur'an overcomes the negative Greco-Roman and Biblical-Judaic implications that woman was the cause of evil and damnation."[35]

The women *salaf*'s robust participation in public activities of all kinds as documented particularly in early biographical and historical literature is upheld by the modernists as establishing a model for later women and meant to be encouraging of their active presence in the public realm today.[36] 'A'isha bint Abi Bakr's energetic role in *hadith* transmission, Qur'an interpretation, and political affairs are stressed as mimetic precedents to legitimate Muslim women's participation in all aspects of public life. The fact that she and other women Companions related *hadith* from the Prophet and that their individual testimony concerning the validity of these statements was accepted by scholars has additional legal significance. These instances are adduced as evidence that a woman's testimony was equal to a man's in religious scholarship where the highest standards of public witnessing had to be maintained. Such a deduction undermines the position of those who would maintain that Qur'an 2:282 mandates that a woman's testimony is always valued at half of a man's. If this verse, the modernists argue, was understood to have such a general applicability rather than referring to a very specific context involving loan transactions as the verse indicates, then the early scholars could not possibly have accepted the *hadith* narrations of so many first generation women on their own authority.[37]

The case of women Companions like Umm 'Umara, our valiant warrior, and Umm Waraqa, who led her mixed household in prayer on account of her superior knowledge of the Qur'an (mentioned in the previous chapter), are cited by the modernists as exemplifying the gender egalitarianism that prevailed in the early period. Historical scrutiny allows modernists to interrogate later sources such as Ibn Hajar's biographical dictionary which tend to minimize women's public roles and compare them to earlier works. Such comparisons reveal later sources as skewing on occasion the earlier accounts in order to promote a culturally conditioned socially inferior position for women in contravention of more egalitarian Islamic attitudes which prevailed in the early period. Certain *hadith*s of dubious reliability which promote misogynist views are similarly dismissed by modernists as reflective of post-prophetic cultural mores and specific socio-political circumstances[38] and thus betraying the gender egalitarian ideals of early Islam as manifested in the Qur'an and corroborated by the historical record.

Some modernists have called for critical scrutiny of the actual texts of *hadith* in addition to the more conventional analysis of their chains of transmission (*isnad*) in order to more rigorously determine the reliability of reports. The Azhar-trained twentieth-century scholar Muhammad al-Ghazali, for example, advocates this form of analysis in his book *al-Sunna al-Nabawiyya*,[39] which has encountered severe criticism in conservative scholarly circles, notably in Saudi Arabia.

The nature of jihad

Modernists find the radical Islamist conception of *jihad* to be anathema and also have trouble with a considerable portion of the classical juridical conception of *jihad* and related concepts. It was mentioned earlier that the distinguished jurist al-Shafi'i divided the world into three realms of war, peace, and treaty/armistice and that he did so on his own initiative without any scriptural basis. Modernists point to this as an example of independent *ijtihad* on al-Shafi'i's part in order to make sense, from an Islamo-centric point of view, of the conflict-ridden world that he inhabited, which has no bearing on the contemporary world.[40]

Muslim reformists have pointed to the diversity of opinions throughout the classical and post-classical period to point to the contested and historically contingent nature of many of the classical pronouncements on *jihad* and related issues. Once again, modernists and reformists have turned to accounts of the views and practices of the *salaf* that have a bearing on these topics to challenge the legitimacy of the Islamist position, particularly in its radical form. A favorite example of modernists drawn from the first century of Islam is the treatment of the Christian Abyssinians by the Prophet and various Muslim administrators after him. The Christian Abyssinians under the devout Negus became famous in early Islam for having harbored a group of destitute Muslims fleeing from the persecution of the pagan Meccans before the migration to Medina by Muhammad and his followers in 622. As a consequence of this exceptional act of good will and religious fellowship, various Muslim authorities in the early period, following the example of the

Prophet, exempted the Abyssinians from the payment of any taxes (*jizya*) that would otherwise be expected and automatically considered them to be part of the abode of treaty/peace. The Nubians of North Africa, despite being non-Muslims, were also exempted from the *jizya* and not considered *dhimmis* ("protected people"). Instead they entered into a trade agreement (*baqt*) with the Muslims according to the terms of which they mutually traded goods.[41] Furthermore, the Prophet's gracious reception of the Christians of Najran in Medina, where he allowed them to pray in his mosque and affirmed the continuing protection of their churches, set a new standard for inter-faith relations.[42] Modernist Muslims invoke these concrete historical instances to bolster their argument that in an era of an international commonwealth of nations subscribing to shared values of human rights and peaceful coexistence, these examples of Muslim and non-Muslim interaction yield a much more pertinent and appropriate model for inter-cultural relations today. It further underscores the fact that relations with non-Muslims are governed not on the basis of religious affiliation but on the good will and peaceableness of the people involved.

Jizya or the head-tax, they point out, was not always consistently imposed on non-Muslims. Women, the elderly, the poor, religious clerics and monks were routinely exempted from its payment. There are also instances when non-Muslims requested to pay the *zakat*, the poor-tax enjoined on Muslims, in lieu of the *jizya* and the request was granted. Thus, 'Umar ibn al-Khattab exempted the Christian tribe Banu Taghlib from the *jizya* when the latter protested its imposition on them and allowed them to pay *zakat* instead; the Christians of Tanukh were treated similarly by him. The Jarajima tribe agreed to serve in the military in lieu of paying the *jizya*.[43] Modernists point to these historical instances to underscore the contingent nature of *jizya* and its imposition.

They also point to the early, magnanimous 'Umar as exemplifying the tolerance and kindness enjoined upon Muslims toward Jews and Christians in particular and decry his later incarnation as a far less tolerant figure who compromised these values.[44] The division of the world into dichotomous hostile spheres requiring the subjugation of one by the other is regarded as being obsolete by the modernists. Thus Muhammad 'Abduh and Rashid Rida recognized that the bipolar division of the world had been defunct for centuries and explicitly affirmed that peaceful co-existence was the normal state of affairs between Islamic and non-Islamic nations.[45]

Mahmud Shaltut (d. 1963), the reformer who like Abduh became the rector of al-Azhar University, expressed a similar conviction. He further stated that Muslims and non-Muslims were equal with regard to rights and duties in a Muslim-majority state, and that only defensive wars are permissible in response to external aggression.[46]

Modernists also wish to highlight the spiritual and social reformist aspects inherent in *jihad* and restore its full semantic purview, compromised by hawkish medieval jurists who were reacting to a violent, adversarial world that was part real, part imaginary. They reject the abrogating status of the so-called sword verses, which would result in the abrogation (*naskh*) of numerous Qur'anic verses that counsel peace and reconciliation.[47] Besides emphasizing the multiple significations of the term *jihad* in the Qur'an, modernists point to the broad range of views among the early *salaf* on what constitutes *jihad* and martyrdom. Thus modernists stress various reports recorded in early *hadith* collections like the *Musannaf* of 'Abd al-Razzaq which define *jihad* in terms of striving daily to live righteously through acts of worship, earning a licit livelihood, and serving one's family, in addition to military defense of Islamic realms.[48] These reports are adduced by them as proof-texts to support their position that the multi-faceted aspects of *jihad* informed the lives of the early *salaf* and that the monolithic, military conception of *jihad* promoted by many of the classical jurists was a historically contingent development and lacking in normativeness today.[49] The position of contemporary radical Islamists that *jihad* refers to unrelenting military activity against all those unlike them, Muslim and non-Muslim, until the latter come around to their view of things is regarded by modernists as a desperate and grotesque distortion of a noble and morally uplifting concept, whose reclamation from the extremists is necessary and long overdue.

Assessment of Islamist and
Modernist Views

In this work, we began with a survey of the times and circumstances attendant at the beginning of Islam in the early seventh century to the middle of the
ninth century of the Common Era, spanning the three generations of the
Pious Forbears. In the last two chapters, we focused on the appropriation of
the *salaf al-salih* as paradigmatic role models by particularly hard-line
Islamists and modernists in the articulation and legitimization of specific
responses to modernity and globalization, two processes essentially spear-
headed by a largely secular and seemingly hegemonic West. We have documented some of the principal positions of both groups on key issues which
reveal contesting constructions of the *salaf*. This allows us to make the following observations regarding which camp is the more credible in their
"ownership" of the Pious Forbears with regard to our four main topics.

THE "ISLAMIC STATE"

The Islamists maintain that the "Islamic State" was fully conceived of during
the prophetic period and available for emulation during the Rashidun period,
a position that we would now recognize, even on the basis of our all-too-brief
survey, as rather ahistorical. None of the pre-modern sources – the Qur'an,
hadith, historical works, exegeses – refers to the recurrent fundamental
Islamist terms of *al-Dawla al-Islamiyya* ("the Islamic State"), *al-Hukuma*

al-Islamiyya ("the Islamic Government"), or *al-hakimiyya*. In reference to the Prophet's life and the succeeding Rashidun period, the term *umma* is predominantly used in early sources to refer to the Muslim community and polity. Furthermore, the Qur'anic term *umma* is not restricted to the Muslim community, but also refers to Christian and Jewish communities, and to other nations long vanished. This early expansive meaning of *umma* is reflected in the Constitution of Medina drawn up by the Prophet in which the term included the Jewish communities of Medina.

The term *dawla* (lit. "a turn," "a revolving") is first used in reference to the 'Abbasid revolution and then used subsequently in the relevant literature to indicate the various dynasties.[1] Thus *al-dawla al-'abbasiyya* and *al-dawla al-fatimiyya* refer to the 'Abbasid and Fatimid dynasties respectively. In regard to the Islamist term *al-Hakimiyya*, it stems rather from the slogan of the first-/seventh-century Khawarij. The Khawarij were the "secessionists" who broke ranks with 'Ali and his supporters who had wished to resort to reasoned negotiation in order to settle their differences with Mu'awiya, the Umayyad contender for the caliphate. The Khawarij insisted that "judgment/arbitration belongs only to God" and proceeded to brand other Muslims as lapsed on account of not subscribing to their extremist platform – a chilling harbinger of today's militant Islamism. It should be noted that the Khawarij themselves, however, did not use the term *al-hakimiyya*.

There is no evidence at all in the early sources that the Companions invoked a supposedly divinely mandated blueprint for an "Islamic Government" or an "Islamic State" in the election of the Prophet's first successor. As we have seen, the sources, primarily (Sunni) historical and biographical works, relate rather that the earliest Muslims were caught by surprise and thrown into confusion at Muhammad's sudden death in Medina in 632. The selection of Abu Bakr as the first caliph during the *saqifa* episode in Medina immediately after the Prophet's death was later tellingly described by 'Umar as a *"falta,"* an ad hoc unpremeditated response by the early Muslims to this exceptional circumstance. This term and the description of the events leading to Abu Bakr's appointment essentially highlight the non-sacral, contingent nature of political administration in this early period subject to the deliberations of human reasoning and considerations of public utility and welfare. Furthermore, the fact that the Prophet did not name a successor to himself (according to the majority of Muslims) or decree a specific mode of governance after him clearly suggest that political administration was not regarded as being regulated by specific religious precepts and, therefore, was a matter in which humans could exercise their independent reasoning, according to the exigencies of their situation.

The majority of the sources report that the passionate debates regarding the appointment of the first caliph were predicated, as we have already observed, on the broad Qur'anic concepts of precedence (*sabiqa*) and excellence (*fadila*), which provided general guidelines for defining legitimate leadership. These principles were further powerfully illustrated in the institution of the *diwan*, the register of pensions established by 'Umar, the second caliph, shortly after Muhammad's death. As discussed previously, the *diwan* set up a system whereby the precedence of each Muslim became an important criterion in determining the amount of stipend that he or she would be awarded from the state treasury. The establishment of the *diwan* was a highly innovative step on 'Umar's part, there being no precedent for it during the Prophet's lifetime. As the sources tell us, 'Umar borrowed this institution from the Persians, recognizing it as the potential instrument to implement the Qur'anic paradigm of precedence and excellence as a basic socio-political and economic organizational principle. The *diwan* was controversial even in his time, its establishment and function being regarded by some as being in violation of the Qur'an's basic egalitarianism, since it set up a system of preference, albeit on the basis of moral excellence, as previously mentioned.[2] What is worth underscoring here is that 'Umar did not claim to be following a prophetic practice (which it was not), nor did he claim that the setting up of the register of pensions was the *only* valid way to implement the broad Qur'anic organizational principles of precedence and excellence. 'Uthman, his successor, saw fit to continue the institution of the *diwan* on the basis of these principles, but 'Ali, the last of the Rightly-Guided Caliphs, did not, believing rather that the Qur'anic intent of creating a polity of equal believers was best served by a non-preferential system of pension distribution in his time. Through the specific example of the *diwan* and its different modes of organization, the first four caliphs emerge as being personally innovative in reacting to their specific historical and political circumstances. Invoking the same scripture and prophetic precedent, they arrived at different interpretations based on independent reasoning, later recognized by the polity as equally valid in their given historical circumstances.

In chapter 7, we traced the varying exegeses of Qur'an 4:59 starting from the Umayyad period and commented on how the understanding of the phrase *ulu 'l-amr* ("those possessing authority") can be traced to changing notions of leadership in different historical circumstances. In the previous chapter, we discussed Rashid Rida's exegesis of this critical term and discovered that his understanding of the term refers broadly to people possessing knowledge and expertise of different kinds and reflects the early eighth-century exegete Mujhad ibn Jabr's exegesis of this term as referring to "people of knowledge and understanding" in general.

The criticisms we are leveling here at hard-line Islamist conceptions of political authority and the "Islamic State" closely echo the modernist critique of their position. It is a critique born of a close scrutiny of various kinds of early sources – historical, biographical, exegetical, and *hadith* works – in addition to a close reading of the Qur'anic text itself. All these sources taken together do not support the notion of a reified "Islamic State" or of an a priori scriptural mandate for a specific form of "Islamic Government." It is, after all, significant that Abu Bakr, according to our sources, was called *Khalifat Rasul Allah* ("successor to the Messenger of God"), which sobriquet does not encode any pretensions to being God's representative or deputy. 'Umar, when he succeeded Abu Bakr, was called both *Khalifat Abi Bakr* ("successor of Abu Bakr") and *Amir al-Mu'minin* ("leader of the faithful"). Later Umayyad and 'Abbasid adoption of the title *Khalifat Allah* ("God's deputy") represents a radical departure from the early tradition and reflects the growing Hellenic and Persian influence on notions of political governance and social hierarchy, particularly in the 'Abbasid period.[3]

It is on the basis of such documentation that modernists reject the extreme politicization of Islam to which hard-line Islamists resort. They in fact credibly perceive the radical Islamist project of imbricating faith in political power as a dangerous hijacking of Islam's transcendence as a faith tradition and inveigh against its reduction to a mere political ideology. While most modernist Muslims would maintain that religious values have a significant role to play in the public sphere, they would deny that religious precepts themselves mandate any particular mode of governance and other specific forms of political behavior. Rather, political administration (*siyasa*) has to do with secular concerns, a realization that occurred fairly early in Islamic realms and became reflected in actual practice.[4]

As we saw in the last chapter, modernists also tend to maintain that there is much in the Islamic tradition that may be understood to be consonant *mutatis mutandis* with the premises and objectives of a modern democratic system that has a due regard for religious and rational morality. The principles of *shura*, *bay'a*, and *ijma'* are all capable of being aggrandized and adapted to conform to modern democratic requirements of electoral systems, popular ratification, and canvassing of the popular will. Our own foray into the past allows us to endorse this modernist optimism which is more firmly anchored – vis-à-vis the hard-line Islamist position – in the historical trends of the early community. The early history of the community points to the consultative nature of government, both as an ideal and reality. Over time, the ideal would remain while reality departed considerably from it. There remained, however, a diversity of thought regarding the necessity of government and the nature of the Islamic political tradition through time (see below). It is this very eclectic nature which augurs well for the future, pointing the way to a similar creative and innovative engagement on the part of Muslims today with the challenges of modern political systems.

THE PERVASIVENESS OF THE RELIGIOUS LAW AND ITS SCOPE

From even our perfunctory treatment of the growth and function of the religious law, Islamist views on the absolute nature of the *shari'a* and its scope appear to be at odds at the very least with early attitudes toward legal decision-making and pre-modern juridical concepts of legal objectives (*maqasid*) and the common good (*maslaha*). Moreover, there is very little appreciation on the part of hard-line Islamists of the actual historical context of legal practices and the application of specific rulings. We have referred to the oft-quoted example of al-Shafi'i who resorted to fresh *ijtihad* when he moved from Iraq to Egypt, since the new social and cultural specificities of Egypt required such a legal reformulation.

One of the most (if not the most) distinguishing features of most Islamist discourses is their insistence on the inextricable intertwining of religion with politics (or the indivisibility of what is termed church and state in the Christian context) on the assumption that such a combination replicates the reality of the early years of the polity. Our review of the formative period of the Muslim polity however challenges this assertion. As our discussion to date will have made evident, the *shari'a* is largely apolitical, which leaves the political sphere wide open to devices of human ingenuity in formulating administrative systems and modes of political authority that do not violate broad moral imperatives, such as justice and egalitarianism. Even in the first centuries of Islam, political and administrative spheres had primarily to do with what we would otherwise call secular and temporal matters, with very little intervention from the religious law. Moral and practical counsel in such matters might be sought from religious sources to the extent that it was applicable but also from existing administrative and advice manuals of non-Islamic origin, such as the Kalila and Dimna fables available in translation in Baghdad since the eighth century, which often incorporated the wisdom and practices of pre- and non-Islamic societies. Hard-line Islamists, in fact, tend to reject the pre-modern vibrant humanistic tradition spawned by the great translation movement of the ninth century (depicted in chapter 8) as something that is extraneous to the Islamic tradition and ultimately corrupting of it. Typically, modernists celebrate the humanistic tradition as endogenous to the Islamic tradition and point to the cultural efflorescence under the 'Abbasids as a manifestation of the tradition's receptivity to what is spiritually, aesthetically, and intellectually enriching of human life, regardless of its origin.

Thus Greece, Persia, India, China, and the ancient Near East proved to be rich shores for Muslims who embarked on often arduous trips in pursuit of knowledge (rihlat talab al-'ilm), having taken to heart the counsel of their Prophet, "Seek knowledge even as far as China!" The search for beauty was never far from the search for truth; neither could it be circumscribed by political or sectarian boundaries.[5]

We have already discussed at length the Rashidun period and the lack of evidence for any notion of sacralized politics in this period. The authority exercised by the early caliphs was primarily political and epistemic, that is, based on their administrative acumen and possession of knowledge. Their authority to interpret the law was shared by other prominent Companions, such as 'Abd Allah ibn 'Abbas, Ibn Mas'ud, 'A'isha, and others. In the post-Rashidun period, political administration as such came to be termed siyasa, a non-Qur'anic Arabic term that had to do with the temporal and worldly realm only. Siyasa referred to an overarching system of administrative and penal laws mostly of non-religious provenance, which was sometimes in contention with fiqh, the religiously derived legislation.[6] Such a delimitation of siyasa from fiqh in fact testifies to the recognition in medieval circles of the bifurcation of the religious and political spheres to a considerable extent. Thus the historian Ira Lapidus has commented:

Despite the common statement (and the Muslim ideal) that the institutions of state and religion are unified, and that Islam is a total way of life which defines political as well as social and family matters, most Muslim societies did not conform to this ideal, but were built around separate institutions of state and religion. The majority of Muslim societies through time have in fact continued to observe this de facto separation between state and religion.[7]

Other than offering broad moral guidelines on public accountability and exhorting to frequent consultation (*shura*) on private and public matters, the Qur'an and the *sunna* have very little to say about the actual mode and mechanics of political governance. The modernist scholar, Fazlur Rahman, has bluntly described slogans about the inseparability of religion and politics in Islam as being "employed to dupe the common man into accepting that, instead of politics or the state serving the long-range objectives of Islam, Islam should come to serve the immediate and myopic objectives of party politics."[8]

In the formative period, according to most sources, there was no universal consensus regarding a *religious* mandate (as opposed to a political mandate born out of pragmatism) to elect or appoint a ruler for the polity. A number of Muslims in this period remained unconvinced that they needed a ruler or any form of government at all to contain disorder. Among the Mu'tazila of the eighth century, al-Asamm and al-Nazzam thought that a caliph was unnecessary as long as the Muslims adhered to the Qur'an and followed the example of their Prophet. Others subscribed to the opinion that more than one ruler or even a ruling body could just as effectively, if not more so, maintain law and order. As the Islamic realm did in fact become fragmented in the eighth century with two rival caliphs reigning (the 'Abbasid caliph based in Baghdad and the Umayyad caliph based in Andalusia or Muslim Spain), pre-modern political theorists were forced to acknowledge the changed political reality and concede the legitimacy of more than one caliph at a time.[9]

The diversity of opinions in the first three centuries of Islam is attested to by the eleventh-century Mu'tazili theologian 'Abd al-Jabbar (d. 1095), who identifies three broad trends of thought still prevalent in his time on the issue of the caliphate. The first, a minority, held that the caliphate was not necessary; the second believed that it was required on the basis of reason; and the third maintained that it was necessary according to the religious law.[10] This range of thought testifies to the active engagement of many thinkers with the critical issues of sound governance and socio-political administration, unfettered by an assumed religious mandate for a specific political institution. Their suggestions and solutions were clearly the product of rational deliberation and moral reflection, based on the needs of their own times and circumstances. It was not until the tenth century that the famous Sunni theologian al-Ash'ari (d. 935) would formulate the doctrine that the caliphate (or the imamate as it was often called) was a requirement of the religious law. But even in this period and beyond, there were Muslim thinkers who continued to believe that leadership devolved from practical concerns rather than from religious dictates. Thus the fourteenth-century scholar 'Adud al-Din al-Iji (d. 1355) continued to maintain that popular consensus and social utility rather than religious doctrine had established the necessity of the caliphate.[11]

STATUS OF WOMEN

A number of scholars have documented the progressive diminution in women's public roles in pre-modern Islamic societies compared to the earliest period and the reflection of this trend in specific social and legislative acts. In our comparison of the portrayals of women Companions in early and later biographies in chapter 9, we established that the later biographers had to "doctor" to a certain extent the early accounts of the lives of the women Companions since, unedited, they conveyed an image somewhat seditiously different from the desired one. The reason for this is readily obvious: early biographical works such as Ibn Sa'd's *al-Tabaqat al-Kubra* contain examples of women Companions who were anything but cloistered beings residing in grand seclusion in their homes. According to the fulsome descriptions we have of many of them, some of them were stalwart combatants in battle, others determinedly took part in relief and humanitarian work on the battlefield and in the Prophet's mosque, and assumed leadership roles in the dissemination of religious knowledge and in worship.

What were later male biographers to make of this phenomenon? The more enterprising ones, like the Mamluk biographer Ibn Hajar, as we have seen, simply excised potentially subversive details that might induce the women of his time to seek greater visibility and influence in the public realm, based on the precedents set by their famous Forbears. His editorial skills are particularly apparent in the case of the Companion Umm Waraqa bint 'Abd Allah ibn al-Harith, who, the earlier biographer Ibn Sa'd records, had led her household in prayer with the express approval of the Prophet. Her selection as the prayer leader was on account of her superior knowledge of the Qur'an vis-à-vis other members of her family. The implication is clear: a male relative could not trump her in this regard simply by virtue of being male. Whereas certain religious functions and authority became cast in highly gendered terms after the eighth century and were understood to ontologically inhere in the knowledgeable male, the principle of *sabiqa* or priority which is in evidence in the report concerning Umm Waraqa allowed the individual with the greatest religious precedence – a woman in this case – to assume this leadership position in the first century of Islam. The later biographer, Ibn Hajar, although retaining the reference to Umm Waraqa's memorization of the Qur'an – a laudable achievement for any Muslim, male or female – makes no mention of the fact that the Prophet had designated her the prayer leader of her household on account of this accomplishment. Ibn Hajar appears to be conceding that religious knowledge may not be denied to the female, of course, but she must not develop "uppity" notions on account of it – believing herself in this case to be on a par with men and serving as the *imam* of her mixed household. Elision of this inconvenient fact in regard to Umm Waraqa allows Ibn Hajar to document the life of this female *salaf* without allowing her to set a dangerous precedent for what appears by his time to be impermissible feminine activity.

Ibn Hajar, in fact, excelled in the artful reconfiguring of the women *salaf*'s lives so as to render them in full compliance with later cultural sensibilities regarding the "proper" position of women. Another woman Companion who fell victim to Ibn Hajar's editorial intrepidity is our valiant warrior, Umm 'Umara, as we have shown. In comparison with Ibn Sa'd, Ibn Hajar grants her scant recognition and leaves out any reference to the Prophet's fulsome praise for her heroic conduct. Instead, Ibn Hajar ingeniously tries to establish that early permission granted to women to join the men in the battlefield had been later rescinded on the basis of a weak and dubious report.[12]

Close reading of such micro-discourses is thus very revealing of shifts in attitudes toward the public roles of women through time. The subtle and not-so-subtle editing of the women *salaf*'s lives to make them "politically correct" in the later period drives home the central importance of the Pious Forbears as moral exemplars for Muslims. With regard to some of the women *salaf* in particular, their lives had to be reconfigured by the later biographers to bring them into line with late medieval constructions of virtuous feminine identity. Sexual segregation that characterized Muslim societies in the later period and the attendant attenuation in women's public roles could then be regarded as being based on the social mores established by the Pious Forbears themselves, in accordance with their correct interpretation of religious prescriptions. It is not surprising, therefore, that later authors like Ibn Hajar and Ibn Qayyim al-Jawziyya rather than Ibn Sa'd are consulted more often by conservative *Salafi*s, particularly on the issue of women's public roles.[13]

THE NATURE OF *JIHAD*

Our preceding discussion has established that the term *jihad* in Qur'anic usage is a term with multiple meanings and, as even a cursory reading of some of the related literature reveals, was understood as such by early religious authorities and scholars. *Jihad* in the Qur'an is a broad umbrella term which means "struggle" and "striving." The fuller term, as usually occurs, is *al-jihad fi sabil Allah* ("striving in the path/for the sake of God"). This striving is an ongoing effort to "enjoin good and forbid wrong," an essential and basic moral imperative for the believer. In Qur'anic usage, the word *jihad* alone does not refer to armed combat. The specific term used for armed combat is *qital*, which can be a means of enjoining good and forbidding wrong in specific circumstances. Another important means of striving in the way of God is through patient forbearance (*sabr*), which is always required of the believer under all circumstances. As mentioned in chapter 7, exegetical glosses from the early period on the full Qur'anic phrase *al-jihad fi sabil Allah* explain this moral imperative as referring to a wide array of activities: for example, embarking on the pursuit of knowledge, giving alms, and earning a licit livelihood, in addition to military defense of Islamic realms.[14]

Thus the early *hadith* compilation of 'Abd al-Razzaq al-San'ani (d. 826), one of the Successors to the Successors, contains reports which refer to *jihad* in their multiple significations. 'Abd al-Razzaq records a report attributed to the famous Successor al-Hasan al-Basri (d. 728), who valorizes the struggle inherent in daily life and worship as the central and more important meaning of *jihad*. In this report al-Hasan says, "There is nothing more arduous or exacting (*ajhad*) for a man than the money which he spends honestly or for a right cause and the prayer that he says deep in the middle of the night."[15] The Arabic superlative *ajhad* is related etymologically to the term *jihad* and underscores the greater merit accruing from doing daily ordinary activities well. Reports such as these highlight the general signification of *jihad* as striving to better oneself and contributing to the welfare of one's family and society.

But 'Abd al-Razzaq also records a report attributed to the same Successor al-Hasan al-Basri, in which the latter relates that the Prophet had stated, "Embarking upon the path of God or returning from it is better than all the world and what it contains. Indeed, when one of you stands within the battle ranks, then that is better than the worship of a man for sixty years."[16] In this report, "embarking upon the path of God" clearly refers to military activity. These reports do not contradict one another; rather they illuminate for us the various dimensions and means of striving in the path of God in variegated circumstances. Early reports like these collectively record for us the rich polysemy of the concept of *jihad* and the dialectics conducted between various groups who wished to privilege certain strands of meaning over others. "Hawkish," pro-establishment groups emphasized the combative aspects of *jihad* which could (and did) justify statist goals of territorial expansion, while "dovish," pietistic circles stressed the non-combative moral and reformist aspects of *jihad* as part of the individual's daily personal and social struggle to realize God's will.

Likewise, early extra-Qur'anic literature (exegesis and *hadith*) also records various perspectives on martyrdom (*shahada*, a term which does not occur in the Qur'an in this sense) that reflect the multiple meanings of the term *jihad*. A number of early *hadith*s affirm that an individual who met death while struggling in any licit and noble pursuit during one's mundane existence on earth could be regarded as a "martyr." Thus, once again, the *Musannaf* of 'Abd al-Razzaq contains a number of early reports which relate competing definitions of the non-Qur'anic term *shahid*, as already discussed in chapter 7. These reports assign martyrdom to, for example, pious people who die quietly in their beds after a life spent in worship and from painful illnesses and injuries, in addition to dying in defense of the faith.

Historical accounts further testify to significant changes in the semantic trajectory of the term *jihad*. We referred earlier to a highly significant clause in the "Constitution of Medina" which describes the military defense of the Islamic polity as a common enterprise between the Muslims and Jews of Medina. The Arabic verb used to describe this joint venture in the Constitution is *jahadu* from which the verbal noun *jihad* is derived. Additionally, certain historical sources refer to military campaigns waged by armies consisting of both Muslims and Christians in the early period.[17] Such historical instances highlight the glaring difference between the early conceptualization of *jihad*, when referring to "armed combat," as military defense in which people of different faith traditions may take part in a common moral endeavor to prevent corruption on earth (*al-fasad fi 'l-ard*; cf. Qur'an 5:32), and the modern extremist notion in which an elect few designated as the "true Muslims" take up the sword against all others, Muslim and non-Muslim. The Qur'an after all underscores the Muslim's duty to come to the aid of oppressed people everywhere, regardless of their religious affiliation and specifically exhorts Muslims (Qur'an 22:40) to defend all places of worship in which God's name is exalted – churches, synagogues, monasteries, and mosques. Qur'an 22:40, widely believed to be the first verse to permit fighting, unambiguously articulates the objective of the combative *jihad* to be the defense of all righteous people, not only of confessional Muslims, who are wronged.

The extremist notion of *jihad* as relentless militancy is predicated on the concept of *takfir* which refers to the branding of others as unbelievers on the basis of assumed doctrinal differences. These views make radical Islamist factions today the logical heirs of the seventh-century deviant group the Khawarij, who, as previously mentioned, repudiated other Muslims who would not support their militant platform, a process they called *bara'a* ("to be free of"). To guard against the dangerously divisive consequences of the notion of *takfir* and to prevent specific tenets of dogma from becoming fractious litmus tests of faith, the majoritarian Muslim community in the early premodern period came to gradually endorse the principle of *irja'*, as previously discussed. *Irja'* literally means "postponement" or "deferral." Most commonly associated with Abu Hanifa and later becoming the defining characteristic of Sunni Muslims, this principle counsels the deferral of a categorical pronouncement on the legitimacy or illegitimacy of a particular action or turn of events regarding which there is no explicit scriptural injunction. The underlying assumption is that such matters are known only to God and humans need not exercise themselves in seeking a definitive assessment of their moral valence, especially when such evaluative efforts would lead to communal dissension.

An example of such a matter is the recognition of 'Uthman as the third Rightly-Guided Caliph, whose rule had become controversial on the basis of his alleged nepotism. A consensus would slowly emerge that 'Uthman was entitled to this title and that the majoritarian community would desist from judging the moral propriety of specific actions of his in the absence of certain criteria for forming such a judgment. At the same time, the consensus slowly emerged that 'Ali was the fourth Rightly-Guided Caliph. This allowed for the creation of a broad-based coalition among various early groups who had differing opinions on the caliphate.[18]

Several *hadiths* found in authoritative collections stress that a minimal confession of faith in the one God is sufficient for remaining a Muslim. In one such *hadith* related by 'Uthman, the Prophet states, "Whoever dies while acknowledging that there is no god but God will enter heaven." In a variant report related by the Companion Mu'adh ibn Jabal, the Prophet announces, "For those among the faithful who bear witness that there is no god but God and that Muhammad is His servant and Messenger, God will prohibit the Fire for them."[19] This minimalist doctrinal position remained an ideal for most Muslims, even if not always subscribed to, and prevented subsequent permanent cleavages on dogmatic issues, at least among Sunnis.

The notorious practice of branding others as infidels (*takfir*), as practiced by radical Islamist groups today, appear to go back to the writings of the fourteenth-century scholar Ibn Taymiyya (d. 1328), who had declared the Mongols to be unbelievers in spite of their formal declaration of Islam. On this basis, they could then be legitimately fought against. Ibn Taymiyya was in many ways a maverick thinker who saw himself free to frequently step outside the majoritarian consensus on a number of issues. His bellicose pronouncements against the Mongols reflect the unhappy experiences of his youth when he and his family were forced to flee from Damascus before their depredations. Ibn Taymiyya's opinions on political authority and what constitutes fidelity to Islam thus occasionally represent a rupture *from* rather than a continuity *with* mainstream Islamic thought.[20] It should be pointed out though that, except in reference to the Mongols for whom he had conceived a deep personal animus, Ibn Taymiyya maintained in general that *takfir* among Muslims was a deplorable practice.[21]

The principle of *takfir* and the concept of *jihad* as unrelenting military activity waged against unbelievers as formulated by militant groups today represent a gross departure from well-established, majoritarian Muslim practices of accommodation and consensus-making. The greatest irony inherent in radical Islamism is that, for all its claims to be reviving authentic Qur'anic, prophetic, and *salafi* thought and practice, it betrays a clear debt to the ideologies of sectarian and deviant factions that it otherwise (purportedly) regards with disdain.

Conclusion

On the basis of our foregoing survey and comparison, it is quite clear that those whom we call "modernists" today are in fact much closer to the *salaf al-salih* in their world-view, as reflected in the early sources. In their receptivity to accountable, participatory modes of government, enhanced public roles for women, tolerant attitudes toward religious minorities, and emphasis on the adaptability of the religious law, modernists may be shown to draw upon the examples set by, apart from the Prophet himself, the Rashidun caliphs, many intrepid women Companions, and early pious scholars and authorities, such as al-Hasan al-Basri, Rabi'a al-'Adawiya, and Sufyan al-Thawri from the generation of the Successors. Paradoxically then, we are justified in calling the modernists the true *salafi*s or even "fundamentalists" in a positive vein on account of their focus on retrieving the fundamentals of their religious tradition and the earliest most historically reliable information regarding the *salaf*, shorn of the later interpolations and constructions which have generated on occasion skewed codes of conduct and legislation.

In contrast, Islamists often construct their Pious Forbears from late premodern sources, especially from the Mamluk period, which have tarred them to a considerable extent with an illiberal brush. Ibn Hajar's creative reconstruction of some of the women Companions' lives fits well with Islamist notions of women's restricted public roles, and Ibn Taymiyya's notions of *jihad* and *takfir, mutatis mutandis*, allow militant Islamists to legitimize the concept of a relentless bloody, global *jihad* against mainstream Muslims and non-Muslims. When claiming early Islamic parallels, radical

Islamist notions of *jihad* and *takfir* are discovered to conform to deviant notions of militancy and intolerance as prevailed among the Khawarij rather than among majoritarian Muslims or to conform to pre-modern statist, non-scriptural conceptions of *jihad* emanating from realpolitik concerns.

The reconstruction of the history of the formative period of Islam from the early sources concerns radical Islamists very little because such a project would undermine the claimed historicity of their ideology and political agenda. Thus, a fairly recent article tries to posit a first-century provenance for the term and concept of *al-hakimiyya* but, for obvious reasons, fails in this attempt.[1] The Islamists' articulation of political Islam as an "authentic" reading of Islam is of recent vintage and distorts the historical trajectory of a currently much-beleaguered faith tradition in whose name they claim to speak. Such a highly politicized version of Islam could not, in fact, have arisen earlier than the twentieth century, that is before the concatenation of specific historical circumstances that abetted the rise of Islamism – primarily the abolition of the caliphate by the republican Turks in 1924 and the disarray in much of the Islamic world under Western colonial occupation. A heightened sense of "Islamicness" reactively conceived in primarily political terms at a time of great vulnerability was – and remains – *a* compensatory response to the political supremacy of the modern West.

In recent times, the term *Salafiyya* has been claimed by many as a badge of pride and hurled by some at others as a term of opprobrium. In its neutral usage, it is a lofty sobriquet that points to the believer's basic admiration for the First Muslims, the first three generations of believers who were the closest to their Prophet, who had witnessed (in the case of the Companions) his very acts and listened to his very speech, and who carried with them vivid memories of their precious encounters with him. The First Muslims or the *Salaf* could not but be the best exemplars for succeeding generations of the faithful. The *Salafiyya*, by their very designation, are committed to replicating the spirit and world-view of these Pious Forbears, if not their very acts when feasible, adapted to their contemporary circumstances.

How the *salaf* are constructed thus has a very important bearing on the modern Muslim's perceptions of the world and his or her conduct in it. When the *salaf* are viewed through an illiberal prism, as through some of the later sources, the resulting *Salafiyya* can be (and have been) intolerant and repressive in their social and political policies. The *salaf*, when viewed through a liberal lens, as through quite a number of early and now modernist sources, can generate *Salafi*s who are (and have been) tolerant, magnanimous, and boldly innovative while attempting to remain true to certain core Islamic principles and their spirit. Thus, through the illiberal prism, some of the statements of the Companion Abu Hurayra (whose reports were often impugned for lack of reliability) are privileged, in which he asserts that, according to the Prophet, the ruler must always be obeyed, even if he is morally reprobate, so as to promote a politically authoritarian culture. When they wish to justify their curtailing of women's rights, illiberal *salafi*s show a preference for Ibn Hajar's later account of the lives of the women Companions over the earlier one of Ibn Sa'd. And if they wish to discriminate against non-Muslims, they invoke the later spurious Pact of 'Umar rather than the treaty signed by the Prophet with the Christians of Najran or that concluded by 'Umar with the residents of Jerusalem in the seventh century.

From the liberal perspective, Abu Bakr's inaugural speech recorded in early sources, in which he promises to consult with the people, asserts his accountability to them, and invites them to correct him if he should deviate, is understood as being supportive of and requiring consultative, democratic forms of government in Islamic societies today. Concerning the rights of women, the liberals point to early biographical and historical sources, which preserve accounts of women's robust participation in religious and humanitarian activities, as evidence of the gender egalitarian thrust of the early period. With regard to inter-faith relations and treatment of non-Muslims, the spirit of inclusiveness that prevailed in the early community toward Jews and Christians and the state's solicitude toward their poor and disadvantaged, as documented by the early scholar Abu Yusuf (d. 798) for example, are the instances which the liberal camp tends to underscore. The examples on both sides of the divide could go on. To some degree, how one "reads" the *salaf* is contingent on the kind of sources one chooses to consult and how one proceeds to interpret them.

For the believing Muslim, this historical-hermeneutic project remains a worthwhile and even urgent endeavor today. Given the fact that Islam's formative period remains contested among many, reclamation of this past in a responsible and historically defensible way must remain part and parcel of every contemporary reformist project that wishes to gain broad legitimacy and acceptance. Even a brief critical survey of the early sources and their comparison with later ones, as undertaken in this present study, allows us to remark that this project of reclamation is being done more credibly today by those we have termed "modernist" and/or "reformist" Muslims (called "liberal" or "moderate" by others) than by hard-line Islamists. These modernists have imbibed more than a drop of their illustrious forbears' penchant for robust faith, creative thinking, and fidelity to the core principles of their religion. In contrast, the illiberal and radical Islamists, for all their protestations to the contrary, have to a large degree undermined these core principles and betrayed the legacy of the earliest Muslims in their nihilistic quest for political power.

We conclude our book by affirming the continuing relevance of the lives of the First Muslims in the contemporary world wherever Muslims live, perhaps never more so than now. Will the modernists carry the day or their nemeses? Given that so much is at stake, this is no longer merely an academic question nor a question we can pose dispassionately. Careful, meticulous study of the legacy of the Pious Forbears and what it means will continue to have important repercussions for the behavior and world-view of most (observant) Muslims. It is hoped that this book will make a contribution to this passionate and remarkable conversation already underway.

Endnotes

INTRODUCTION

1. Another term identical with *muslim* in this broad non-confessional sense is *hanif*, a term applied to one who is an upright monotheist in a primordial sense, such as Abraham (for example, Qur'an 2:135; 6:79).

2. *Qur'anic Studies: Sources and Methods of Scriptural Interpretation* (Oxford, 1977); *The Sectarian Milieu: Content and Composition of Islamic Salvation History* (Oxford, 1978).

3. For this particular criticism and others, see Neal Robinson, *Discovering the Qur'an: A Contemporary Approach to a Veiled Text* (London, 1996), 51–59.

4. Michael Cook and Patricia Crone, *Hagarism: The Making of the Islamic World* (Cambridge, 1977), 3.

5. Among such amateurs is an anonymous person by the name of Ibn Warraq who appears to delight in using gratuitously offensive language. For critical reviews of some of his "edited" works, see, for example, Fred Donner's review of Ibn Warraq's *The Quest for the Historical Muhammad* (New York, 2000) in the *Middle East Studies Association Bulletin* 35 (2001):75; and my review of the same title in the *Journal of the American Oriental Society* 121 (2001):728–29.

6. See, for example, William Graham's review of *Qur'anic Studies*, in the *Journal of the American Oriental Society* 100 (1980):137–41.

7. See Fazlur Rahman's critique in his *Major Themes of the Qur'an* (Minneapolis, 1994), 55–56.

8. The collection of articles in *The Biography of Muhammad: The Issue of the Sources*, ed. Harald Motzki (Leiden, 2000), for example, indicates that the rejectionist attitude of the revisionists toward the sources is rather excessive. A number of the articles in this collection use early *hadith* works such as 'Abd al-Razzaq's *al-Musannaf* and Ibn Abi Shayba's *al-Musannaf* to point to the early provenance of a number of reports and thus their historical value for reconstructing the past; see, for instance, Gregor Schoeler, "Musa b. 'Uqba's Maghazi," 67–97. Many of the reports contained in 'Abd al-Razzaq's *al-Musannaf* have been carefully assessed and dated to roughly the

late seventh century by Harald Motzki in his article "The Musannaf of 'Abd al-Raz-zaq al-San'ani as a source of authentic ahadith of the first century A.H.," in *Journal of Near Eastern Studies* 50 (1991):1–21.

9. For a preliminary report, see Gerd-R. Puin, "Observations on Early Qur'an Manuscripts in San'a'," in *The Qur'an as Text*, ed. Stefan Wild (Leiden, 1996), 107–11; cf. the article "Manuscripts of the Qur'an," *Encyclopaedia of the Qur'an*, ed. Jane McAuliffe (Leiden, 2003), 3:255–62.

10. C. H. M Versteegh has produced an erudite study of a number of these early works; see his *Arabic Grammar and Qur'anic Exegesis in Early Islam* (Leiden, 1993).

11. Mujahid ibn Jabr, *Tafsir Mujahid*, ed. 'Abd al-Rahman al-Tahir b. Muhammad al-Surta (Cairo, n.d.).

12. Cf. Harald Motzki, "The collection of the Qur'an," *Der Islam* 78 (2001):1–35, in which he marshals new evidence which point to the early redaction of the Qur'an.

13. See my *Excellence and Precedence: Medieval Islamic Discourse on Legitimate Leadership* (Leiden, 2002).

14. For an extensive discussion of *sabiqa* and its role as a socio-political organizational principle, see ibid., 36–79.

15. See, for example, Leila Ahmed, *Women and Gender in Islam* (New Haven, 1992), 41–78; and my article, "Reconstituting Women's Lives: Gender and the Poetics of Narrative in Medieval Biographical Works," *The Muslim World* 92 (2002): 461–80.

16. See, for example, Fazlur Rahman, *Islamic Methodology in History* (Karachi, 1965); the articles in the previously mentioned *The Biography of Muhammad*, edited by Harald Motzki; A. A. Duri, *The Rise of Historical Writing among the Arabs*, trans. Lawrence I. Conrad (Princeton, 1983); and Fred Donner, *Narratives of Islamic Origins: The Beginnings of Islamic Historical Writing* (Princeton, 1998).

CHAPTER 1

1. See, for example, W. Montgomery Watt, *Muhammad at Mecca* (Oxford, 1953).

2. See Martin Lings, *Muhammad: His Life Based on the Earliest Sources* (Cambridge, 1995), 31–32 (first published in Great Britain in 1983 by George Allen and Unwin).

3. Ibid., 272.

4. M. M. Bravmann, *The Spiritual Background of Early Islam: Studies in Ancient Arab Concepts* (Leiden: 1972), 67.

5. See the excellent study by Toshihiko Izutsu, *Ethico-religious concepts in the Qur'an* (Montreal, 1966).

6. Lings, *Muhammad*, 104. This genre of literature is believed by a number of scholars to have influenced Dante's *Inferno*.

7. See his *Muhammad at Medina* (Oxford, 1956), 225.

8. Ibn Hisham, *al-Sira al-nabawiyya* ("The Prophet's Biography"), ed. Suhayl Zakkar (Beirut, 1992), 1:350.

9. For the full text of the Constitution and an analysis of its main tenets, see Watt, *Muhammad*, 221–25. I am slightly adapting Watt's translation in parts. For the Arabic original, see Ibn Hisham, *Sira*, 1:351 ff.

10. R. B. Serjeant, "The Constitution of Medina," *The Islamic Quarterly* 8 (1964), 3–16; idem, "The Sunnah Jami'ah, Pacts with the Yathrib Jews and the *Tahrim* of Yathrib: Analysis and Translation of the Documents Comprised in the So-Called 'Constitution of Medina,' " *Bulletin of the School of Oriental and African Studies* 41 (1978), 1–42.

11. We will discuss in some detail the Qur'anic ethics of war and peace and the classical juridical treatment of this topic in a later chapter.

12. According to the details given by Ibn Ishaq (as recorded by Ibn Hisham), the Prophet set up the equivalent of an ad hoc tribunal and secured the agreement of all to abide by a decision to be made, not personally by him, but by a third party from an allied tribe. These terms were acceptable to all sides. Sa'd ibn Mu'adh's decision was in accordance with the Old Testament concept of justice to be meted out to those vanquished in a battle and does not represent an exercise in mere retaliation; see Ibn Hisham, *Sira*, 2:713 ff.

For a different view altogether by an author who argues on the basis of a close analysis of the narratives regarding this incident and the lack of Qur'anic reference to it that these events may not have occurred at all and are the product of a literary imagination, see W. N. Arafat, "New Light on the Story of Banu Qurayza and the Jews of Medina," *Journal of the Royal Asiatic Society of Great Britain and Ireland* (1976):100–107. Among the points worth considering are that Ibn Ishaq, who is the main source of this story, was inclined to accept tales more for their narrative appeal than their probable veracity and was dubbed a liar on account of this by other more punctilious scholars. Furthermore, the Qurayza stories are full of topoi similar to those of other Jewish stories and myths, such as the Masada story, and strongly suggest that Ibn Ishaq reported fanciful details related by his contemporary Jewish sources.

13. See Lings, *Muhammad*, 268.

14. For example, see Mark R. Cohen, *Under Crescent and Cross: The Jews in the Middle Ages* (Princeton, 1994), esp. 30–74.

15. Ibn Hisham, *Sira*, 2:783 ff.

16. Lings, *Muhammad*, 258–59.

17. Al-Tabari, *Jami' al-bayan 'an ta'wil ay al-qur'an* ("The Compendium of Eloquence concerning Interpretation of the Verses of the Qur'an") (Beirut, 1977), 14:435–36.

18. This view is expressed in a *hadith* in which the Prophet states, "Not one of those who pledged their allegiance under the tree will enter the Fire." According to A. J. Wensinck, *Concordance et Indices de la Tradition musulmane* (Leiden, 1969),

7:37, this *hadith* is recorded by Muslim, Abu Da'ud, and Ahmad ibn Hanbal. Another report recorded by Ibn Hanbal from Jabir quotes the Prophet as saying, "Any man who witnessed Badr and al-Hudaybiyya will not enter the Fire," reported in 'Abd al-Ghani al-Nabulsi, *Ahl al-janna wa-ahl al-nar* (Cairo, 1983), 28.

19. Ibn Hisham, *Sira*, 2:787.

20. See Lings, *Muhammad*, 302.

21. Ibid., 303.

22. Ibid., 326.

23. Ibn Hisham, *Sira*, 2:1027.

24. Ibid.

25. Ibn Sa'd, *Al-Tabaqat al-kubra*, 1:259–261, ed. Muhammad 'Abd al-Qadir 'Ata (Beirut, 1997); cf. Lings, *Muhammad*, 291–92.

26. Ibn Hisham, *Sira*, 2:1023–24. Translation based on http://islamicity.com/articles/Articles.asp?ref=IC0107-322

27. Cf. Abdulaziz Sachedina, *The Islamic Roots of Democratic Pluralism* (Oxford, 2001), 32–35.

28. Sunni *hadith* compilers who include this report include al-Tirmidhi, Ibn Maja, and Ibn Hanbal; for this discussion, see Afsaruddin, *Excellence and Precedence*, 158 ff.

29. See Afsaruddin, *Excellence and Precedence*, 165–69.

30. Abu Nu'aym al-Isbahani, *Dala'il al-nubuwwa* ("The Signs of Prophethood") (Hyderabad, 1950), 139.

31. Annemarie Schimmel, *And Muhammad is His Messenger* (Chapel Hill, 1985), 25.

32. Muslim, *Sahih Muslim* ("The Sound Collection of Muslim") (Beirut, 1995), 4:1464, #140; for variant *hadiths*, see also ibid., #139, 141,

33. Translated and quoted by Schimmel, *And Muhammad*, 46.

34. For a recent assessment of the Prophet's legacy in such a vein, see Tariq Ramadan, *In the Footsteps of the Prophet: Lessons from the Life of Muhammad* (Oxford, 2007), esp. 211–16.

35. Thus 'Abd al-Karim al-Jili wrote a work entitled *al-Insan al-Kamil*, translated by R. J. Nicholson in his *Studies in Islamic Mysticism* (Cambridge, 1921).

36. Translated by Arthur Jeffrey, *A Reader on Islam* (The Hague, 1962), 610.

CHAPTER 2

1. See 'Abd al-Jalil Razi, *Kitab al-naqd* ("Book of Criticism"), ed. S. Jalal al-Din Muhaddith (Tehran, 1952), 656–64; Muhammad Dja'far Mahdjoub, "The Evolution of Popular Eulogy of the Imams among the Shi'a," in *Authority and Political Culture in Shi'ism*, ed. Said Amir Arjomand (Albany, 1988), 54.

2. Qur'an 9:40 runs: "... the second of the two, when they were in the cave, he said to his companion, 'Be not distressed, for indeed God is with us.' Then God sent down His tranquility upon him and strengthened him with forces which you could not see, and made the word of those who disbelieved the most base while the word of God became the loftiest, and God is Almighty, All-Wise."

3. Al-Nasa'i, *Fada'il al-sahaba* ("Excellences of the Companions"), ed. Faruq Hamada (Casablanca, 1984), 55–56.

4. Al-Tabari, *Ta'rikh al-umam wa-'l-muluk* ("The History of Nations and Kings") (Beirut, 1997), 2:242–43. Other versions of this famous speech occur in various sources.

5. 'Amr ibn Bahr al-Jahiz, *Risalat al-'uthmaniyya* ("The Treatise of the 'Uthmaniyya"), ed. 'Abd al-Salam Harun (Cairo, 1955), 202.

6. Ibid., 43 ff.

7. Al-Ya'qubi, *Kitab al-ta'rikh* ("History"), ed. M. T. Houtsma (Leiden, 1883), 2:137; Afsaruddin, *Excellence and Precedence*, 29–30.

8. It should be pointed out that the appellation Bakriyya is used with some imprecision in our literature and appears to have been applied to two primary groups of different provenance. The first reference is to an earlier amorphous group from the seventh century which is said to have sprung up immediately after the Prophet's death and which proclaimed Abu Bakr's greater precedence in claiming the caliphate. For a fuller account of the Bakriyya, see my article "In Praise of the Caliphs: Recreating History from the *Manaqib* Literature," *International Journal of Middle East Studies* 31 (1999):329–50.

9. Ibn Abi 'l-Hadid, *Sharh nahj al-balagha* ("Commentary on 'The Path of Eloquence'"), ed. Muhammad Abu 'l-Fadl Ibrahim (Cairo, 1959–64), 11:48–50, 338.

10. Roy Mottahedeh, *Loyalty and Leadership in an Early Islamic Society* (Princeton, NJ, 1980), 98–104.

11. It is necessary to qualify this, however, by noting that someone who possessed *hasab* (*hasib*) could also be an individual who had acquired individual merit without an illustrious lineage; see the article "Hasab wa-Nasab," in *Encyclopaedia of Islam*, new edn., ed. H. Gibb et al. (Leiden and London, 1960–2002; henceforth to be referred to as *EI²*), 4:239.

12. This trend is well-documented by Louise Marlow in her *Hierarchy and Egalitarianism in Islamic Thought* (Cambridge, UK, 1997), passim.

13. Al-Jahiz, *'Uthmaniyya*, 196.

14. Cited by Muhammad Baqir al-Majlisi, *Bihar al-anwar: al-jam'a li-durar akhbar al-a'imma al-athar* ("The Seas of Lights: the Collection of Pearls of Sayings of the Pure Imams") (Tehran, 1956–83), 7:241–42.

15. ʿAli ibn Ibrahim al-Qummi, *Tafsir* ("Exegesis"), ed. Tayyib al-Musawi al-Jaraʾiri (Najaf, 1966), 2:94; al-Majlisi, *Bihar al-anwar*, 7:239.

16. Al-Qummi, *Tafsir*, 2:94.

17. Other verses that make this equation between righteous deeds and "inheriting" the earth, explicitly or implicitly, are Qurʾan 7:69; 7:169; 17:38; 57:7; 6:133; 4:133; 14:19; 28:5–6; and 35:16.

18. Cf. Martin Hinds, "Kufan Political Alignments and Their Background in the Mid-Seventh Century A.D.," *International Journal of Middle East Studies* 2 (1971):347.

19. Cf. Marlow, *Hierarchy and Egalitarianism*, 14.

20. See this discussion in Afsaruddin, *Excellence and Precedence*, 75–79.

21. Thus the pro-ʿAlid historian Ahmad al-Yaʿqubi relates that Abu Bakr once ruefully remarked that he wished he had asked the Prophet who would succeed him; see his *Taʾrikh al-Yaʾqubi* (Beirut, n.d.), 2:137.

22. Cf. Fred Donner, "La Question de Messanisme dans l'Islam primitif," *Revue du Monde Musulman et de la Mediterranée* (forthcoming); Mahmoud M. Ayoub, *The Crisis of Muslim History: Religion and Politics in Early Islam* (Oxford, 2003), 145.

CHAPTER 3

1. Cf. Ibn ʿAbd al-Barr, *Jamiʾ bayan al-ʿilm wa-fadlihi* ("Compendium on the Exposition of Knowledge and Its Merits") (Medina, n.d.), 2:85; 102; ʿAbd al-Jabbar, *Tathbit dalaʾil al-nubuwwa* ("Confirming the Signs of Prophethood") (Beirut, 1966), 227–28.

2. For this version of the *hadith*, see Muslim, *Sahih*, 4:1491, #33; al-Nasaʾi, *Sunan* ("Reports [of the Prophet]"), ed. Hasan Muhammad al-Masʿudi (Cairo, 1930), 6:6.

3. Al-Jahiz, *ʿUthmaniyya*, 81.

4. Al-Jahiz, "Istihqaq al-imama" ("Qualifications for leadership of the polity"), in *Rasaʾil al-Jahiz* ("Treatises of al-Jahiz"), ed. ʿAli Bu Milhim (Beirut, n.d.), 158.

5. Al-Jahiz, *ʿUthmaniyya*, 24.

6. See M. A. Shaban, *Islamic History: A New Interpretation* (Cambridge, UK, 1971), 18–19; and Fred Donner, *The Early Islamic Conquests* (Princeton, 1981), 84–85.

7. Articles which discuss the identity of these early Qurʾan reciters/readers include G. H. A. Juynboll, "The *Qurraʾ* in Early Islamic History," *Journal of Economic and Social History* 16 (1973): 113–29; Norman Calder, "The *Qurraʾ* and the Arabic Lexicographical Tradition," *Journal of Semitic Studies* 36 (1991):305; and my "The Excellences of the Qurʾan: Textual Sacrality and the Organization of Early Islamic Society," *Journal of the American Oriental Society* 122 (2002):13–18.

8. Al-Khazin al-Baghdadi, *Lubab al-ta'wil* ("The Essence of Interpretation") (Cairo, 1961), 2:54. See also 'Abd al-Jabbar, *Tathbit*, 418, where 'Ali expresses special approval for Abu Bakr's decision not to give in to the rebels.

9. Ibn Abi Da'ud, *Kitab al-masahif* ("Book of the Qur'an Copies"), ed. Arthur Jeffrey (Leiden, 1937), 5–10.

10. Ibn Taymiyya, *Risala fi tafdil al-shaykhayn 'ala mu'asir al-sahaba* ("Treatise on the Superiority of the Two Shaykhs [sc. Abu Bakr and 'Umar] over the [Other] Companions"), Ms. Istanbul Universitesi Kutuphanesi, catalog no. A2882, fol. 9.

11. Muslim, *Sahih*, 7:108.

12. 'Abd al-Razzaq, *al-Musannaf* ("The Indexed Collection"), ed. Ayman Nasr al-Din al-Azhari (Beirut, 2000), 5:266.

13. Ahmad ibn Hanbal, *Fada'il al-sahaba* ("The Excellences of the Companions"), ed. Wasi Allah ibn Muhammad 'Abbas (Mecca, 1983), 1:239, #295.

14. Ibn Taymiyya, *Minhaj al-sunna al-nabawiyya* ("The Way to the Prophet's Normative Practices"), ed. Muhammad Rashad Salim (Saudi Arabia, 1986), 7:120–21.

15. From *The Saints: A Concise Biographical Dictionary*, ed. John Coulson (New York, 1957).

16. Al-Muhibb al-Tabari, *Al-Riyad al-nadira fi manaqib al-'ashara* ("The Verdant Gardens Concerning the Excellences of the Ten [Companions]") (Cairo, 1327), 1:199; Al-Dhahabi, *Siyar a'lam al-nubala'* ("Lives of the Noble Luminaries"), ed. Shu'ayb al-Arna'ut (Beirut, 1998), volume entitled "Siyar al-Khulafa' al-Rashidun," 76.

17. As translated by Lings, *Muhammad*, 86.

18. Ibid., 86–87.

19. Al-Dhahabi, *Siyar a'lam al-nubala*, vol. "al-Khulafa' ", 74–75.

20. Ibn Sa'd, *al-Tabaqat al-kubra* ("The Great Generations") (Beirut, 1998) 3:294–304; al-Baladhuri, *Futuh al-buldan* ("The Conquests of Countries"), ed. M. J. de Goeje (Leiden, 1866), 448 ff.; Abu 'Ubayd Ibn Sallam, *Kitab al-nasab* ("The Book of Lineage") (Beirut, 1989), 74–78; Abu Yusuf, *Kitab al-kharaj* ("The Book of Land-Tax"), ed. Ihsan 'Abbas (Beirut and Cairo, 1985), 140–44.

21. Ibn al-Jawzi, *Sirat 'umar ibn al-khattab* ("The Life of 'Umar ibn al-Khattab") (Cairo, n.d.), 53.

22. According to one report, each of the Prophet's wives was given 12,000 dirhams as opposed to 5,000 dirhams for each Migrant and Helper who had participated in Badr; see, for example, Abu Yusuf, *Kitab al-kharaj*, 141.

23. *Al-Fisal fi 'l-milal wa-'l-ahwa' wa-'l-nihal*, ("Divisions in Communities, Trends, and Creeds"), ed. 'Abd al-Rahman Khalifa (Cairo, 1928), 4:91, and also 4:94, where he refers to Qur'an, 33:6, which states, "The Prophet is closer to the faithful than themselves and his wives are their mothers." In Ibn Hazm's understanding, the

companionship of the wives to the Prophet is thus endowed with a special quality denied to the rest of the Companions. Reports which state that 'A'isha headed the register of pensions are, therefore, far more credible than reports which state that al-'Abbas, the Prophet's uncle and a late convert to Islam, was at the top of the list; cf., Ibn al-Jawzi, *Sirat 'Umar*, 53.

24. Ibn Sa'd, *Tabaqat*, 3:213 ff; al-Maqrizi, *Kitab al-khitat al-maqriziyya* ("Maqrizi's Book of Topography") (Lebanon, 1959), 1:163–67. For a pro-kinship, pro-'Abbasid report, see Abu Yusuf, *Kitab al-kharaj*, 143–44.

25. Abu 'Ubayd Ibn Sallam, *Kitab al-amwal* ("The Book of Revenues"), ed. 'Abd al-Amir 'Ali Sahanna (Beirut, n.d.), 268.

26. Ibid., 267; see also Abu Yusuf, *Kitab al-kharaj*, 140.

27. *Kitab al-kharaj*, 140.

28. Al-Maqrizi, *al-Khitat*, 1:163–67.

29. Ibid., 165.

30. Ibid.

31. Ibn Taymiyya, *Minhaj al-sunna*, 6:101 ff.

32. See al-Bukhari, *al-Sahih* ("The Sound Collection") (Cairo, 1973–90), 6:389, #3692; Muslim, *Sahih*, 3:1109, #57.

33. See Abu Yusuf, *Kitab al-Kharaj*, 142–43, which reports that 'Abd Allah ibn 'Umar protested to 'Umar, his father, when he found out that the latter had given him a stipend smaller than that of another Companion, Usama ibn Zayd. 'Umar justified this by saying, "Indeed, the father of Usama [sc. Zayd ibn al-Harith, Muhammad's adopted son] was more beloved of the Messenger of God, peace and blessings be upon him, than your father, and Usama was more beloved of the Messenger of God, peace and blessings be upon him, than you."

34. For example, Ibn Sa'd, *Tabaqat*, 3:213; al-Tabari, *Ta'rikh*, 2:569.

35. Julius Wellhausen, *The Arab Kingdom and Its Fall*, trans. M. G. Weir (Calcutta, 1927), 138; and Shaban, *Islamic History*, 57.

36. Al-Tabari, *Ta'rikh*, 2:569. See further my discussion of these various titles and what they connoted in *Excellence and Precedence*, 160, f.n. 56.

37. Ibn 'Abd al-Barr, *al-Riyad al-nadira*, 1:190.

38. Ibn Taymiyya, *Minhaj al-sunna*, 6:96 ff.

39. Cf. for example, Malik ibn Anas, *al-Muwatta'* ("The Smooth Path"), ed. Bashshar 'Awad Ma'ruf and Mahmud Muhammad Khalil (Beirut, 1993), 2:15 ff.

40. Muhammad Asad, *The Message of the Qur'an* (Gibraltar, 1980), 150.

41. Al-Tabari, *Ta'rikh*, 2:570.

42. Ibn Abi Da'ud, *Kitab al-masahif*, 50–52; 85–87.

43. Ibid., 53–54.

44. Al-Tabari, *Jami' al-bayan*, 14:438–39.

45. I am borrowing this term from Wael B. Hallaq, *The Origins and Evolution of Islamic Law* (Cambridge, 2005), 165.

46. Al-Baladhuri, *Kitab futuh al-buldan* ("The Book of the Conquests of the Lands"), trans. by Philip Hitti as *The Origins of the Islamic State* (New York, 1916), 211.

47. Quoted in Bernard Lewis, *The Arabs in History*, rev. edn. (New York, 1966), 58.

48. Quoted in T. W. Arnold, *The Preaching of Islam* (New York, 1913), 54.

49. For a useful review of these various interpretations, see Fred M. Donner, *The Early Islamic Conquests* (Princeton, 1981), 3–9.

50. For this discussion, see Barbara Freyer Stowasser, "The *Hijab*: How a Curtain Became an Institution and a Cultural Symbol," in *Humanism, Culture and Language in the Near East: Studies in Honor of Georg Krotkoff*, eds. Asma Afsaruddin and A. H. Mathias Zahniser (Winona Lake, IN, 1997), 87–104.

51. Ibid., 90 ff.

52. Reported, for example, by al-Shawkani, *Fath al-qadir: al-jami' bayna fannay al-riwaya wa-'l-diraya min 'ilm al-tafsir* ("The Opening for the Capable: the Book that Combines Narrative Reports and Reflection with regard to Knowledge of Exegesis") (Beirut, 1996), 1:563.

53. Al-Dhahabi, *Siyar a'lam al-nubala*, vol. "al-Khulafa' ", 76.

54. Our discussion in chapters 7 and 8 regarding the appropriation of the Pious Forbears as paradigmatic figures by both the modernists and hard-line Islamists will refer to this issue again.

55. Al-Turtushi, *Siraj al-Muluk* ("The Lamps of the Kings"), ed. Ja'far Bayati (London, 1990), 229–30.

56. Mark R. Cohen refers to these medieval regulations as Byzantine Christian-Roman Jewry law; see his *Under Crescent and Cross*, 55.

57. A. S. Tritton, *The Caliphs and Their Non-Muslim Subjects* (London, 1930), 8 ff.

58. This is an ancient name for Jerusalem.

59. Slightly modified from Arnold's translation, *Preaching*, 56.

60. See al-Tabari, *Ta'rikh*, 2:449.

61. Arnold, *Preaching*, 57.

62. Cf. the *hadith* in which the Prophet states, "I am the guardian of a person who has no guardian;" recorded by al-Tirmidhi, *al-Jami'a al-sahih* ("The Sound Compendium"), ed. Kamal Yusuf al-Hut (Beirut, n.d.), 4:367.

63. Abu Yusuf, *Kitab al-kharaj*, 122.

64. Ibid., 126.

65. In the early period, *sadaqa* was the catch-all term for all obligatory alms or taxes paid by the Muslims, and used usually synonymously with *zakat*.

66. Abu Yusuf, *Kitab al-kharaj*, 144.

67. See Robert Schick, *The Christian Communities of Palestine from Byzantine to Islamic*

Rule (Princeton, 1995), 77–80, 96–7; Michael Morony, *Iraq after the Muslim Conquest* (Princeton, 1984), 332–83.

68. Morony, *Iraq*, 68–74.

69. Zafar Ishaq Ansari, "Islamic Juristic Terminology before Shafiʻi: A Semantic Analysis with Special Reference to Kufa," *Arabica* 19 (1972): 255–300.

70. As pointed out by Bravmann, *Spiritual Background*, 138–39. See further the discussion of these concepts and their interchangeability in the early period by Wael B. Hallaq, *A History of Islamic Legal Theories: An introduction to Sunni usul al-fiqh* (Cambridge, 1999), 46–52.

71. See his *Tafsir al-Qurtubi* ("The Qur'an Commentary of al-Qurtubi") (Cairo, n.d.), 2:1491–92.

72. Ibid., 2:1491.

CHAPTER 4

1. See the entry on ʻUthman in Ibn Saʻd, *Tabaqat*, 3:53–79.

2. Shaban, *Islamic History*, 63.

3. Mentioned by Bravmann, *Spiritual Background*, 126–29.

4. A detailed recounting of the recension of the Qur'an under ʻUthman is given by Ibn Abi Da'ud, *Kitab al-masahif*, 18–26; see also al-Bukhari, *Sahih al-Bukhari*, ed. Qasim al-Shammaʻi al-Rifaʻi (Beirut, n.d.), 6:580–86 (subsequent references to al-Bukhari's *Sahih* will refer to this edition only); al-Suyuti, *al-Itqan fi ʻulum al-Qur'an* ("Certitude concerning the Sciences of the Qur'an"), ed. Mustafa Dib al-Bugha (Damascus, 1993), 1:157–58.

5. Ibn Abi Da'ud, *Kitab al-masahif*, 11–12.

6. Al-Bukhari, *Sahih*, 6:582–84.

7. *The Cambridge History of Arabic Literature: Arabic Literature to the End of the Umayyad Period*, ed. A. F. L. Beeston et al. (Cambridge, 1983), 243.

8. Al-Baladhuri, *Ansab al-ashraf*, ed. S. Goitein (Jerusalem, 1936), 5:36.

9. For a discussion and comparison of the "cave" vs the "decoy" event, see Afsaruddin, *Excellence and Precedence*, 183–96.

10. Ibid., 52–79.

11. Shaban, *Islamic History*, 72–78.

12. See the article "Imama," *EI²*, 3:1164.

13. See Muhammad Qasim Zaman, *Religion and Politics under the Early ʻAbbasids: The Emergence of the Proto-Sunni Elite* (Leiden, 1997), 171 ff.

14. Al-Bukhari, *Sahih*, 6:79. This is a widely quoted *hadith* in later Sunni works; see, for example, Ahmad al-Khallal, *al-Sunna* (Riyadh, 1994), pt. 2, 371, #507.

15. Abu Da'ud, *Sahih Sunan Abi Da'ud* ("Sound *Hadith*s of Abu Da'ud"), ed. Muhammad Nasir al-Din al-Albani (Beirut, 1989), 3:876, #3870; #3871.

16. Muhammad ibn Yusuf al-Kindi, *Wulat misr* ("The Governors of Egypt") (Beirut, 1959), 39, 42; Montgomery Watt, *The Formative Period of Islamic Thought* (Edinburgh, 1973), 77; Wilferd Madelung, *The Succession to Muhammad* (Cambridge, 1997), 153 ff.

17. Josef van Ess, *Frühe mu'tazilitische Häresiographie: zwei Werke des Nasi' al-Akbar* (Beirut and Wiesbaden, 1971), 60–61.

18. Watt, *Formative Period*, 77; also 333–34.

19. Cf. al-Khallal, *Sunna*, pt. 2, 378–83.

20. For a discussion of these views, see Saleh Said Agha, "A Viewpoint of the Murji'a in the Umayyad Period: Evolution through Application," *Journal of Islamic Studies* 8 (1997):36. For the Murji'a, see the article "Murdji'a," *EI²*, 7:605–607.

21. Al-Baghdadi, *al-Farq bayna 'l-firaq* ("The Division among the Sects"), ed. Muhammad 'Uthman al-Khusht (Cairo, n.d.), 302.

22. According to a report not found in the six authoritative Sunni *hadith* works, there were ten Companions, which included the Rashidun caliphs, who were promised Paradise by the Prophet. For a discussion of the possible political implications of this report, see Maya Yazigi, "*Hadith al-'ashara* or the Political Uses of a Tradition," *Studia Islamica* 86 (1997):159–67.

23. This is, in all likelihood, a reference to the Treaty of Hudaybiyya concluded in 628.

24. Al-Baghdadi, *Farq*, 303–34; also reported by al-Suyuti, *Ta'rikh al-khulafa'* ("History of the Caliphs") (Beirut, 1969), 41. Al-Baghdadi, however, excepts a man called Quzman from the list of those who participated at Uhud, for he committed suicide.

25. Al-Baghdadi, *Farq*, 1:62.

CHAPTER 5

1. Ibn Sa'd, *Tabaqat*, 2:376. For Ibn Sa'd's role, as well as that of some of his contemporaries, in the articulation of a distinctive Sunni Islam, see the recent comprehensive study by Scott C. Lucas, *Constructive Critics, Hadith Literature, and the Articulation of Sunni Islam: The Legacy of the Generation of Ibn Sa'd, Ibn Ma'in, and Ibn Hanbal* (Leiden, 2004).

2. See also the article " 'Abd Allah b. al-'Abbas," *EI²*, 1:40–41.

3. Al-Fasawi, *Kitab al-ma'rifa wa-'l-ta'rikh* ("The Book of Knowledge and History"), ed. Akram Diya' al-'Asmari (Baghdad, 1976), 1:495.

4. Abu Nu'aym, *Hilyat al-awliya' wa-tabaqat al-asfiya'* ("The Ornaments of the Friends [of God] and Generations of the Pure"), ed. Mustafa 'Abd al-Qadir 'Ata (Beirut, 1997), 1:389.

5. See *EI²*, 1:40–41.

6. Ibn Abi Da'ud, *Kitab al-masahif*, 21–23; *The Cambridge History of Arabic Literature: Arabic Literature to the End of the Umayyad Period*, ed. A. F. L. Beeston et al. (Cambridge, 1993), 1:236 ff.

7. Rashid Ahmad, "Qur'anic exegesis" in *Islamic Quarterly* 12 (1960):80.

8. Abu Nu'aym, *Hilyat al-awliya'*, 1:388.

9. For a general account of his life, see Ibn Sa'd, *Tabaqat*, 3:150–161; article "Ibn Mas'ud," *EI²*, 3:873–75.

10. Ibn Sa'd, *Tabaqat*, 3:151–57.

11. Ibn Abi Da'ud, *Kitab al-masahif*, 13–18; al-Baladhuri, *Ansab al-ashraf*, 5:36.

12. *Cambridge History of Arabic Literature: Arabic Literature to the End of the Umayyad Period*, 1:238.

13. See *EI²*, 3:874–75.

14. Ibn Sa'd, *Tabaqat*, 8:53.

15. Ibn Sa'd, *Tabaqat*, 8:63, 66; Ibn Hajar, *al-Isaba fi tamyiz al-sahaba* ("Correct Comprehension of the Distinction of the Companions") (Beirut, n.d.), 8:140.

16. Ibn Sa'd, *Tabaqat*, 8:58–62; Ibn Hajar, *Isaba*, 8:139.

17. Abu Nu'aym, *Hilyat al-awliya'*, 2:55.

18. Nabia Abbott, *Aishah, the Beloved of Mohammed* (London, 1998), 67–68.

19. Abu Nu'aym, *Hilyat al-awliya'*, 2:54.

20. Ibn Sa'd, *Tabaqat*, 8:63–64; with a variant list given in ibid., 8:65; also in Ibn Hajar, *al-Isaba*, 8:141.

21. Ibn Hisham, *Kitab sirat rasul Allah* ("The Book of the Life of the Messenger of God"), ed. F. Wüstenfeld (Göttingen, 1858–60; repr. Frankfurt, 1961), 1:731–40; al-Waqidi, *Kitab al-maghazi* ("The Book of Military Expeditions"), ed. Marsden Jones (London, 1965), 2:427–40.

22. Abbott, *Aishah*, 175, citing al-Tabari, *Ta'rikh* ("Annales"), ed. M. J. de Goeje (Lugduni Batavorum, 1879–1901), 1:3185.

23. Ibid., 165–76.

24. Reported by Ibn Hajar al-'Asqalani, *Tahdhib al-tahdhib* (roughly "Superior Instruction") (Beirut, 1996), 5:623.

25. For this discussion, see Abbott, "Women and the State in Early Islam," *Journal of Near Eastern Studies* 1(1942):121–24; Fatima Mernissi, *The Veil and the Male Elite: A Feminist Interpretation of Women's Rights in Islam* (Reading, MA, 1991), 49–61.

26. Ibn Sa'd, *Tabaqat*, 8:66; Ibn Hajar, *Isaba*, 8:140.

27. Abbott, *Aishah*, 203.

28. Aisha Geissinger, "The Exegetical Traditions of 'A'isha: Notes on their Impact and Significance," *Journal of Qur'anic Studies* 6 (2004):1–17.

29. Ibn Hajar, *Isaba*, 8:140

30. Ibid.; also in Ibn 'Abd al-Barr, *Kitab al-isti'ab fi ma'rifat al-ashab* ("The Book of Comprehension regarding Knowledge of the Companions"), ed. 'Ali Muhammad Mu'awwad and Jum'a Tahir al-Najjar (Beirut, 1995), 4:437.

31. Abu Nu'aym, *Hilyat al-awliya'*, 2:57–58.

32. Ibn Sa'd, *Tabaqat*, 8:66.

33. Muhammad ibn Bahadur al-Zarkashi, *al-Ijaba li-irad ma istadrakathu 'A'isha 'ala al-sahaba* ("A Presentation of 'A'isha's Elucidation of Certain Matters to the Companions") (Cairo, 1965), 20 ff.

34. Ibn Sa'd, *Tabaqat*, 8:73–74.

35. Ibid., 8:412–416.

36. Ibid., 8:413.

37. Ibid., 8:416.

38. Ibid., 3:233.

39. Abu Nu'aym, *Hilyat al-awliya'*, 1:199.

40. Ibn Sa'd, *Tabaqat*, 3:236.

41. Abu Nu'aym, *Hilyat al-awliya'*, 1:202.

42. Ibn Qutayba, *Ta'wil mukhtalif al-hadith* ("Explanation of Differences in Hadiths"), ed. 'Abd al-Qadir Ahmad 'Ata (Cairo, 1982), 39, 61.

43. For a survey of the literature on 'A'isha and her changing image through time, see Denise Spellberg, *Politics, Gender and the Islamic Past: The Legacy of 'A'isha bint Abi Bakr* (New York, 1994).

44. Pro-Mu'awiya sentiment flourished during the 'Abbasid period; see Charles Pellat, "Le culte de Mu'awiya au IIIe siecle de l'hegire," *Studia Islamica* 6 (1956):53–66.

45. Al-Tabarani, *al-Mu'jam al-awsat* ("The Middle Compendium"), ed. Tariq ibn 'Iwad Allah ibn Muhammad and 'Abd al-Muhsin ibn Ibrahim al-Husayni (Cairo, 1995), 3:339, #3336.

46. 'Abd al-Mun'im Salih al-'Ali, *al-Difa' 'an Abi Hurayra* ("In Defense of Abu Hurayra") (Beirut, 1973).

CHAPTER 6

1. See particularly Bulliet's two works *Conversion to Islam in the Medieval Period: An Essay in Quantitative History* (Cambridge, MA, 1979); and *Islam: the View from the Edge* (New York, 1994); cf. idem, *The Case for Islamo-Christian Civilization* (New York, 2004), 16–26. For the situation in Iraq in particular, see Morony, *Iraq after the Muslim Conquest*, passim; and for Palestine, Gil, *A History of Palestine*, passim.

2. Bulliet, *Islam: the View from the Edge*, 39–40. Cf. Jamsheed K. Choksy, *Conflict and Cooperation: Zoroastrian Subalterns and Muslim Elites in Medieval Iranian Society* (New York, 1997).

3. Schick, *Christian Communities of Palestine*, 158.

4. Gerald Hawting, *The First Dynasty of Islam: the Umayyad Caliphate AD 661–750*, 2nd edn (London, 2000), 106.

5. Al-Tabari, *Ta'rikh*, 3:298.

6. Al-Suyuti, *al-La'ali 'l-masnu'a fi 'l-ahadith al-mawdu'a* ("The Artificial Pearls concerning Fabricated Reports") (Beirut, n.d.), 1:293.

7. For a fuller discussion of this topic, see Werner Ende, *Arabische Nation und islamische Geschichte. Die Umayyaden im Urteil arabischer Autoren des 20 Jahrhunderts* (Beirut, 1977).

8. See article "Mukhtar ibn Abi 'Ubayd," *EI²*, 7:521–24.

9. Cf. al-Tabari, *Ta'rikh*, 3:476–78; Shaban, *Islamic History*, 95–6.

10. Cf. Steven M. Wasserstrom, *Between Muslim and Jew: the Problem of Symbiosis in Early Islam* (Princeton, 1995), 47–71.

11. For a detailed study of the Kaysaniyya, see Wadad al-Qadi, *Al-Kaysaniyya fi 'l-ta'rikh wa-'l-adab* ("The Kaysaniyya in History and Literature") (Beirut, 1974).

12. See Shaban, *Islamic History*, 180 ff.

13. The Khariji poet 'Amr ibn Dhukayna warned 'Umar ibn 'Abd al-'Aziz against emphasizing kinship over personal piety; see James Bellamy, "The Impact of Islam on Early Arabic Poetry," in *Islam: Past Influence and Present Challenge*, eds. Welch and Cachia (New York, 1977), 141–67.

14. Some scholars have suggested that this may have represented an Umayyad attempt to build a counter-sanctuary to the Ka'ba under Ibn al-Zubayr's control. While this on the surface seems plausible, it is highly unlikely that 'Abd al-Malik would have embarked on such a venture on the basis of such a motivation which would have further eroded the legitimacy of the Umayyads in the eyes of the general population. Given the broad-based popular support for Ibn al-Zubayr, it is clear that the people longed for a government which ruled according to acknowledged Islamic principles. Such a government would continue to connect them to the prophetic and the Rashidun past, now acquiring the mythic contours of an almost irretrievable "Golden Age."

15. For a brief account of his reign, see Shaban, *Islamic History*, 155–60.

16. Ibid.

17. See article "Ghaylan ibn Muslim Abu Marwan al-Dimashqi al-Qibti," *EI²*, 2:1026.

18. Cf. Josef van Ess, *Anfänge muslimischer Theologie. Zwei antiqadaritische Traktate aus dem ersten Jahrhundert der Hiğra* (Beirut, 1977).

19. For still popular studies of the 'Abbasid revolution, see Wellhausen's previously cited *The Arab Kingdom and Its Fall*; and M. Sharon, *Black Banners from the East: the Incubation of a Revolt* (Jerusalem, 1983). But also see the more recent work by Saleh Said Agha, *The Revolution Which Toppled the Umayyads: Neither Arab nor 'Abbasid* (Leiden and Boston, 2003), esp. 274–325, which nuances some of the positions of the earlier authors.

20. See further *Akhbar al-dawla al-'abbasiyya* ("Information regarding the 'Abbasid Dynasty"), ed. 'Abd al-'Aziz al-Duri and 'Abd al-Jabbar al-Muttalibi (Beirut, 1971), p. 282 ff.

21. For a comprehensive depiction of 'Umar II's life, see Ibn al-Jawzi, *Sirat 'Umar ibn 'Abd al-'Aziz* ("The Life of 'Umar ibn 'Abd al-'Aziz") (Cairo, 1331).

22. Ibid., 173 ff.

23. Nabia Abbott, *Studies in Arabic Literary Papyri, vol. II: Qur'anic Commentary and Tradition* (Chicago, 1967), 26.

24. Ibn Taghribirdi, *Nujum al-Zahira fi muluk misr wa-'l-qahira* ("The Resplendent Stars regarding the Rulers of Egypt and Cairo") (Cairo, 1963), 1:238.

25. The German historian R. J. H. Gottheil doubted whether the intolerant edicts attributed to 'Umar II really emanated from him; see his *Dhimmis and Moslems in Egypt* (Old Testament and Semitic Studies in memory of William Rainey Harper; vol. 2) (Chicago, 1908), 358–59.

26. For a brief, accessible biography of al-Hasan in English, see the *Shorter Encyclopedia of Islam*, ed. H. A. R. Gibb and J. H. Kramers (Leiden, 1974), 136. See also Ibn Khallikan, *Wafayat al-a'yan* ("Obituaries of the Notables"), ed. Ihsan 'Abbas (Beirut, n.d.), 2:69–73.

27. Ibn Sa'd, *Tabaqat*, 7:163–65.

28. For a recent study of al-Hasan al-Basri as a historical and mythical figure, see Suleiman Ali Mourad, *Early Islam between Myth and History: Al-Hasan al-Basri (d. 110H/728 CE) and the Formation of His Legacy in Classical Islamic Scholarship* (Leiden, 2006), 19–120.

29. Ibn Khallikan, *Wafayat al-a'yan*, 2:72.

30. For a brief biographical sketch, see Moojan Momen, *An Introduction to Shi'i Islam* (New Haven and London, 1985), 38–39; and article "Dja'far al-Sadik," *EI²*, 2:374–75.

31. See al-Mizzi, *Tahdhib al-kamal fi asma' al-rijal* ("The Perfect Instruction regarding the Names of Hadith Transmitters"), ed. Bashshar 'Awwad Ma'ruf (Beirut, 1992), 5:77.

32. Such an ecumenical tendency became even more pronounced under the Mongols; see Alessandro Bausani, "Religion under the Mongols," in *The Cambridge History of Iran*, ed. J. A. Boyle (Cambridge, 1968), 5:538–49.

33. For al-Baqir's thought, see Arzina R. Lalani, *Early Shi'i Thought: The Teachings of Imam Muhammad al-Baqir* (London, 2000).

34. Al-Majlisi, *Bihar al-anwar*, 27:167.

35. For a thorough-going discussion of the rise of jurisprudence, see Hallaq, *Origins and Evolution*, esp. 29–56.

36. Al-Fasawi, *Kitab al-ma'rifa*, 1:471.

37. See article "Abu Hanifa," *EI²*, 1:123–24; and the entry on him in Ibn Khallikan, *Wafayat al-a'yan*, 5:405–415, on which this account is based.

38. For a treatment of the Maturidi school of thought, see article "Maturidiyya" in *EI²*, 6:847–48.

39. The rationalist influence is evident in several works by Muhammad 'Abduh, such as his *Risalat al-tawhid* ("Treatise on the Unity of God"), and his *Tafsir al-manar* ("Commentary of the Beacon").

40. For example, al-Nawawi, *Tahdhib al-asma'* ("Correction of Names"), ed. F. Wustenfeld (Gottingen, 1842–47), 531.

41. See article "Malik b. Anas," *EI²*, 6:264–65; and Yasin Dutton, *The Origins of Islamic Law: The Qur'an, the Muwatta' and Medinan 'Amal* (Richmond, 1999), 11–21.

42. For a study of this work, see Dutton, *Origins of Islamic Law*, 22 ff.

43. Hallaq, *Origins and Evolution*, 105.

44. Ibid., 106.

45. Dutton, *Origins of Islamic Law*, 37 (I have slightly modified his translation in parts).

CHAPTER 7

1. It was certainly not optimistic for everyone; the Shi'i minority, for example, had good reason to be disheartened in the aftermath of the 'Abbasid revolution.

2. For a comprehensive description of Baghdad during this time, see Guy le Strange, *Baghdad during the Abbasid caliphate* (Oxford, 1924).

3. This strong Persian nationalist identity would find expression between the eighth and the tenth centuries in a movement known as the Shu'ubiyya, which expressed anti-Arab but not anti-Islamic sentiments; see the noteworthy article by Roy P. Mottahedeh, "The Shu'ubiyah Controversy and the Social History of Early Islamic Iran," *International Journal of Middle East Studies* 7 (1976):161–82.

4. These are the only instances when the word *harb* is employed in the Qur'an, and, therefore, does not represent a common Qur'anic usage as Reuven Firestone maintains in his *Jihad: The Origin of Holy War in Islam* (Oxford, 1999), 140, n. 23.

5. These traditional sources were used by the editors of the standard 1924 Cairo edition of the Qur'an to determine a chronology of Qur'anic verses and chapters that is widely accepted. For a useful account of Qur'anic chronology, see Hanna Kassis, *A Concordance of the Qur'an* (Berkeley, 1983), xxxv–xxxix.

6. See A. J. Wensinck, *Concordance et indices de la tradition musulmane* (Leiden, 1936–69), 3:242.

7. For traditional accounts of these events rendered into highly accessible English, see Lings, *Muhammad*, 43 ff.

8. These were four specific months deemed sacred in the pre-Islamic period during which fighting was prohibited.

9. Mujahid, *Tafsir*, 169; Muqatil, *Tafsir*, 3:130.

10. See al-Tabari, *Jami 'al-bayan*, 2:202–206; al-Wahidi, *al-Wasit fi tafsir al-qur'an al-majid* ("The Middle Compendium in Exegesis of the Glorious Qur'an"), ed. 'Adil Ahmad 'Abd al-Mawjud et al. (Beirut, 1994), 3:281.

11. Muqatil, *Tafsir*, 2:157, where he specifically identifies the polytheists as "the unbelievers among the people of Mecca."

12. Al-Tabari, *Jami' al-bayan*, 3:18, where he cites a *hadith* to this effect related by the Companion al-Dahhak.

13. See further Sohail Hashmi, "Interpreting the Islamic Ethics of War and Peace," in *The Ethics of War and Peace*, ed. Terry Nardin (Princeton, 1996), 146–66; Asma Afsaruddin, "Competing Perspectives on *Jihad* and Martyrdom in Early Islamic Sources," in *Witnesses for the Faith: Christian and Muslim Perspectives on Martyrdom*, ed. Brian Wicker (Aldershot, UK, 2006), 15–31.

14. Afsaruddin, "Competing Perspectives," 22–29.

15. Roy Mottahedeh and Ridwan al-Sayyid, "The Idea of the Jihad in Islam before the Crusades," in *The Crusades from the Perspective of Byzantium and the Muslim World*, ed. Angeliki E. Laiou and Roy Parviz Mottahedeh (Washington, DC, 2001), 23–29.

16. Ibid., 26.

17. Ibid, 25–27.

18. See, in general, Khalid Yahya Blankinship, *The End of the Jihad State: The Reign of Hisham Ibn 'Abd al-Malik and the Collapse of the Umayyads* (Albany, 1994).

19. For an extensive discussion of this controversial topic, see al-Tabari, *Jami' al-bayan*, 3:15–19; also 'Abd al-Rahman Ibn al-Jawzi, *Nawasikh al-Qur'an* ("The Abrogating Verses of the Qur'an") (Beirut, n.d.), 93–94.

20. Al-Tabari, *Jami' al-bayan*, 3:18.

21. Ibn al-Jawzi, *Nawasikh*, 93.

22. See Ibn al-'Arabi, *al-Nasikh wa'l-mansukh fi 'l-qur'an al-karim* ("The Abrogating and Abrogated Verses of the Noble Qur'an") (Beirut, 1997), 61; Ibn al-Jawzi, *Nawasikh*, 94.

23. Al-Shafi'i, *Kitab al-umm* ("The Source Book") (Cairo, 1321), 4:103–4.

24. Al-Shafi'i, *al-Risala* ("The Treatise"), ed. Ahmad Shakir (n.pl., 1891), 430–32.

25. Majid Khaddûri, *War and Peace in the Law of Islam* (Baltimore, 1955), 64–65; cf. the eleventh-century Shafi'i jurist and political theorist al-Mawardi's (d. 1058)

famous treatise *The Ordinances of Government*, trans. Wafaa H. Wahba (Reading, UK, 1996), 16–17.

26. See *The Islamic Law of Nations: Shaybani's Siyar*, trans. and ed. Majid Khadduri (Baltimore, 1966), 12–13; Khadduri, *War and Peace*, 145.

27. As did the Hanafi jurist Ahmad al-Tahawi (d. 933) in his *Kitab al-Mukhtasar*, ed. Abu 'l-Wafa al-Afghani (Cairo, 1950), 281; cited by Khadduri, *Islamic Law*, 58.

28. For a discussion of this, see Khadduri, *Islamic Law*, 61.

29. 'Abd al-Razzaq, *al-Musannaf* ("The Indexed Collection"), ed. Ayman Nasr al-Din al-Azhari (Beirut, 2000), 5:189.

30. Cited by Majid Khadduri, *War and Peace*, 65–66.

31. Al-Tabari, *Jami' al-bayan*, 3:25.

32. Ibn Kathir, *Tafsir al-qur'an al-'azim* ("Exegesis of the Glorious Qur'an") (Riyad, 1998), 1:416–17.

33. Al-Tabari, *Ikhtilaf al-fuqaha'* ("Differences of the Jurists") (Cairo, 1933), 1–21.

34. Al-Suyuti, *Itqan*, 2:706–712, where he lists all the verses from the second chapter believed to have been abrogated but does not list 2:256.

35. It should be pointed out that the Qur'an uses the term *shahid* as an eye-witness for both God and humans; in relation to God, see Qur'an 3:98; 6:19; 41:53, etc.

36. *Contra* Michael Bonner who suggests that the direction of influence went the other way. He, however, does not take into consideration the lack of Qur'anic attestation for the concepts of "martyr" and "martyrdom." See his *Aristocratic Violence and Holy War: Studies in the Jihad and the Arab-Byzantine Frontier* (New Haven, 1996), 10.

37. Arthur Jeffrey, *The Foreign Vocabulary of the Qur'an* (Baroda, 1938), 187; Keith Lewinstein, "The Reevaluation of Martyrdom in Early Islam," in *Sacrificing the Self: Perspectives on Martyrdom and Religion* (Oxford, 2002), 78–79. This relationship needs to be better studied and further documented. On this topic, see also the still useful article by A. J. Wensinck, "The oriental doctrine of the martyrs," in his *Semietische Studiën uit de nalatenschap* (Leiden, 1941), 91–113, which establishes striking parallels between Christian and post-Qur'anic Muslim concepts of martyrdom; and the article by Etan Kohlberg, "Shahid," in *EI²*, 9:104.

38. 'Abd al-Razzaq, *Musannaf*, 5:181.

39. Ibid., 5:183.

40. Ibid., 5:182–83.

41. Al-Bukhari, *Sahih*, 2:420–21.

42. Malik ibn Anas, *al-Muwatta'*, 1:366–67.

43. 'Abd al-Razzaq, *Musannaf*, 5:183.

44. Wensinck, *Concordance*, 1:389.

45. Ibid., 5:455.

46. Ibid., 1:389.

47. Cited by A. J. Wensinck, "Oriental doctrine," 95.

48. Al-Bukhari records a *hadith* in which the Prophet relates that God forbade Paradise to a man who took his own life after being badly wounded in a battle; see the *Sahih of Imam al-Bukhari*, trans. Muhammad Muhsin Khan (Medina, 1971) vol. 4, Bk. 56, #669.

49. Louise Marlow, *Hierarchy and Egalitarianism in Islam* (Cambridge, 1997).

50. See Afsaruddin, *Excellence and Precedence*, chapter 5.

51. Al-Jahiz, *'Uthmaniyya*, 202.

52. For example, see Ibn Qutayba, *'Uyun al-akhbar* ("The Fount of Information") (Cairo, 1963), 2:115, where a certain Sudayf laments that under the 'Abbasids, political leadership was no longer consultative and had become despotic.

53. Mujahid ibn Jabr, *Tafsir Mujahid*, ed. 'Abd al-Rahman al-Surta (Islamabad, n.d.), 1:162–63.

54. Muqatil ibn Sulayman, *Tafsir Muqatil*, ed. 'Abd Allah Mahmud Shihata (Cairo, 1969?), 1:246.

55. Ibid.

56. Al-Tabari, *Jami' al-bayan*, 4:152.

57. Ibid.

58. Ibid.

59. See the article "Sultan," in *EI²*, 9:849–51. As this article points out, the word "*sultan*" occurs in the Qur'an and *hadith* only in the sense of "power" and "authority." Not until about the tenth century would the word acquire the secondary meaning of "someone who holds power and authority."

60. Al-Tabari, *Jami' al-bayan*, 4:150–51.

61. For an extensive discussion of this topic, see my "Obedience to Political Authority: An Evolutionary Concept," in *Islamic Democratic Discourse: Theory, Debates, and Directions*, ed. Muqtedar Khan (Lanham, MD, 2006), 37–60.

62. Al-Jahiz, *'Uthmaniyya*, 115 ff.

63. 'Ali ibn Muhammad al-Mawardi, *Al-Ahkam al-Sultaniyya* ("The Governmental Ordinances") (Beirut, 1996), 13.

64. Ibid., 13–14.

65. See, for example, Ibn Qutayba, *Kitab ta'wil ikhtilaf al-hadith* ("The Book of Interpretations of Differences in *Hadith*") (Cairo, 1982), 39, 61, where it is reported that 'Umar, 'Uthman, and 'A'isha (the Prophet's wife) tended to reject Abu Hurayra's reports.

66. See Lewis' *The Political Language of Islam* (Chicago, 1988), 91. See further my article "Obedience to Political Authority," 53–54, which takes issue with his misreading. For similar ill-considered views, see Elie Kedourie, *Democracy and Arab Political Culture* (London, 1994), 7. In the post-September 11 milieu, these

views have gained greater currency in the popular media and policy-making circles, since they are being successfully peddled by influential ideologues and polemicists.

CHAPTER 8

1. See George Makdisi, *The Rise of Colleges: Institutions of learning in Islam and the West* (Edinburgh, 1981); Richard Bulliet, *The Case for Islamo-Christian Civilization* (New York, 2004), 26–27. See also Makdisi, *The Rise of Humanism in Classical Islam and the Christian West* (Edinburgh, 1990), where he argues that Classical Islam appears to have provided the model for Italian Renaissance humanism.

2. Philip Hitti, *History of the Arabs* (London, 1953), 306 ff.

3. See the article "Kaghad," *EI²*, 4:419.

4. Hitti, *History*, 309.

5. Ibn Khaldun, *al-Muqaddima* ("The Prolegomena") (Cairo, 1867), 401.

6. Ibn al-Nadim, *al-Fihrist* ("The Index"), ed. G. Flügel (Leipzig, 1872), 243.

7. For an insightful analysis of this dream episode and its far-reaching implications, see Dimitri Gutas, *Greek thought, Arabic culture: the Graeco-Arabic translation movement in Baghdad and early 'Abbasid society (2nd–4th / 8th–10th centuries)* (London and New York, 1998), 95–104.

8. Ibid., 8.

9. See the article "Hunayn b. Ishaq," *EI²*, 2:177–178.

10. Hitti, *History*, 310–16.

11. Ibid., 315.

12. Al-Mas'udi, *Muruj al-dhahab* ("Meadows of Gold"), ed. Charles Pellat (Beirut, 1965–79), 741; cited by Gutas, *Greek Thought*, 89.

13. Gutas, *Greek Thought*, 90. It is highly ironic that Pope Benedict XVI in a provocative speech would use the words of a fourteenth-century Byzantine emperor to redirect the same accusation at Muslims in the twenty-first century; see the transcript of his address given at the University of Regensburg, Germany, September 12, 2006, on the Vatican website, for example.

14. For an extensive treatment of his life and works, see J. D. Latham, "Ibn al-Muqaffa' and Early 'Abbasid Prose" in *The Cambridge History of Arabic Literature: 'Abbasid Belles-Lettres*, ed. Ashtiany et al. (Cambridge, 1990; henceforth referred to as *CHAL*), 48–77.

15. For more details, see H. T. Norris, "Shu'ubiyyah in Arabic Literature," *CHAL*, 31–47.

16. This was a term devised by Marshall Hodgson which has had limited currency;

see his *The Venture of Islam: Conscience and History in a World Civilization* (Chicago, 1974), 1:58–59.

17. Tarif Khalidi, *Classical Arab Islam: The Culture and Heritage of the Golden Age* (Princeton, 1985), 57.

18. This is a phrase used by Muhammad Arkoun in his *L'humanisme arabe au IVe/IXe siècle, Miskawayh, philosophe et historien* (Paris, 1982), 357.

19. This classification was developed by Michael G. Carter in his chapter, "Humanism in Medieval Islam," in *Humanism, Culture, and Language in the Near East*, ed. Asma Afsaruddin and Mathias Zahniser (Winona Lake, IN, 1997), 27–38. For a wide-ranging study of various types of humanism in the Islamic milieu, see Lenn E. Goodman, *Islamic Humanism* (Oxford, 2003); cf. also Marcel Boisard, *Humanism in Islam* (Bloomington, IN, 1987).

20. Ibn Qutayba, *Kitab al-shi'r wa-l-shu'ara'* ("The Book of Poetry and Poets"), ed. M. J. de Goeje (Leiden, 1902), 560; S. A. Bonebakker, "Adab and the Concept of Belles-Lettres," *CHAL*, 26.

21. Cited in *CHAL*, 26.

22. Many of the following details are taken from the article "al-Shafi'i," *Shorter Encyclopedia of Islam*, 512–15; *EI²*, 9:181–85.

23. See further Wael B. Hallaq, "Was al-Shafi'i the Master Architect of Islamic Jurisprudence?", *International Journal of Middle East Studies* 25 (1993):593 ff.

24. Ibid., 599.

25. Wael B. Hallaq, *A History of Islamic Legal Theories: An introduction to Sunni usul al-fiqh* (Cambridge, 1999), 34.

26. For more on Ibn Surayj and his legal activities, see Christopher Melchert, *The Formation of the Sunni Schools of Law, 9th–10th Centuries C.E.* (Leiden, 1997), 87–115.

27. See this discussion in al-Matroudi, *The Hanbali School of Law and Ibn Taymiyyah: Conflict or Conciliation* (London and New York, 2006), 5–6.

28. See further the article "Ahmad b. Hanbal," *EI²*, 1:272–77.

29. Ibn Hanbal's travails during al-Ma'mun's reign are described in Michael Cooperson's *Classical Arabic Biography: the Heirs of the Prophets in the Age of al-Ma'mun* (Cambridge, 2000).

30. For a discussion of this issue, see al-Matroudi, *Hanbali School*, 8–13.

31. For an accessible treatment of the rise of contemporary intolerant and militant movements ideologically linked to Wahhabism, see John L. Esposito, *Unholy War: Terror in the Name of Islam* (Oxford, 2002), esp. 45–68.

32. For example, see my article, "The Excellences of the Qur'an: Textual Sacrality and the Organization of Early Islamic Society," *Journal of the American Oriental Society* 122 (2002):13–18.

33. Martin Lings, *What is Sufism?* (Berkeley, 1975), 48.

34. Ibid., 45.

35. Ibid.

36. Cf. Ibn Taymiyya, *Majmu'a al-fatawa* ("Collection of Legal Responsa"), ed. 'Amir al-Jazzar and Anwar al-Baz (Riyadh, 1998), 293–94.

37. Al-'Attar, *Tadhkirat al-Awliya'* ("Notes of the Intimates of God"), ed. R. A. Nicholson (London, 1905), 59.

38. Ibid., 61 ff.; for a monograph-length study of Rabi'a, see Margaret Smith, *Rabi'a the Mystic and her Fellow-Saints in Islam* (Cambridge, 1928), 1 ff.

39. *Muslim Saints and Mystics: Episodes from the Tadhkirat al-Auliya' by Farid al-Din Attar*, trans. A. J. Arberry (London, 1966), 47.

40. Smith, *Rabi'a*, 21.

41. Abu Talib al-Makki, *Qut al-qulub* ("Nourishment of the Hearts") (Cairo, 1310), 1:156–57.

42. Al-'Attar, *Tadhkirat*, 71.

43. Al-Dhahabi, *Siyar a'lam al-nubala'*, 8:241–243; idem, *al-'Ibar fi khabar man ghabara* ("Wise counsel concerning those who have departed"), ed. Muhammad al-Sa'id ibn Bassiyuni Zaghlul (Beirut, n.d.), 1:214

44. Al-Jahiz, *al-Bayan wa-'l-tabyin* ("The Plainly Evident and [Its] Elucidation") (Cairo, 1332), 3:66.

45. See my article "Knowledge, Piety, and Religious Leadership: Re-Inserting Women into the Master Narrative," in *Sisters in Faith: Women, Religion and Leadership in Christianity and Islam*, ed. Scott Alexander (Lanham, MD, forthcoming).

CHAPTER 9

1. Albert Hourani, *Arabic Thought in the Liberal Age: 1798–1939* (Cambridge, 2003), 149.

2. See Rashid Rida, *Yusr al-Islam wa-usul al-tashri' al-'amm* ("The Ease of Islam and the Sources of General Legislation") (Cairo, 1956), 7.

3. Ibn Hanbal, *Musnad*, 1:225, 227; cited by Wensinck, *Concordance*, 2:505.

4. Lings, *Muhammad*, 165.

5. Al-Waki', *Akhbar al-qudat* ("Information Regarding Judges") (Beirut, n.d.), 2:189.

6. Al-Tabari, *Jami' al-bayan*, 1:66.

7. Al-Suyuti, *Sawn al-mantiq wa-'l-kalam 'an fann al-mantiq wa-'l-kalam* ("Preservation of Logic and Speech from the Art of Logic and Speech"), ed. 'Ali Sami al-Nashad (Cairo, 1947), 32.

8. Ibn al-Athir, *al-Lubab fi tahdhib al-ansab* ("Essential Knowledge concerning Genealogies") (Beirut, 1994), 2:126.

9. Ibn Taymiyya, *Majmu'a al-fatawa*, 5:111.

10. For a general treatment of Afghani's and 'Abduh's thought, see Hourani, *Arabic Thought*, 103–61; Malcolm Kerr, *Islamic Reform: The Political and Legal Theories of Muhammad Abduh and Rashid Rida* (Berkeley, 1966).

11. Or like a lighthouse, *al-Manar* in Arabic. This was the name 'Abduh gave to the periodical he ran with his disciple Rashid al-Rida and to his exegetical work, entitled in full *Tafsir al-Manar*.

12. See, for example, Khaled Abou el Fadl, *Conference of the Books: The Search for Beauty in Islam* (Lanham, MD, 2001), passim; Tariq Ramadan, *Islam, the West and the Challenges of Modernity* (Leicester, 2001), 108–10; idem, *Western Muslims and the Future of Islam* (Oxford, 2004), 89–92.

13. See G. H. A. Juynboll, *The Authenticity of the Tradition Literature: Discussions in Modern Egypt* (Leiden, 1969), 18.

14. For a rather scathing account of these developments, see Hamid Algar, *Wahhabism: A Critical Essay* (New York, 2002), esp. 4–5, 46–47, 67–68.

15. Other authors have used other terms to designate these two camps. Recently, Khaled Abou el Fadl expressed a preference for the terms "moderates" vs "puritans" to describe these contending factions; see his *The Great Theft: Wrestling Islam from the Extremists* (New York, 2005). Note that we are not dealing with Shi'i Islamism, which merits a separate study.

16. For an account of the *Ikhwan*, see Richard Mitchell, *The Society of Muslim Brothers* (New York, 1969).

17. For a comprehensive and engaging account of Mawdudi's life and thought, see Vali Nasr, *Mawdudi and the Making of Islamic Revivalism* (Oxford, 1996).

18. For a broad introduction to the rise of political Islam and its various manifestations, see John L. Esposito, *Islam and Politics*, 3rd rev. edn (Syracuse, 1991). For an overview of al-Banna's, Mawdudi's, and Qutb's thought in relation to one another, see idem, *Unholy War*, 47–64.

19. Olivier Roy, *Globalized Islam: The Search for a New Ummah* (New York, 2004), 250.

20. See Rahman, *Modernist Islam 1840–1940: A Sourcebook*, ed. Charles Kurzman (Oxford, 2002), 294.

21. For this line of analysis, see, for example, Roxanne Euben, *The Enemy in the Mirror: Islamic Fundamentalism and the Limits of Modern Rationalism* (Princeton, 1999).

22. For an excellent, comprehensive introduction to the development of Islamic modernism, see Fazlur Rahman *Islam & Modernity: Transformation of an Intellectual Tradition* (Chicago, 1982); also *Modernist Islam 1840–1940*, 3–27.

23. See al-Mawdudi, *The Process of Islamic Revolution* (Lahore, 1979), 13.

24. Ibid., 13–14. He repeats these ideas in his *al-Hukuma al-Islamiyya* ("The Islamic Government") (Cairo, 1980), 15–20.

25. Qutb, *Ma'alim fi 'l-tariq* ("Signposts along the Road") (Beirut, 1982), 105.

26. Ibid.

27. Ibid.

28. Mawdudi, *Al-Islam wa-'l-madaniyya al-haditha* ("Islam and Modern Civilization") (Cairo, 1978), 42.

29. Mawdudi, *Al-'Adala al-Ijtima'iyya fi 'l-Islam* ("Social Justice in Islam") (Cairo, 1949), 107–8.

30. For further discussion of Qutb's thought as developed in this particular work, see William Shepard, "The Development of the Thought of Sayyid Qutb as Reflected in Earlier and Later Editions of 'Social Justice in Islam,' " *Die Welt des Islams* 32 (1992): esp. 217 ff.

31. See Vali Nasr's analysis of Mawdudi's "Islamic State" in his *Mawdudi and the Making of Islamic Revivalism* (Oxford, 1996), esp. 80–106.

32. Quintan Wiktorowicz, *The Management of Islamic Activism: Salafis, the Muslim Brotherhood, and State Power in Jordan* (Albany, 2001), 111–20.

33. S. Abu'l-A'la Mawdudi, *Political Theory of Islam*, ed. and trans. Khurshid Ahmad (Lahore [Pakistan], 1976), 31.

34. This kind of anti-intellectualism is excoriated by Khaled Abou el-Fadl in his *Speaking in God's Name: Islamic Law, Authority and Women* (Oxford, 2001), esp. 170–208. See further Tamara Albertini, "The seductiveness of certainty: the destruction of Islam's intellectual legacy by the fundamentalists," *Philosophy: East and West* 53 (2003):455–71.

35. Cf. William Shepard, "Islam as a 'System' in the Later Writings of Sayyid Qutb," *Middle Eastern Studies* 25 (1989):31–50; also Nasr, *Mawdudi*, 80–106.

36. See the discussion of this concept in Qutbian Islamist thought in my article "Obedience to Political Authority," 45–46.

37. Some scholars, quite persuasively, have detected the influence of Western fascist thought on Qutb's conceptualization of the utopian totalitarian government, notably that of the German Catholic right-wing philosopher Carl Schmitt (d. 1985); see Aziz al-Azmeh, *Islam and Modernities* (London, 1996), 77–101; Abou el-Fadl, *Great Theft*, 83.

38. Muhammad Mutawalli al-Sha'rawi, *Qadaya al-mar'a al-muslima* ("The Case of the Muslim Woman") (Cairo, 1982), 18 ff.

39. Barbara Freyer Stowasser, "Religious Ideology, Women, and the Family: The Islamic Paradigm," in *The Islamic Impulse*, ed. Barbara Freyer Stowasser (Washington, DC, 1989), 281–82.

40. For an extensive discussion of personal or family law, see John L. Esposito with Natana J. DeLong-Bas, *Women in Muslim Family Law* (Syracuse, NY, 2001).

41. Ibid., 29–30.

42. Ibn al-Jawzi, *Ahkam al-nisa'* ("Regulations Concerning Women"), ed. Ahmad Shuhan (Damascus, 1991), 68–71.

43. Ibid., 70.

44. Ibid., 72.

45. *Akhbar al-nisa'* ("Information about Women"), ed. 'Abd al-Majid Tu'ma (Beirut, 1997), 12. This work's attribution to Ibn Qayyim has been doubted, however.

46. For this discussion, see Spellberg, *Politics, Gender, and the Islamic Past*, 140–49.

47. Ibn Hajar, *Isaba*, 8:306.

48. Ibid., 8:262 ff.

49. Ibid., 8:270 ff.

50. Ibid.

51. Ibn Sa'd, *Tabaqat*, 8:237–238.

52. Cf. Leila Ahmed, *Women and Gender in Islam* (New Haven, 1992), 61. Ahmed points out further that 'A'isha and Umm Salama had acted as prayer leaders for women during the Prophet's lifetime. 'Umar, the second caliph, however, saw fit to appoint a male prayer leader for the women during his reign.

53. The usage of this word here evokes Qur'an 33:33, "*wa-qarna fi buyutikunna* ..." commonly translated as "remain in your (f. pl.) homes." The imperative *qarna* remains problematic, however, since it is irregular and in its present conjugated form in the imperative cannot categorically be linked to the verbs *qarra* or *waqara*, which would connote "to remain" and "to behave with dignity" respectively. For a brief discussion of this, see Barbara Stowasser, *Women in the Qur'an, Traditions, and Interpretation* (Oxford, 1994), 172, n. 79.

54. Ibn Hajar, *Isaba*, 8:289.

55. This position is reflected in the *tafsir* literature in general; cf. for example, Ibn Kathir (d. 1373), *Tafsir al-Qur'an al-'azim* ("Commentary on the Glorious Qur'an") (Beirut, 1990), 3:464, where he interprets Qur'an 33:33 as counseling the Prophet's wives "to remain in their homes."

56. The standard Islamist work on this is Mawdudi's *al-Islam wa al-Jahiliyya* ("Islam and the Age of Ignorance") (Beirut, 1980). For a discussion of Sayyid Qutb's understanding of *Jahiliyya*, see the article by William Shepard, "Sayyed Qutb's Doctrine of Jahiliyya," *International Journal of Middle East Studies* 35 (2003):521–45.

57. S. Abu'l-A'la Mawdudi, *Jihad in Islam* (Salimiah, Kuwait, 1977), 5.

58. For a broad range of views on this topic among Islamists in Jordan, for example, see Quintan Wiktorowicz, "The Salafi Movement in Jordan," *International Journal of Middle East Studies* 32 (2000):222–26.

59. See further my monograph *Striving in the Path of God: Discursive Traditions on Jihad and the Cult of Martyrdom*, in progress.

60. See further the article "Takfir" in *Oxford Encyclopedia of the Modern Islamic World*, ed. John L. Esposito (New York and Oxford, 1995), 4:178–79.

61. Even though we pointed out earlier that many Islamists eschew the interpretations of the pre-modern jurists based on independent reasoning for which method they claim to have scant regard, they have embraced, however, this particular Shafi'i postulate, despite its not having a Qur'anic nor sunnaic antecedent, since it accords very nicely with their "fundamentalist" Manichaean view of the world. As perceptively observed by Marty and Appleby, religious fundamentalists in general resort to "a selective retrieval of doctrines, beliefs, and practices from a sacred past ... [which] are refined, modified, and sanctioned in a spirit of shrewd pragmatism;" see *Fundamentalism Observed*, ed. Martin Marty and R. Scott Appleby (Chicago, 1991), 835. Such a shrewd pragmatism is clearly evident in this instance.

62. See further my article, "Competing Perspectives on *Jihad* and Martyrdom," 15–31.

63. This *hadith*, which appears to have emanated from Sufi circles, is recorded by al-Ghazali, "The book of invocation," *Ihya' 'ulum al-din*, translated by Kojiro Nakamura as *Ghazali on Prayer* (Tokyo, 1975), 167. For further attestations of this *hadith*, see John Renard, "*Al-Jihad al-Akbar*: Notes on a Theme in Islamic Spirituality," in *Muslim World* 78 (1988):225–42.

64. For an account of general tension between Sufis and Islamists as well as traditionalists, see Julian Johansen, *Sufism and Islamic Reform in Egypt: the Battle for Islamic Tradition* (Oxford, 1996), passim. See further Carl W. Ernst, *The Shambhala Guide to Sufism* (Boston, 1997), 211–14.

CHAPTER 10

1. See my article, "The 'Islamic State': Genealogy, Facts, and Myths," in *Journal of Church and State* 48 (2006):153–73.

2. For a general discussion of these principles and their invocation as building-blocks for democratic systems, see Ahmad S. Moussalli, *The Islamic Quest for Democracy, Pluralism, and Human Rights* (Gainesville, 2001), chapter 1; also John L. Esposito and John O. Voll, *Islam and Democracy* (New York, 1996), esp. 25–30.

3. The Tunisian activist Rachid Ghannouchi (see his *al-Hurriya al-'amma fi al-dawla al-islamiyya* ["Public Freedom in the Islamic State"] (Beirut, 1993)); Muhammad 'Imara (see his *al-Islam wa al-sulta al-diniyya* ["Islam and Religious Authority"] (Cairo, 1979)); Sa'id al-Ashmawy (his views are primarily expressed in the important work *al-Islam al-siyasi* ["Political Islam"](Cairo, 1987) mentioned below); Azizah al-Hibri ("Islamic Constitutionalism and the Concept of Democracy," *Case*

Western Reserve Journal of International Law 1 (1992):1–27); and Tariq Ramadan (*Islam, the West and the Challenges of Modernity*, 81–91), for example, see no problems with recasting and aggrandizing *shura* as the organizational principle for a modern democratic polity. Among the cluster of choices available to modern Muslims, they regard democracy as the system of government that offers the best opportunity for consultative and collective political decision-making.

4. For a thorough discussion of the application of democratic principles in the Islamic context and the kind of discussion such a project engenders, see the various essays in Khaled Abou el-Fadl, *Islam and the Challenge of Democracy* (Princeton, 2003). See also in this context Feisal Abdul Rauf, *What's Right with Islam: a New Vision for Muslims and the West* (San Francisco, 2004).

5. See, for example, the online article "Islamic Viewpoint on Voting," posted by Muslim Professionals, UK at http://www.muslimprofessionals.org.uk/uk_elections_2005/uk_elections_2005/voting_in_islam_2005041139/, April 11, 2005; and Michael Wolfe, "Islam: The Next American Religion?" posted at http://www.beliefnet.com/story/69/story_6982_1.html.

6. M. Y. Faruqi, "The Development of *Ijma'*: the Practices of the *Khulafa' al-Rashidun* and the Views of the Classical *Fuqaha'*," *American Journal of Islamic Social Sciences* 9 (1992):173–87.

7. Al-Ghazali, *al-Mustasfa min 'ilm al-usul* ("Selections from Knowledge of the Sources") (Beirut, 1997), 1:171, where he defines *ijma'* as an agreement of the Muslim community on a particular religious issue.

8. For this view of *ijma'*, see, for example, Fakhr al-Din al-Razi, *al-Mahsul fi 'ilm usul al-fiqh* ("The Harvested Knowledge concerning Principles of Jurisprudence"), ed. Taha al-Alwani (Beirut, 1992), 4:20.

9. Such sentiments are already prefigured in the well-known *hadith*, "My community will never agree on error." For a brief and excellent discussion of *ijma'* as a juridical principle, see Wael Hallaq, *A History of Islamic Legal Theories: An Introduction to Sunni Usul al-Fiqh* (Cambridge, 1997), 75–81.

10. See A. Hasan, *The Doctrine of Ijma' in Islam: A Study of the Juridical Principle of Consensus* (Islamabad, 1984), 228.

11. Among modernist writers on political Islam who have vigorously and convincingly challenged the notion of *hakimiyyat Allah* and its presumed Qur'anic lineage is Muhammad Sa'id al-Ashmawi, who in his work *al-Islam al-siyasi*, states that this concept is actually un-Islamic and contrary to the Qur'an and *sunna*. Similar views were expressed earlier by Hasan al-Hudaybi, *Du'ah la qudah* ("Summoners not Judges") (Cairo, 1965). On al-Hudaybi, see Abou El Fadl, *Great Theft*, 84–85.

12. See his article "The Islamic Concept of State," in *Islam in Transition: Muslim Perspectives*, ed. John J. Donohue and John L. Esposito (New York and Oxford, 1982), 264.

13. Muhammad 'Abduh, *Tafsir al-manar* (Beirut, 1999), 5:147. For a brief discussion of "the people who loosen and bind," see, for example, Abou el Fadl, *Islam and the Challenge of Democracy*, 11–12. For a discussion of its overlap with the Qur'anic concept of *ulu 'l-amr*, see Afsaruddin, "Obedience to Political Authority," 42–46.

14. 'Abduh, *Tafsir*, 5:150.

15. Ibid., 5:152. We must not forget that Rida was the editor of the highly regarded periodical *al-Manar* and his mentor Muhammad 'Abduh was one of the key figures associated with the influential journal *al- 'Urwa al-wuthqa*; no doubt he was including himself and 'Abduh among the *ulu 'l-amr*.

16. Cf. Robert D. Crane, "Shari'ah: Legacy of the Prophet: the Role of Human Rights in Islamic Law," *The American Muslim*, January–March 2005 issue, online at http://www.theamericanmuslim.org/; Ramadan, *Western Muslims*, 147–52; Abou el Fadl, *Speaking in God's Name*, 27–30; Sachedina, *Islamic Roots*, 109–12. For a comprehensive discussion of justice in Islamic thought, see Majid Khadduri, *The Islamic Conception of Justice* (Baltimore, 1984).

17. Abou el Fadl, *The Place of Tolerance in Islam* (Boston, 2002), 11–23.

18. For an excellent discussion of this legal principle and its rootedness in historical practice, see Hallaq, *History of Islamic Legal Theories*, 83–95.

19. Muhammad Sa'id al-'Ashmawi, "Shari'a: the Codification of Islamic Law" in *Liberal Islam: A Sourcebook*, ed. Charles Kurzman (Oxford, 1998), 52–54.

20. Muhammad Shahrour, *al-Kitab wa-'l-Qur'an qira'a mu'asira* ("The Book and the Qur'an: a Contemporary Reading") (Damascus, 1990), 454–64.

21. Ramadan, *Western Muslims*, 31–61.

22. Fazlur Rahman, *Major Themes of the Qur'an* (Minneapolis, 1980), 47.

23. Wael Hallaq, "Juristic Authority vs. State Power: The Legal Crises of Modern Islam," *Journal of Law and Religion* 19 (2004): 246.

24. See Wael Hallaq, "Logic, Formal Arguments and Formalization of Arguments in Sunni Jurisprudence," *Arabica* 37 (1990): 317–18.

25. For a detailed study of al-Shatibi, see Khalid Masud, *Islamic Legal Philosophy: A Study of Abu Ishaq al-Shatibi's Life and Thought* (Islamabad, Pakistan, 1977).

26. See Muqtedar Khan, "The Politics, Theory, and Philosophy of Islamic Democracy," in *Islamic Democratic Discourse*, 149–71.

27. The well-known women's and human rights advocate Aziza al-Hibri refers to the multiple inferences that may be drawn from this anecdote; see her "Islamic Constitutionalism and the Concept of Democracy," *Case Western Reserve Journal of International Law* 24 (1992): 24–25.

28. See Rashid Rida, *Yusr al-Islam*, 12–23; also Wael Hallaq, *History of Islamic Legal Theories*, 214–20.

29. For an extensive discussion of this, see Wael Hallaq, "The Primacy of the

Qur'an in Shatibi's Legal Theory," in *Islamic Studies Presented to Charles J. Adams* (Leiden, 1991), 69–90.

30. An extensive hermeneutic treatment of this type is reflected in Asma Barlas's *Believing Women in Islam: Unreading Patriarchal Interpretations of the Qur'an* (Austin, TX, 2002).

31. Ibid., 189–92.

32. See his *Islamic Methodology in History* (Karachi, 1965), 81.

33. Daniel Brown, *Rethinking Tradition in Modern Islamic Thought* (Cambridge, 1996), 11; and sources cited therein.

34. For this fascinating discussion, see Stowasser, *Women in the Qur'an*, "The Chapter of Eve," 25–38.

35. See her *Qur'an and Woman: Rereading the Sacred Text from a Woman's Perspective* (Oxford, 1999), 24–25.

36. See, for example, Leila Ahmed, *Women and Gender*, 41–63.

37. See the article by Muhammad Fadel, "Two Women, One Man: Knowledge, Power, and Gender in Medieval Sunni Legal Thought," *International Journal of Middle East Studies* 29 (1997):185–204; and Abdulaziz Sachedina, "Woman, Half-the-Man? The Crisis of Male Epistemology in Islamic Jurisprudence," in *Intellectual Traditions in Islam*, ed. Farhad Daftary (London and New York, 2001), 82–97.

38. Fatima Mernissi, *The Veil and the Male Elite* (Reading, MA, 1991), 49–61.

39. The full title of this work is *al-Sunna al-Nabawiyya bayna ahl al-fiqh wa ahl al-hadith* ("The Prophetic Sunna among the Jurisprudents and Traditionists") (Cairo, 1989).

40. For example, Mohammad Talaat al-Ghunaimi, *The Muslim Conception of International Law and the Western Approach* (The Hague, 1968), 104.

41. Majid Khadduri, *War and Peace*, 257–61.

42. See, for example, Ramadan, *In the Footsteps*, 114–17.

43. Khadduri, *War and Peace*, 197–99.

44. Sachedina, *Islamic Roots*, 64–69.

45. *Oxford Encyclopedia of the Modern Islamic World*, ed. John Esposito (Oxford, 1995), 2:369–73.

46. See Kate Zebiri, *Mahmud Shaltut and Islamic Modernism* (Oxford, 1993), 68.

47. Al-Suyuti, *Itqan*, 2:714, where he says that the sword verse would effectively abrogate 124 conciliatory verses.

48. See Abou El Fadl, *Great Theft*, 220–49; Afsaruddin, "Competing Perspectives," 15–31.

49. See the articles "The Myth of a Militant Islam," by David Dakake and "Recollecting the Spirit of Jihad," by Reza Shah-Kazemi in *Islam, Fundamentalism, and the*

Betrayal of Tradition: Essays by Western Muslim Scholars, ed. Joseph E. B. Lumbard (Bloomington, IN, 2004), 3–38; 121–42.

CHAPTER 11

1. See the article "Dawla," in *EI²*, 2:177–78.
2. See, for example, the eighth-century author Abu Yusuf, *Kitab al-Kharaj*, 140.
3. Louise Marlow, *Hierarchy and Egalitarianism in Islamic Thought* (Cambridge, 1997).
4. The Egyptian philosopher Hasan Hanafi in his book entitled *Islam in the Modern World* (Cairo, 1995) maintains that Islam is secular at its core.
5. This embrace of beauty and truth as natural corollaries is lyrically conveyed by Abou el Fadl in his *Conference of the Books*, passim.
6. See al-Maqrizi, *Khitat* (Cairo, 1934), 2:220. See further the article on "Siyasa Shar'iyya," *EI²*, 9:694–96.
7. See his "State and Religion in Islamic Societies," *Past and Present* 151 (1996):24. For similar views, see also Sami Zubaida, *Islam, the People and the State* (London, 1989).
8. Stated in his *Islam and Modernity: Transformation of an Intellectual Tradition* (Chicago, 1982), 140.
9. For a more extended discussion of some of these points, see my article "The 'Islamic State,'" 153–73.
10. See his *al-Mughni fi al-'Adl wa al-Tawhid* ("The Indispensable Source on Justice and Unity [of God]"), ed. 'Abd al-Halim Mahmud and Sulayman Dunya (Cairo, n.d.), 20:16. I owe this reference to Hayrettin Yucesoy; see his (unpublished) paper "Is Political Leadership Necessary? Religious and Rational Morality in Islamic Political Thought," delivered at the conference of the Middle East Studies Association, Anchorage, AK, November, 2003.
11. See his *al-Mawaqif fi 'ilm al-kalam* ("Postulates regarding Theology") (Cairo, 1983), 396–97.
12. See my article "Reconstituting Women's Lives," 461–80.
13. Cf. Abou El Fadl, *Great Theft*, 152.
14. See my article, "Competing Perspectives," 15–31, for a fuller treatment of the broad spectrum of views in the early period.
15. *Musannaf*, 10:142.
16. Ibid., 5:175.
17. Donner, *Early Islamic Conquests*, 200.
18. For a more detailed account of this process, see my article "In Praise of the Caliphs: Recreating History from the *Manaqib* Literature," *International Journal of Middle East Studies* (1999).

19. For these and similar *hadiths*, see Muslim, *Sahih*, section on Iman ("Faith"), 1:60–65.

20. Donald Little, "Did Ibn Taymiyya Have a Screw Loose?" *Studia Islamica* 41 (1975):93–111.

21. Sulayman b. 'Abd al-Wahhab, *al-Sawa'iq al-ilahiyya* ("The Divine Flashes"), 48–49; cited by Abou el Fadl, *Great Theft*, 296, f.n. 34. Sulayman was the brother of Muhammad ibn 'Abd al-Wahhab, the founder of Wahhabism, but he held a pretty dim view of his brother's reactionary ideas.

CHAPTER 12

1. See Sayed Khatab, "*Hakimiyyah* and *Jahiliyyah* in the Thought of Sayyid Qutb," *Middle Eastern Studies* 38 (2002):145–70.

Select Bibliography

PRIMARY SOURCES

'Abd al-Jabbar ibn Ahmad al-Asadabadi. *Al-Mughni fi abwab al-tawhid wa-'l-'adl*. Eds 'Abd al-Halim Mahmud et al. Cairo, 1900.

———. *Tathbit dala'il al-nubuwwa*. Ed. 'Abd al-Karim 'Uthman. Beirut, 1966.

'Abd al-Razzaq al-San'ani. *Al-Musannaf*. Ed. Ayman Nasr al-Din al-Azhari. Beirut, 2000.

'Abduh, Muhammad. *Tafsir al-manar*. Beirut, 1999.

Abu Da'ud Sulayman. *Sahih sunan Abi Da'ud*. Ed. Muhammad Nasir al-Din al-Albani. Beirut, 1989.

Abu Yusuf, Ya'qub. *Kitab al-kharaj*. Ed. Ihsan 'Abbas. London, 1985.

Al-'Attar, Farid al-Din. *Tadhkirat al-awliya'*. Eds R. A. Nicholson and Mirza Muhammad Qazwini. London, 1905.

———. *Muslim Saints and Mystics: Episodes from the* Tadhkirat al-Awliya'. Tr. A. J. Arberry. London, 1966.

Al-Baghdadi, 'Abd al-Qahir. *Al-Farq bayna 'l-firaq wa-bayan al-firqa al-najiya minhum*. Ed. Muhammad 'Uthman al-Khusht. Cairo, n.d.

Al-Baladhuri, Ahmad ibn Yahya. *Kitab futuh al-buldan*. Ed. M. J. de Goeje. Leiden, 1866.

———. *Ansab al-ashraf*. Ed. M. J. de Goeje. Leiden, 1866.

Al-Bukhari, Muhammad b. Isma'il. *Sahih*. Ed. Qasim al-Shamma'i al-Rifa'i. Beirut, n.d.; Cairo, 1973–90.

Al-Fasawi, Ya'qub b. Sufyan. *Kitab al-ma'rifa wa-'l-ta'rikh*. Ed. Akram Diya' al-'Asmari. Baghdad, 1976.

Al-Ghazali, Abu Hamid. *Al-Mustasfa min 'ilm al-usul*. Ed. Muhammad Sulayman Ashqar. Beirut, 1997.

Ibn 'Abd al-Barr, Yusuf ibn 'Abd Allah. *Al-Isti'ab fi ma'rifat al-ashab*. Cairo, n.d.

———. *Kitab al-isti'ab fi ma'rifat al-ashab*. Ed. 'Ali Muhammad Mu'awwad and Jum'a Tahir al-Najjar. Beirut, 1995.

Ibn al-'Arabi, Muhammad ibn 'Abd Allah. *Al-Nasikh wa-al-mansukh fi 'l-qur'an al-karim*. Ed. 'Umayrat, Zakariya. Beirut, 1997.

Ibn al-Athir, 'Izz al-Din. *Al-Lubab fi tahdhib al-ansab*. Ed. 'Abd al-Karim ibn Muhammad Sam'ani. Beirut, 1994.

———. *Usd al-ghaba fi ma'rifat al-sahaba*. Ed. Shihab al-Din al-Najafi. Tehran, n.d.

Ibn al-Hadid, Abu Hamid ibn Hibat Allah. *Sharh nahj al-balagha*. Ed. Muhammad Abu 'l-Fadl Ibrahim. Cairo, 1959–64.

Ibn Hajar al-'Asqalani, Ahmad ibn 'Ali. *Tahdhib al-tahdhib*. Ed. 'Adil Murshid. Beirut, 1996.

———. *Al-Isaba fi tamyiz al-sahaba*. Cairo, 1907.

Ibn al-Jawzi, Abu al-Faraj 'Abd al-Rahman ibn 'Ali. *Sirat 'Umar ibn al-Khattab*. Cairo, n.d.

———. *Nawasikh al-Qur'an*. Beirut, 1985.

Ibn Kathir, Isma'il b. 'Umar. *Tafsir al-Qur'an al-'Azim*. Ed. Muhammad Ibrahim Banna. Riyadh, 1998.

Ibn Khaldun. *Al-Muqaddima*. Cairo, 1867.

Al-Khallal, Ahmad ibn Muhammad. *Al-Sunna*. Ed. 'Atiya Zahrani. Riyadh, 1994.

Ibn Khallikan. *Wafayat al-A'yan*. Cairo, 1881.

Ibn Qutayba, 'Abd Allah ibn Muslim. *Kitab ta'wil mukhtalif al-hadith*. Ed. 'Abd al-Qadir Ahmad 'Ata. Cairo, 1982.

Ibn Qutayba, *Kitab al-shi'r wa-'l-shu'ara'* ("The Book of Poetry and Poets"). Ed. M. J. de Goeje. Leiden, 1902.

Ibn Sa'd, Muhammad. *Al-Tabaqat al-kubra*. Ed. Muhammad 'Abd al-Qadir 'Ata. Beirut, 1997.

Ibn Sallam, Abu 'Ubayd al-Qasim. *Kitab al-nasab*. Beirut, 1989.

———. *Kitab al-amwal*. Ed. 'Abd al-Amir 'Ali Sahanna. Beirut, n.d.

Ibn Taymiyya, Taqi al-Din. *Majmu'a al-fatawa*. Eds 'Amir al-Jazzar and Anwar al-Baz. Riyadh, 1998.

———. *Minhaj al-sunna al-nabawiyya*. Ed. Muhammad Rashad Salim. Riyadh, 1986.

Al-Isbahani, Abu Nu'aym. *Dala'il al-nubuwwa*. Hyderabad, 1950.

———. *Hilyat al-awliya; wa-tabaqat al-asfiya'*. Beirut, 1997.

Al-Jahiz, 'Amr b. Bahr. *Risalat al-'Uthmaniyya*. Ed. 'Abd al-Salam Harun. Cairo, 1955.

Khan, Muhammad Muhsin. *Sahih al-Bukhari: The Translation of the Meanings of Sahih al-Bukhari*. Medina, 1971.

Al-Khatib al-Baghdadi. *Ta'rikh baghdad aw madinat al-salam*. Cairo, 1931.

Al-Khazin, 'Ali ibn Muhammad al-Baghdadi. *Lubab al-ta'wil fi ma'ani al-tanzil*. Ed. al-Husayn ibn Mas'ud Baghawi. Cairo, 1961.

Al-Kindi, Abu 'Umar Muhammad ibn Yusuf and Nassar, Husayn. *Wulat misr.* Beirut, 1959.

Al-Lalaka'i, Hibat Allah ibn al-Hasan. *Sharh usul i'tiqad ahl al-sunna wa-al-jama'a min al-kitab wa al-sunna wa-ijma' al-sahaba wa-'l-tabi'in min ba'dihim.* Ed. Ahmad ibn Sa'd ibn Hamdan. Riyadh, 1994.

Majlisi, Muhammad Baqir ibn Muhammad Taqi. *Bihar al-anwar: al-jam'a li-durar akhbar al-a'imma al-athar.* Tehran, 1956–83.

Al-Makki, Abu Talib Muhammad ibn 'Ali. *Qut al-qulub fi mu'amalat al-mahbub wa-wasf tariq al-murid maqam al-tawhid.* Cairo, 1892.

Al-Mawardi, 'Ali ibn Muhammad. *Al-Ahkam al-sultaniyya wa-'l-wilaya al-diniyya.* Beirut, 1996.

———. *The Ordinances of Government: Translation of al-Ahkam al-Sultaniyya wa 'l-Wilayat al-Diniyya.* Tr. Wafaa Hassan Wahba. Reading, UK, 1996.

Malik b. Anas. *Al-Muwatta'.* Ed. Bashshar 'Awad Ma'ruf and Mahmud Muhammad Khalil. Beirut, 1994.

Al-Muhibb al-Tabari. *Al-Riyad al-nadira fi manaqib al-'ashara.* Cairo, 1327.

Mujahid ibn Jabr. *Tafsir Mujahid.* Ed. 'Abd al-Rahman al-Tahir b. Muhammad al-Surta. Islamabad, n.d.

Muqatil ibn Sulayman al-Balkhi. *Tafsir Muqatil ibn Sulayman.* Ed. 'Abd Allah Mahmud Shihatah. Cairo, 1969?.

Al-Nasa'i, Ahmad b. Shu'aib. *Fada'il al-sahaba.* Ed. Faruq Hamada. Casablanca, 1984.

———. *Sunan.* Ed. Hasan Muhammad al-Mas'udi. Cairo, 1930.

Al-Qummi, 'Ali ibn Ibrahim. *Tafsir.* Ed. Al-Sayyid Tayyib al-Musawi al-Jara'iri. Najaf, 1966.

Al-Qurtubi, Muhammad ibn Ahmad. *Tafsir al-Qurtubi.* Ed. Tawfiq Hakim. Cairo, n.d.

Qutb, Sayyid. *Al-'Adala al-ijtima'iyya fi 'l-islam.* Cairo, 1949.

Al-Razi, Fakhr al-Din. *Al-Mahsul fi 'ilm usul al-fiqh.* Ed. Taha al-Alwani. Beirut, n.d.

Rida, Muhammad Rashid. *Yusr al-islam wa-usul al-tashri' al-'amm.* Cairo, 1956.

Al-Shafi'i, Muhammad ibn Idris. *Al-Risala.* Ed. Ahmad Shakir. 1891.

——— . *Kitab al-umm.* Cairo, 1903.

Al-Shawkani. *Fath al-qadir: al-jami' bayna fannay al-riwaya wa-'l-diraya min 'ilm al-tafsir.* Beirut, 1996.

Al-Shaybani, Muhammad ibn al-Hasan. *The Islamic Law of Nations: Shaybani's Siyar.* Tr. Majid Khadduri. Baltimore, 1966.

Al-Suyuti, Jalal al-Din 'Abd al-Rahman. *Al-Itqan fi 'ulum al-qur'an.* Ed. Mustafa Dib al-Bugha. Damascus, 1993.

———. *Sawn al-mantiq wa-'l-kalam 'an fann al-mantiq wa-'l-kalam.* Ed. 'Ali Sami al-Nashad. Cairo, 1947.

Al-Tabarani, Sulayman ibn Ahmad. *Al-Mu'jam al-awsat.* Eds Abu Mu'adh Tariq ibn 'Iwad Allah ibn Muhammad and 'Abd al-Muhsin ibn Ibrahim al-Husayni. Cairo, 1995.

Al-Tabari, Muhammad ibn Jarir. *Ikhtilaf al-fuqaha'.* Cairo, 1933.

——. *Jami' al-bayan 'an ta'wil ay al-Qur'an.* Beirut, 1997.

——. *Ta'rikh al-umam wa 'l-muluk.* Beirut, 1997.

Al-Tirmidhi, Muhammad ibn 'Isa. *Sunan al-Tirmidhi.* Beirut, 1965.

Al-Wahidi, 'Ali ibn Ahmad. *Al-Wasit fi tafsir al-qur'an al-majid.* Ed. 'Adil Ahmad 'Abd al-Mawjud et al. Beirut, 1994.

Waki', Muhammad ibn Khalaf ibn Hayyan. *Akhbar al-Qudat.* Beirut, n.d.

Al-Ya'qubi, Ahmad b. Ishaq. *Kitab al-ta'rikh.* Ed. M. T. Houtsma. Leiden, 1883.

——. *Ta'rikh al-Ya'qubi.* Beirut, n.d.

SECONDARY SOURCES

Abbott, Nabia. *Aishah, the Beloved of Mohammad.* London, 1998.

Abou el-Fadl, Khaled. *Speaking in God's Name: Islamic Law, Authority and Women.* Oxford, 2001.

——. *Conference of the Books: The Search for Beauty in Islam.* Lanham, MD, 2001.

——. *The Place of Tolerance in Islam.* Boston, 2002.

——. *Islam and the Challenge of Democracy.* Princeton, 2003.

——. *The Great Theft: Wrestling Islam from the Extremists.* New York, 2005.

Afsaruddin, Asma. *Excellence and Precedence: Medieval Islamic Discourse on Legitimate Leadership.* Leiden, 2002.

——. "Competing Perspectives on *Jihad* and Martyrdom in Early Islamic Sources." In *Witnesses for the Faith: Christian and Muslim Perspectives on Martyrdom.* Ed. Brian Wicker. Aldershot, UK, 2006.

——. "Obedience to Political Authority: An Evolutionary Concept." In *Islamic Democratic Discourse: Theory, Debates, and Directions.* Ed. Muqtedar Khan. Lanham, MD, 2006.

——. "Reconstituting Women's Lives: Gender and the Poetics of Narrative in Medieval Biographical Collections," *Muslim World* 92 (2002): 461–80.

——. "The 'Islamic State:' Genealogy, Facts and Myths," *Journal of Church and the State* 48 (2006): 153–73.

Agha, Saleh Said. *The Revolution Which Toppled the Umayyads: Neither Arab nor 'Abbasid.* Leiden, 2003.

Ahmed, Leila. *Women and Gender in Islam: Historical Roots of a Modern Debate.* New Haven, 1992.

Arnold, Thomas Walker. *The Preaching of Islam: A History of the Propagation of the Muslim Faith*. New York, 1913.

Asad, Muhammad. *The Message of the Qur'an*. Gibraltar, 1980.

Barlas, Asma. *Believing Women in Islam: Unreading Patriarchal Interpretations of the Qur'an*. Austin, TX, 2002.

Bravmann, M. M. *The Spiritual Background of Early Islam: Studies in Ancient Arab Concepts*. Leiden, 1972.

Brown, Daniel. *Rethinking Tradition in Modern Islamic Thought*. Cambridge, UK, 1996.

Bulliet, Richard W. *Conversion to Islam in the Medieval Period: An Essay in Quantitative History*. Cambridge, US, 1979.

———. *Islam: The View from the Edge*. New York, 1994.

———. *The Case for Islamo-Christian Civilization*. New York, 2004.

The Cambridge History of Arabic Literature: 'Abbasid Belles-Lettres. Eds Julia Ashtiany, et al. Cambridge, UK, 1990.

The Cambridge History of Arabic Literature: Arabic Literature to the End of the Umayyad Period. Eds A. F. L. Beeston et al. Cambridge, UK, 1993.

Carter, Michael G. "Humanism in Medieval Islam." In *Humanism, Culture, and Language in the Near East*. Eds Asma Afsaruddin and Mathias Zahniser. Winona Lake, IN, 1997.

Dakake, David. "The Myth of a Militant Islam." *Islam, Fundamentalism, and the Betrayal of Tradition: Essays by Western Muslim Scholars*. Ed. Joseph E. B. Lumbard. Bloomington, IN, 2004.

DeLong-Bas, Natana J. and John L. Esposito. *Women in Muslim Family Law*. Syracuse, 2001.

Donner, Fred McGraw. *The Early Islamic Conquests*. Princeton, 1981.

Dutton, Yasin. *The Origins of Islamic Law: The Qur'an, the Muwatta' and Medinan 'Amal*. Richmond, 1999.

Encyclopedia of Islam (EI²). New edn. Ed. H. Gibb et al. Leiden and London, 1960–2000.

Esposito, John L. *Unholy War: Terror in the Name of Islam*. New York, 2002.

——— and John Voll. *Islam and Democracy*. New York, 1996.

Fadel, Muhammad. "Two Women, One Man: Knowledge, Power, and Gender in Medieval Sunni Legal Thought." *International Journal of Middle East Studies* 29 (1997).

Geissinger, Aisha. "The Exegetical Traditions of 'A'isha: Notes on their Impact and Significance." *Journal of Qur'anic Studies* 6 (2004).

Gil, Moshe. *A History of Palestine, 634–1099*. Cambridge, 1992.

Al-Ghunaimi, Mohammad Talaat. *The Muslim Conception of International Law and the Western Approach*. The Hague, 1968.

Gutas, Dimitri. *Greek thought, Arabic culture: the Graeco-Arabic translation movement in Baghdad and early 'Abbasid society (2nd–4th / 8th–10th centuries)*. London and New York, 1998.

Hallaq, Wael B. *A History of Islamic Legal Theories: An Introduction to Sunni Usul al-Fiqh*. Cambridge, UK, 1999.

———. "Juristic Authority vs. State Power: The Legal Crises of Modern Islam," *Journal of Law and Religion* 19 (2004).

———. *The Origins and Evolution of Islamic Law*. Cambridge, 2005.

Hashmi, Sohail. "Interpreting the Islamic Ethics of War and Peace." *The Ethics of War and Peace: Religious and Secular Perspectives*. Ed. Terry Nardin. Princeton, 1996.

Al-Hibri, Azizah. "Islamic Constitutionalism and the Concept of Democracy," *Case Western Reserve Journal of International Law* 1 (1992).

Hitti, Philip Khuri. *History of the Arabs: from the Earliest Times to the Present*. London, 1953.

Hodgson, Marshall. *The Venture of Islam: Conscience and History in a World Civilization*. Chicago, 1974.

Hourani, Albert. *Arabic Thought in the Liberal Age: 1798–1939*. Cambridge, UK, 2003.

Humanism, Culture, and Language in the Near East: Studies in Honor of Georg Krotkoff. Eds Asma Afsaruddin and Mathias Zahniser. Winona Lake, IN, 1997.

Islam, Fundamentalism, and the Betrayal of Tradition: Essays by Western Muslim Scholars. Ed. Joseph E. B. Lumbard. Bloomington, IN, 2004.

Islamic Democratic Discourse: Theory, Debates, and Philosophical Perspectives. Ed. M. A. Muqtedar Khan. Lanham, MD, 2006.

Izutsu, Toshihiko. *Ethico-Religious Concepts in the Qur'an*. Montreal, 1966.

Kerr, Malcolm H. *Islamic Reform: The Political and Legal Theories of Muhammad Abduh and Rashid Rida*. Berkeley, 1966.

Khadduri, Majid. *War and Peace in the Law of Islam*. Baltimore, 1955.

Khalidi, Tarif. *Classical Arab Islam: The Culture and Heritage of the Golden Age*. Princeton, 1985.

Khan, Muqtedar. "The Politics, Theory, and Philosophy of Islamic Democracy." *Islamic Democratic Discourse: Theory, Debates, and Philosophical Perspectives*. Ed. Muqtedar Khan. Lanham, MD, 2006.

Liberal Islam: A Sourcebook. Ed. Charles Kurzman. Oxford, 1998.

Lings, Martin. *Muhammad: His Life Based on the Earliest Sources*. Cambridge, UK, 1995 (first published in Great Britain in 1983 by George Allen and Unwin).

———. *What is Sufism?* Berkeley, 1975.

Lucas, Scott C. *Constructive Critics, Hadith Literature, and the Articulation of Sunni*

Islam: The Legacy of the Generation of Ibn Sa'd, Ibn Ma'in, and Ibn Hanbal. Leiden, 2004.

Makdisi, George. *The Rise of Colleges: Institutions of Learning in Islam and the West.* Edinburgh, 1981.

Marlow, Louise. *Hierarchy and Egalitarianism in Islamic Thought.* Cambridge, UK, 1997.

Al-Matroudi, Abdul Hakim I. *The Hanbali School of Law and Ibn Taymiyyah: Conflict or Conciliation.* New York, 2006.

Mawdudi, Syed Abu'l-'Ala. *Al-'Adala al-Ijtima'iyya fi 'l-Islam.* Cairo, 1949.

———. *The Process of Islamic Revolution.* Lahore, 1979.

Modernist Islam 1840–1940: A Sourcebook. Ed. Charles Kurzman. Oxford, 2002.

Momen, Moojan. *An Introduction to Shi'i Islam: the History and Doctrines of Twelver Shi'ism.* New Haven, 1985.

Morony, Michael. *Iraq after the Muslim Conquest.* Princeton, 1984.

Mottahedeh, Roy P. and Ridwan al-Sayyid. "The Idea of the *Jihad* in Islam Before the Crusades." *The Crusades from the Perspective of Byzantium and the Muslim World.* Eds Angeliki E. Laiou and Roy Parviz Mottahedeh. Washington, DC, 2001.

Moussalli, Ahmad S. *The Islamic Quest for Democracy, Pluralism and Human Rights.* Gainesville, 2001.

Nasr, Seyyed Vali Reza. *Mawdudi and the Making of Islamic Revivalism.* Oxford, 1996.

Qutb, Sayyid. *Ma'alim fi 'l-tariq.* Beirut, 1982.

Rahman, Fazlur. "The Islamic Concept of State." *Islam in Transition: Muslim Perspectives.* Eds John J. Donohue and John L. Esposito. New York, 1982.

———. *Major Themes of the Qur'an.* Minneapolis, 1980.

———. *Islam and Modernity: Transformation of an Intellectual Tradition.* Chicago, 1982.

———. *Islamic Methodology in History.* Karachi, 1965.

Ramadan, Tariq. *Islam, the West and the Challenges of Modernity.* Leicester, 2001.

———. *Western Muslims and the Future of Islam.* Oxford, 2004.

———. *In the Footsteps of the Prophet: Lessons from the Life of Muhammad.* Oxford, 2007.

Renard, John. "*Al-Jihad al-Akbar:* Notes on a Theme in Islamic Spirituality." *Muslim World* 78 (1988).

Sachedina, Abdulaziz Abdulhussein. *The Islamic Roots of Democratic Pluralism.* New York, 2001.

———. "Woman, Half-the-Man? The Crisis of Male Epistemology in Islamic Jurisprudence." *Intellectual Traditions in Islam.* Ed. Farhad Daftary. London, 2001.

Schick, Robert. *The Christian Communities of Palestine from Byzantine to Islamic Rule.* Princeton, 1995.

Schimmel, Annemarie. *And Muhammad is His Messenger.* Chapel Hill, 1985.

Serjeant, R. B. "The Constitution of Medina." *The Islamic Quarterly* 8 (1964): 3–16.

Shaban, M. A. *Islamic History: A New Interpretation,* A.D. 600–750. Cambridge, UK, 1971.

Shepard, William. "The Development of the Thought of Sayyid Qutb as Reflected in Earlier and Later Editions of 'Social Justice in Islam'," *Die Welt des Islams* 32 (1992).

———. "Islam as a 'System' in the Later Writings of Sayyid Qutb," *Middle Eastern Studies* 25 (1989).

———. "Sayyed Qutb's Doctrine of *Jahiliyya*," *International Journal of Middle East Studies* 35 (2003): 521–45.

Smith, Margaret. *Rabi'a the Mystic and her Fellow-Saints in Islam.* Cambridge, 1928.

Spellberg, Denise. *Politics, Gender and the Islamic Past: The Legacy of 'A'isha bint Abi Bakr.* New York, 1994.

Shorter Encyclopedia of Islam. Eds H. A. R. Gibb and J. H. Kramers. Leiden, 1974.

Stowasser, Barbara. "The *Hijab*: How a Curtain Became an Institution and a Cultural Symbol." *Humanism, Culture and Language in the Near East: Studies in Honor of Georg Krotkoff.* Eds Asma Afsaruddin and A. H. Mathias Zahniser. Winona Lake, IN, 1997.

———. *Women in the Qur'an, Traditions and Interpretation.* Oxford, 1994.

Wadud, Amina. *Qur'an and Woman: Rereading the Sacred Text from a Woman's Perspective.* Oxford, 1999.

Watt, W. Montgomery. *Muhammad at Mecca.* Oxford, 1953.

———. *Muhammad at Medina.* Oxford, 1956.

Wensinck, A. J. et al. *Concordance et Indices de la Tradition Musulmane.* Leiden, 1969.

Zebiri, Kate. *Mahmud Shaltut and Islamic Modernism.* Oxford, 1993.

Glossary

adab: humanistic literature; humanism; manners and etiquette

ahl al-dhimma (sing. *dhimmi*): "protected people;" referring primarily to Jews and Christians; status also later extended to Hindus and Zoroastrians

ahl al-hall wa 'l-'aqd: lit. "people who dissolve and bind;" also conflated with *ulu 'l-amr* (see below)

ahl al-kitab: People of the Book, referring to Jews and Christians, and later extended to others

Amir al-mu'minin: Counselor/Leader of the Faithful; usual title of the caliph

Ansar: Medinan Helpers

atba' al-tabi'in: Successors to the Successors, the third generation of Muslims

bay'a: pledge of loyalty to the ruler

bid'a: innovation

dawla: dynasty in pre-modern usage; a nation-state in modern usage

diwan: register of pensions established by 'Umar I

fadl/fadila: moral excellence

fiqh: lit: "understanding;" the science of law; jurisprudence

fitna: chaos; civil war

al-Futuh: lit.: "the Openings;" referring to the early conquests

hadd (pl. *hudud*): penalties prescribed for major crimes

hadith: a saying of the Prophet

al-Hakimiyya: concept of "divine sovereignty" espoused by many Islamists

hasab: merit inherited from one's ancestors

hijra: migration to Medina in 622 CE

Hilf al-Fudul: roughly "Alliance of the Virtuous," a pact entered into by the young Muhammad before the rise of Islam

hilm: clemency, self-restraint

hudna: peace, truce

ijma': juridical consensus; one of the four sources of jurisprudence

ijtihad: independent reasoning

'ilm: knowledge; specifically religious, and specialized knowledge

irja': deferment to God's judgment in the hereafter; opposite of *takfir*

islah: reform

Islam: "submission" to God

Jahiliyya: pre-Islamic period in Arabia

jihad: "struggle;" "effort" in the service of God

jizya: a head-tax levied on able-bodied males from the People of the Book in lieu of *zakat* and military service

Khalifat Rasul Allah (*khalifa*): successor to the Messenger of God; regnal title (caliph)

Khalifat Allah: Vicegerent/Deputy of God

Khawarij (sing. *Khariji*): the "seceders;" extremist faction in early Islam

Al-Khulafa' al-Rashidun: the four Rightly-Guided Caliphs, Abu Bakr, 'Umar, 'Uthman, and 'Ali, who collectively ruled between 632–61

madhhab (pl. *madhahib*): school of law

manaqib: virtues; moral excellences

maqasid: objectives (of the *shari'a*)

ma'rifa: knowledge; more specifically "experiential knowledge"

maslaha: common or public good, a principal objective of the *shari'a*

mawali (sing. *mawla*): non-Arab converts to Islam

mawla: "patron," "client" (see also *mawali*)

Muslim: one who submits to God

Muhajirun: Meccan Migrants to Medina

mujaddid: renewer; particularly the centennial renewer

Murji': one who defers or postpones judgment to God of actions and beliefs for which there are no specific textual rulings

Mu'tazila: rationalist school of thought in Islam

mushaf: copy of the Qur'an

nasab: lineage

naskh: abrogation, particularly of a Qur'anic verse

qital: fighting, a component of *jihad*

qiyas: analogical reasoning; one of the sources of jurisprudence

al-Qur'an: lit. "the Reading/Recitation;" revealed scripture of Islam; the first source of jurisprudence

qurra': Qur'an reciters/readers

ra'y: discretionary, personal opinion

sabiqa: precedence or priority in Islam, especially through early conversion

sabr: patience, forbearance; a component of *jihad*

Sahaba: the Companions of the Prophet

Sahifat al-madina: the Constitution of Medina

Sahih: "sound," reliable *hadith*; also a collection of such *hadiths al-salaf al-salih* (*salaf*): the Pious Forbears from the first three generations of Muslims

shahada: basic testimonial of faith; bearing of witness; "martyrdom" in later usage

shahid (pl. *shuhada'*) a legal or eye-witness; a "martyr" in later usage

shama'il: literature in praise of the Prophet Muhammad

al-shari'a: lit. "the Way;" referring to divine guidelines for moral and ethical behavior, usually translated as "religious law"

Shi'i: one who is a partisan of 'Ali and his offspring through Fatima, Muhammad's daughter; denominational minority within Islam

shura: consultation

sira: biography, specifically biography of the Prophet

siyar: law of nations

Sufi: a mystic

sulh: peace; peacemaking; reconciliation

sunna: customs and practices of the Prophet; second source of jurisprudence

Sunni: one who follows the customs of the Prophet; denominational label of the majority of Muslims today

Tabi'un: the Successors (to the Companions)

tafsir: commentary on the Qur'an

tajdid: renewal, particularly of the religion

takfir: labeling someone with whom one disagrees on doctrinal matters an unbeliever

ta'lif al-qulub: "joining of hearts;" reconciliation

tasawwuf: mysticism

ulu 'l-amr: people possessing authority (of different kinds)

umma: trans-national community of Muslims; in early usage referred to Christian and Jewish communities in addition to the Muslim

yusr: ease, particularly in religious practices

zakat: obligatory alms due to the poor, one of the five pillars of Islam

General Index

Banu Jusham 5
Banu Mustalik 67
Banu Nadir 8, 9
Banu Najjar 5, 70
Banu Qaynuqa' 9
Banu Qurayza 9
Banu Taghlib 181
Banu Umayya 12, 78; *see also* Umayyads
Banu Zahra 72
Baqi' 69, 97, 105
baqiyyat xv
baqt 181
bara'a 194
al-barid 84
Barmakids 107
Basra 38, 49, 52, 62, 83, 88, 93, 95, 99
Battle of
    Ajnadayn 29, 38
    'Aqraba 28, 29
    Badr 5, 8, 13, 63, 113, 163, 164
    the Camel 52, 68, 69
    Hunayn 70, 161
    al-Khandaq 8, 9, 63, 113
    Khaybar 161, 162
    Nahrawan 53
    Qadisiyya 38
    Siffin 53
    Uhud 8, 57, 63, 70, 113, 161
    al-Yamama 70, 71, 161, 163
    Yarmuk 38
bay'a 169, 170, 171, 187
Bay'at al-ridwan 11
Bay'at al-shajara 11
Bayazid al-Bistami 143
Bayt al-Hikma 132
Bedouin 7, 63, 160
Ben Yohay 39
Berber 77
bid'a 144, 149
Bilal ibn Rabah 71–3
Bilalian News 73
Bi'r Ma'una 9
Bishr ibn Bara' 10
al-Bukhari 15, 34, 55, 62, 103, 121, 122, 140
Bulliet, Richard 77
al-Bulqini 138
al-Busiri 18

al-Buwayti 138
Byzantine(s) 119, 131
    army 29
    church 38
    coins 84
    expeditions 38
    frontier 92
    rule 38

caliph 20, 22, 27, 28, 30, 32, 40, 43, 44, 47,
    50, 51, 54, 55, 57, 58, 74, 80, 90, 91, 93,
    103, 106, 107, 108, 123, 131, 132, 140,
    160, 189
    primus inter pares 123
Caspian Sea 77
Charlemagne 134
China 188
Chosroes 13
Christ child 12
Christian(s)
    Abyssinians 180–1
    Byzantine 134
    communities 77
    Eastern 72
    Diophysite 38
    Monophysite 38
    Nestorian 38, 131, 133
    of Najran 13, 181, 198
    of Syria 41
    of Tanukh 181
Christianity 13, 134
    Catholic 144
    Orthodox 144
Church of the Resurrection 42
Companions xiii, 18, 33, 36, 41, 49, 59–60,
    62, 66, 69, 72, 73, 74, 76, 80, 81, 101,
    103, 104, 111, 122, 125, 143, 149, 151,
    197; *see also* Sahaba
    sunna of 98
Constantinople 92, 106
Constitution of Medina 9, 193
Cook, Michael xiv, xv
Coptic 77
Copts 38
Cordoba 89
Creation story, Biblical 178
Crone, Patricia xiv, xv

ijma' 98, 169, 171, 187
ijtihad 138, 154, 157, 175, 176, 180, 187
Ikhtilaf al-fuqaha' 120
Ikhwan al-muslimin 153; see also the Muslim
    Brotherhood
'Ikrima 61
'illa 174
'ilm 97, 143, 188
imam 24, 68, 74, 89, 96
Imami / Ithna 'Ashari 98
India 130, 135, 188
Indonesia 139
Iran 88, 150
Iraq 49, 65, 87, 100
    Sawad 49
'irfan 143
irja' 56, 194
irtidad xvii
Ishaq ibn Hunayn 133
islah 150
Islamic Government 155, 156, 184, 184, 186;
    see also al-Hukuma al-Islamiyya
Islamic Revolution 158
    tali'a 158
Islamic State 155, 156, 159, 165, 169, 183,
    184, 186; see also al-Dawla al-islamiyya
"Islamicness" 197
Islamism 153, 197
    hard-line 155
Islamist(s)
    activists 177
    hard-line 152–8, 165, 168, 169, 172, 173,
        175, 186, 187, 199
    militant 153, 166
    moderate 154
    Qutbian 172
    radical 153, 167, 173, 196–7, 199
Isma'il (son of Abraham) 51
Isma'il (son of Ja'far al-Sadiq) 98
Isma'ilis 98
isnad 59, 60, 103, 180
isra'iliyyat 151
istibdad 46
istihsan 98, 138

Jabir ibn Hayyan 96
Jabriyya 140

Ja'far al-Sadiq 24, 89, 96–8, 103, 105, 137
Ja'fari school of jurisprudence 96
al-Jahiliyya 2–3, 165; see also Jahili period
    values of 3
Jahili
    period 79
    values 3
al-Jahiz ('Amr ibn Bahr) 21, 23, 24, 28, 93,
        126, 136, 146
    Risalat al-'Uthmaniyya 21, 22, 126
jahl 2–3
Jahmiyya 99, 101
Jamaat-i Islami 153
Jarajima tribe 181
Jerusalem 4, 42, 44, 84
Jesus 13, 131
Jewish communities 77
Jews 38, 44, 198
    return to Jerusalem 44
(al-)jihad xiii, 5, 6, 108–23, 139, 155, 165–7,
        180, 182, 192, 193, 194, 196
    fi sabil allah 109, 116, 122, 192, 197
    jus ad bellum 112
    jus in bello 113
jizya 39, 42, 181
    verse 114
Jundishapur (Gondishapur) 131
Jurjis ibn Bakhtishu' 131

Ka'ba 31, 72, 80, 83, 84
Kabul 99
Kalb 83
Kalila wa Dimna 108, 135, 188
Karbala' 79, 82, 95
katib 107
al-Kaysaniyya 81
khabar al-wahid 68
Khabbab 31
Khadija (bint Khuwaylid) 2, 3
khalaf 148, 149
Khalid ibn al-Walid 8, 28, 125
khalifa 90, 172
Khalifat Abi Bakr 35, 186
Khalifat Allah 35, 78, 124
Khalifat Khalifat Rasul Allah 35
Khalifat Rasul Allah 29, 78, 186
khalil 30

Mosul 81
Mother(s) of the Believers 66, 68
Mu'adh ibn Jabal 195
mu'adhdhin 36, 71, 72
mu'amalat 174
Mu'awiya (ibn Abi Sufyan) 47, 48, 52, 53, 62,
  69, 78, 80, 184
Mu'awiya (ibn Yazid) 82
mubhamat 61
al-Mudawwana 105
Mughira ibn Shu'ba 78
(al-)Muhajirun 4, 20, 37; *see also* Meccan
  Migrants, Migrant Muslims
  al-awwalun 11
Muhammad 'Abduh 102
Muhammad al-Baqir 96
Muhammad Baqir al-Majlisi 97
Muhammad (ibn 'Abd Allah) Prophet xii, xiii,
  29, 30, 31, 32, 40, 51, 61, 62, 66, 67, 69,
  71, 72, 110, 148, 158, 159, 172, 178,
  180, 184, 185
  Habib Allah 16
  al-insan al-kamil 18
  life of 1–16
  al-Mustafa 16
  remembering the Prophet 16–18
Muhammad ibn al-Hanafiyya 81
Muhammad al-Nafs al-Zakiyya 96
Muhammadans xiv
mujaddid 93
Mujahid ibn Jabr xvi, 95, 125, 186
Mukhtar (ibn Abi 'Ubayd al-Thaqafi) 81, 82,
  83, 88
mulk 78
al-mu'minun 5
al-munafiqun 67
Muqawqis 13
Murji'a 56–7, 101
Muqatil ibn Sulayman (al-Balkhi) 125
Musa ibn Kazim 98
Musaylima 28, 71
mushaf 20, 49, 62
al-mushaf al-'uthmani 49; *see also* 'Uthmanic
  codex
Muslim (ibn al-Hajjaj) 15, 34, 62, 122, 140
Muslim(s)
  modernist(s) 154, 168–82, 196, 199

reformist(s) 154, 168–82, 199
  traditionalist(s) 154, 159, 175, 177
al-mustad'afun 71
mut'a 36
al-Mu'tasim 140
mutawatir 138
al-Mu'tasim 108
al-Mutawakkil 108, 133, 140
Mu'tazila 56, 86, 95, 99, 100, 132, 136, 140,
  189
al-Muzani 138

Nafi' *mawla* 'Abd Allah ibn 'Umar 103
Na'ila bint al-Furafisa 50
nasab 23, 25
nash wa-nasiha 5
al-Nasa'i 140, 141
naskh 117, 182
nass 97
Nasr ibn Sayyar 89
al-Nazzam 189
Negus, Christian ruler of Abyssinia 3, 180
Nishapur 89
North Africa 76, 77, 83, 181
Nubians 181
Nusayba bint Ka'b 70–1, 161
nussak 142

Ottoman(s) 101
  era 139

Pact of 'Umar 41, 198
Pahlavi (Middle Persian) 135
paideia 136
Pakistan 153
Palestine 29, 42, 137
  Asqalan 137
Palmyra 86, 87
paper, introduction of 130
Paul of Tarsus, St. 30
the Penitents 80, 81
People of the Book 114, 117, 133
Pericles 132
Persia 13, 77, 108, 123, 130, 131, 135
Phoenicia 130
Pious Forbears xiii, 148, 151, 152, 158, 168,
  183, 191, 192, 196, 199

Plato 133
   Republic 133
Pledge of 'Aqaba 4
Pledge of Satisfaction 11; *see also Bay'at*
   al-ridwan
Pledge of the Tree 11; *see also Bay'at al-shajara*
proto-Shi'a xvii, 25, 79, 81
proto-Sunni xvii
Ptolemy 133
qadam xvii
qadar 86

Qadariyya 86, 87, 94, 99, 101
qadhf 68
qadi 36, 99
Qadi 'Iyad 17, 141
al-Qa'idun 111
qari' 64
Qasim ibn Muhammad 99
Qatar 141
Qays 83
qibla 130
al-qira'at/qira'a 49, 99
qital 109, 113, 117, 123
qiyas 98, 100, 138, 171
Quda'a, tribe of 163
Queen of Sheba 69
al-Qummi, 'Ali ibn Ibrahim 24
(al-)Qur'an xvi, xviii, 1–4, 16, 26, 31, 37, 40,
   67, 71, 95, 98, 100, 103, 107, 109, 110,
   112, 113, 114, 115, 117, 118, 120, 133,
   134, 136, 137, 138, 140, 141, 149, 154,
   157, 158, 166, 171, 172, 173, 174, 175,
   176, 177, 179, 182, 183, 189, 191, 192,
   194
   collection of 48–50
   uncreated 140
   'Uthmanic codex xix
Qur'an reciters 48, 53
Quraysh 3, 5, 7, 10, 11, 12, 21, 31, 33, 47, 63,
   80, 122, 137
qurra' 48; *see also* Qur'an reciters
al-Qurtubi, Muhammad 45
qussas 142
Qutb, Sayyid 153, 156, 157, 158
   Fi zilal al-qur'an 157
   Ma'alim fi 'l-tariq 156

Rabi'a al-'Adawiyya 143, 144–7, 196
Rahman, Fazlur xv, 172, 178, 189
al-Rashidin al-Mahdiyyin 55
the Rashidun
   caliphate 169
   caliphs 43, 58, 78, 91, 196
   period 170, 171, 183, 184, 188
ra'y 17, 98, 100, 138, 140
al-Razi, Fakhr al-Din 139
Realpolitik 119, 197
religious law 153, 155
Renaissance, in Europe 130
   Italian 132
al-rida min al Muhammad 88
Rida, Rashid 148, 172–3, 176, 181, 186
ridda xvii, 27, 28, 29, 37, 49, 51, 52
the Rightly-Guided Caliph(s) 26, 27, 29, 47,
   55, 57, 58, 59, 60, 91, 156, 169, 170,
   172, 185, 194–5; *see also al-Khulafa' al-*
   Rashidun; the Rashidun caliphs
rihlat talab al-'ilm 188
   legacy of 54–8
rijal 60, 73, 101
riyasa 147
Robinson, Neal xiii
Ruqayya (daughter of the Prophet) 47

Sabians
   in the Qur'an 133–4
   of Harran 133–4
sabiqa xvii, 32, 51, 185, 191
al-sabiqun al-awwalun 11
sabr 111, 192
Sa'd ibn Abi Waqqas 44
Sa'd ibn Jubayr 95
Sa'd ibn Mu'adh 9
Sa'id ibn al-Musayyib 99
sadaqat 43
Safwan ibn al-Mu'attal 67
Sahl ibn Sa'd al-Sa'idi 101
Sahnun 105
Sa'id ibn al-Musayyab 30
Sahaba 18, 73, 74
Sahabiyyat 73; *see also* women Companions
sahifat al-madina 5; *see also* Constitution of
   Medina
Sa'id ibn al-'As 48

women *salaf* 160, 161, 179, 190
wu''az 142

Yahya ibn Sa'id al-Kattan 140
Yahya ibn Yahya al-Masmudi 103
Yathrib 3, 4, 5
Yazid I *see* Yazid (ibn Mu'awiya)
Yazid (ibn Abi Sufyan) 29
Yazid ibn 'Amr 100
Yazid (ibn Mu'awiya) 62, 78, 79, 82
Yazid II 85, 92
Yazid III 85, 86
"Year of the Ash" 36
Yuhanna ibn Masawayh 133

Zab 89
al-Zafarani 138

zakat 27, 28, 43, 181
Zayd ibn 'Ali 96, 99, 103
   Majmu' al-fiqh 99
Zayd ibn Haritha 3
Zayd ibn Thabit 29, 36, 37, 49, 93
Zaydis 24
Zaynab (daughter of the Prophet) 13
Zaynab (wife of the Prophet) 148–9
zawiya 143
Ziyad ibn Abihi 78
Zoroastrian(s) 134
   communities 77
al-Zubayr (ibn al-'Awamm) 44, 52, 68, 82
Zubayrid revolt 84
zuhhad 142
zuhd 100